Between Gay and Straight

Understanding Friendship across Sexual Orientation

LISA M. TILLMANN-HEALY

ALTAMIRA
PRESS

A Division of
ROWMAN & LITTLEFIELD PUBLISHERS, INC.
Walnut Creek • Lanham • New York • Oxford

AltaMira Press
A Division of Rowman & Littlefield Publishers, Inc.
1630 North Main Street, # 367
Walnut Creek, CA 94596
www.altamirapress.com

Rowman & Littlefield Publishers, Inc.
4720 Boston Way
Lanham, Maryland 20706

12 Hid's Copse Road
Cumnor Hill, Oxford OX2 9JJ, England

British Library Cataloguing in Publication Information Available

Library of Congress Cataloging-in-Publication Data

Tillmann-Healy, Lisa M., 1971–
    Between gay and straight : understanding friendship across sexual orientation / Lisa M.
Tillmann-Healy
        p.   cm. — (Ethnographic alternatives book series ; v. 8)
    Includes bibliographical references.
    ISBN 0-7591-0110-8 (cloth : alk. paper) — ISBN 0-7591-0111-6 (pbk : alk. paper)
        1. Gay men—Relations with heterosexuals—United States.   2. Lesbians—Relations with
heterosexuals—United States.   3. Male friendship—United States.   4. Female friendship—
United States.   I. Title.   II. Series.

HQ76.2.U5 T58   2001
305.38'9664—dc21   00-021113

Printed in the United States of America

⊖™ The paper used in this publication meets the minimum requirements of American National
Standard for Information Sciences—Permanence of Paper for Printed Library Materials,
ANSI/NISO Z39.48–1992.

Between Gay and Straight

Ethnographic Alternatives Book Series

Series Editors
Carolyn Ellis
Arthur P. Bochner
(both at the University of South Florida)

About the Series:

Ethnographic Alternatives emphasizes experimental forms of qualitative writing that blur the boundaries between social sciences and humanities. The editors encourage submissions that experiment with novel forms of expressing lived experience, including literary, poetic, autobiographical, multivoiced, conversational, critical, visual, performative, and co-constructed representations. Emphasis should be on expressing concrete lived experience through narrative modes of writing.

We are interested in ethnographic alternatives that promote narration of local stories, literary modes of descriptive scene setting, dialogue, and unfolding action; and inclusion of the author's subjective relations, involvement in the research process, and strategies for practicing reflexive fieldwork.

Please send proposals to:
Carolyn Ellis and Arthur P. Bochner
College of Arts and Sciences
Department of Communication
University of South Florida
4202 East Fowler Avenue, CIS 1040
Tampa, FL 33620-7800
E-mail: cellis@chuma.cas.usf.edu

Books in the Series:
Volume 1, *Composing Ethnography: Alternative Forms of Qualitative Writing,* Carolyn Ellis and Arthur P. Bochner, editors

Volume 2, *Opportunity House: Ethnographic Stories of Mental Retardation,* Michael V. Angrosino

Volume 3, *Kaleidoscope Notes: Writing Women's Music and Organizational Culture,* Stacy Holman Jones

Volume 4, *Fiction and Social Research: By Fire or Ice,* Anna Banks and Stephen B. Banks, editors

Volume 5, *Reading Auschwitz,* Mary Lagerwey

Volume 6, *Life Online: Researching Real Experience in Virtual Space,* Annette N. Markham

Volume 7, *Writing the New Ethnography,* H. L. Goodall Jr.

Volume 8, *Between Gay and Straight: Understanding Friendship across Sexual Orientation,* Lisa M. Tillmann-Healy

Contents

Acknowledgments

Along this journey, I've incurred many debts that cannot be repaid, only honored. My parents, John and Beth Tillmann, have provided me with a lifetime of love and support. For several years, they saw nothing of my mother's salary, which paid for my brothers' and my educations. Their personal sacrifices allowed me to make college my first priority.

I'm beholden to many teachers as well, including Robert Ruberto (retired from Lincoln High School), Lynn Turner (Marquette University), and Helen Sterk (now at Calvin College). Their passion, imagination, and conviction have fueled my own.

I deeply appreciate the individual and collective contributions of my doctoral committee from the University of South Florida's Department of Communication: Barney Downs, who embodies the power of personal narrative; Eric Eisenberg, an inspiring and gifted teacher; Marsha Vanderford, whose unwavering dedication makes *me* a better teacher; and Carolyn Ellis, a strong, loving, and feminist role model. Each continues to shape me as a scholar and a human being.

A special thanks to Jim King for chairing my dissertation defense (the most magical event of my academic life), and for his heartfelt and pointed review of my manuscript.

Art Bochner, my mentor, has given me his passion for stories and for scholarship that aims to make a difference. Both professionally and personally, he and Carolyn Ellis are my second parents. Their presence in my life infuses every page of this book.

I owe this project largely to members of my research community. I'm especially grateful to David Holland for opening the door. Tim Mahn, Rob Ryan, and Pat Martinez will be in my heart forever as brothers.

Words can't express how profoundly the accounts of men like Gordon Bernstein and Al Steel have moved me. Thanks also to Brandon Nolan, Jeff Grasso, Jon Hornish, Chris, Bob, Joe, Kerby, Gregg, Gary, Stewart, Ron, Kem, Scot, Steve Hornsby and the rest of the Monday Night Dinner gang, and all the Suncoast Softball men and women who made this the journey of a lifetime.

Finally, I must acknowledge my husband, Doug Healy, for being my spirit and my best friend. Our love changes everything.

Introduction: Only Us

October 10, 1998: a day of reawakening. I arose early, excited to begin composing a twenty-minute presentation for my Ph.D. dissertation defense, scheduled for the following Friday. With this talk, I would invite the audience inside my fieldwork experience and relationships with a community of gay men in Tampa. I had vivid memories and over three hundred pages of ethnographic stories and analysis—but only twenty minutes. In so little time, how could I communicate the power of the most important and educational journey of my life?

I had been staring at my computer screen for about an hour when I heard the morning paper strike the front porch. Time for a break, I thought.

As I opened the door, a rush of warm autumn air greeted me, and the *St. Petersburg Times* lay on the stoop. I tucked it under my arm and headed back to the office. Reaching my desk, I leisurely unfolded the front page. My body froze when I read the headline: "Gay man clings to life after attack." It was my first introduction to Matthew Shepard.

I remember the slight crinkling sound of the paper; it shook with my hands as I encountered the details. Three days before, at around midnight, Matthew Shepard, age twenty-one, was having a beer at the Fireside, a hangout popular among students at the University of Wyoming. Two men, also age twenty-one, approached.

No one overheard the words exchanged, but some speculated that Matthew Shepard "embarrassed" Russell Henderson and Aaron McKinney by flirting with them. Whatever their motive, Henderson and McKinney lured Matthew Shepard into a truck and began beating him. They drove to a secluded subdivision a mile away. While Matthew Shepard

1

begged for his life, Henderson tied him to a fence, and McKinney pistol-whipped him with a three-pound .357 magnum and set his body on fire. They stole the wallet and shoes of their 5'2", 108-pound victim and left him tied to that fence, where he remained for eighteen hours. When he was found, Matthew Shepard's cheeks were stained with dried rivulets of blood and tears.

Closing my eyes, I tried to imagine his suffering: the raw panic when he first sensed danger, the desperation of his attempts to appease, the brutality of each blow to his skull, the ever deepening cuts to his bound wrists. What was he thinking and feeling as the truck at last sped away? Hope? Despair? Was he conscious as each cruel hour passed without rescue?

I opened my eyes and studied the printed photograph of him. In his young, thoughtful face, I saw the faces of my informants—and my best friends. My tears hit the paper like raindrops on a tin roof, blurring the newsprint. I sat down and forced myself to finish the article; when I read the last word, my hands released the paper. As the section gently settled to the floor, I was overcome by pain like a fist to my stomach.

I clutched the edge of the desk and wept harder than I ever had for someone I didn't know. I cried because so much had changed for me since beginning my fieldwork on friendship in and with a gay male community, and because I could see how much more cultural change was needed. In the wake of this horrific attack, my project seemed of little significance. And of vital significance. Suddenly, I wasn't just defending a dissertation; I was defending a vulnerable class of persons to which my research community—my friends—belonged.

On Monday, October 12, 1998, Matthew Shepard died from massive head trauma. His funeral was picketed by demonstrators from the Westboro Baptist Church of Topeka, Kansas. Led by Reverend Fred Phelps, the group marched with signs reading, "God Hates Fags" and "Matt in Hell."[1]

Fear- and hate-motivated murders of gay men would persist. On February 19, 1999, Billy Jack Gaither, a thirty-nine-year-old gay man from rural Alabama, was beaten to death by Steven Mullins and Charles Monroe Butler. Like Aaron McKinney, Butler offered a "gay panic" account, saying that Billy Jack Gaither started "talking queer stuff" that "set off" a violent reaction. He and Mullins bludgeoned Billy Jack Gaither with an ax handle and cut his throat before throwing his body on a pile of tires and setting it ablaze.[2]

On July 1, 1999, Benjamin Matthew Williams and his younger brother, James Tyler Williams, shot to death Gary Matson and Winfield Mowder as they lay sleeping in their bed in Happy Valley, California. Each suffered multiple bullet wounds; the walls and ceiling of the bedroom they shared were sprayed with blood. The elder Williams considers himself "a Christian martyr" who is guilty not of murder but of "obeying the laws of the creator."[3] Though Benjamin Matthew Williams is believed to be straight, some associates have questioned his sexual orientation. Their suspicions are said to have haunted him.

Columbine High killers Eric Harris and Dylan Klebold (also thought to be straight) frequently were taunted with homophobic slurs. Though Harris and Klebold didn't appear to target gay victims, such cases illustrate the symbolic weight of a homosexual label, particularly for young men. Responding to the infamous "talk-show murder" (in which Scott Amedure died at the hands of Jonathan Schmitz, a man to whom he had revealed a "secret crush" on a never-aired episode of the *Jenny Jones Show*), Gamson argues that some men would rather kill a gay man than be perceived as one.[4]

Just four days after the Happy Valley murders, Calvin Glover used a baseball bat to beat a sleeping fellow soldier into unconsciousness. Barry Winchell died the next day. According to army prosecutors, the victim became a frequent target of antigay remarks when his company learned that he had visited a bar known to be popular among gay men.[5] Two days before the attack, he and Glover were involved in a physical altercation. Barry Winchell defeated Glover, who vowed revenge, telling comrades he would not be beaten by a "faggot."[6]

On March 21, 2000, a man walking in Queens, New York, found a plastic container. Inside were a foot, loose teeth, and a skull inscribed with the words "gay nigger number one." The police notified John Fenrich, whose nineteen-year-old stepson, Steen, had been reported missing. A standoff between police and Fenrich ensued. The stepfather (who is white) allegedly admitted to Steen's murder. Apparently, Fenrich disapproved of his stepson's homosexuality and reacted violently when Steen tried to return home after a breakup with his boyfriend. The seven-hour standoff ended when John Fenrich shot himself to death.[7]

The family is just one context where homophobia lingers. In 1999, GLSEN (the Gay, Lesbian, and Straight Education Network) surveyed 496 gay, lesbian, bisexual, and transgendered students. Ninety-one percent reported hearing terms like "faggot," "dyke," and "queer" regularly at school; 69 percent said they had experienced direct verbal harassment; and 24 percent had been physically assaulted. In addition, 40 percent of runaways and "throwaways" are nonheterosexual, and gay and lesbian youth account for one-third of all teen suicides.[8]

Regarding civil rights, as of June 2000, fifteen states still legally prohibit sodomy. Twelve ban oral and/or anal sex for both mixed- and same-sex relations (though prosecutions of heterosexuals are exceedingly rare). Four states (Arkansas, Kansas, Oklahoma, and Texas) ban sodomy only for same-sex relations, as permitted under *Bowers v. Hardwick* (1986), in which the U.S. Supreme Court upheld the rights of states to prohibit consensual homosexual activity. Penalties range from $200 fines to twenty years' imprisonment. In addition, thirty states (and the federal government) have passed "defense of marriage" legislation, barring legal recognition for same-sex couples.[9] Four states (Arkansas, Florida, Utah, and Mississippi) limit adoption rights for nonheterosexuals, while only eleven states prohibit discrimination based on sexual orientation.[10] At the federal level, hate crimes statutes currently provide enhanced penalties for offenses motivated by the victim's race, color, national origin, or religion; efforts to add sexual orientation are ongoing. Since Matthew Shepard's murder, only three states have enacted or strengthened hate crimes laws inclusive of sexual orientation; similar legislation failed in twenty-two states, including Wyoming.

The recent U.S. cultural terrain has been equally rocky for nonheterosexuals. In February 1999, Jerry Falwell's *National Liberty Journal* deemed the Teletubbies character Tinky Winky "a gay role model." "He is purple," said the warning to parents, "the gay-pride color; and his antenna is [sic] shaped like a triangle—the gay-pride symbol."[11] On August 13, 1999, talk show host Dr. Laura Schlesinger claimed that "a huge portion of the homosexual male populace is predatory on young boys."[12] In 2000, "ex-gay" born-again Christians held the sixth annual Coming Out of Homosexuality Day;[13] and the U.S. Supreme Court overturned a New Jersey State Supreme Court ruling that prohibited the Boy Scouts of America from excluding homosexual members and leaders.

In *Imagine That: Letters from Russell*, gay poet and playwright Russell Harold writes to his straight friend Lydia, "It does seem, at times, that we are on a journey of a hundred miles and are being asked to content ourselves with two steps forward, one step back."[14] Since the murder of Matthew Shepard, I often have experienced the journey toward greater interpersonal and cultural harmony between gay and straight communities in the way Harold describes: a hundred miles, two steps forward, one step back. The steps backward—from hate crimes to heterosexist legislation—have been persistent and frustrating. But there have been notable steps forward as well.

For many, Matthew Shepard's murder was both a wake-up call and a rallying point. It galvanized efforts to add actual or perceived sexual orientation to the classes covered by hate crimes laws.[15] It sparked a town hall discussion on tolerance in Colorado and the creation of the

Matthew Shepard Foundation, which sponsors programs for disenfranchised youth.[16] In addition, his death increased support for, and participation in, organizations like PFLAG (Parents and Friends of Lesbians and Gays), GSA (Gay Straight Alliance), and GLSEN.[17] In fact, the number of local gay–straight coalitions is thought to have doubled in the year following Matthew Shepard's murder, which also inspired the off-Broadway play *The Laramie Project* and the documentaries *Journey to a Hate-Free Millennium* and MTV's *Fight for Your Rights: Take a Stand against Violence.*[18]

New and unexpected alliances have formed. Judy Shepard (Matthew's mother) has become an outspoken gay rights activist. She headlined *Journey to a Hate-Free Millennium*, went on a speaking tour, and taped public service announcements for the Human Rights Campaign and GLSEN. In perhaps the most surprising turn of events of 1999, Jerry Falwell cohosted an antiviolence forum with Mel White (a gay minister who once was Falwell's aide). While not conceding his position that homosexuality is a sin, Falwell told attendees to love all people regardless of sexual orientation and to pray for an end to antigay violence.[19]

Such efforts are aimed at increasing tolerance of differences. Greater tolerance, it is hoped, will reduce the number of hate crimes and promote more hospitable social and cultural environments.

These are laudable goals, to be sure. This book, however, attempts to envision and travel a road *beyond* tolerance, toward a place where differences are seen less as problems to be solved or obstacles to be overcome than as unique opportunities for engagement, understanding, learning, and growth.[20] In that place, we would appreciate the particular standpoints that emerge from our cultural categories (such as gender, race, and sexual orientation). As important, we would recognize these categories as human constructions that often blind us to our fundamental interconnectedness. In that place, there would be no "they" or "them," only *us*.

The Journey

This book chronicles my journey toward such a place. It's a journey into a world once foreign to me as a straight woman, a journey back through my old worlds (but with a new consciousness), and a search for a home somewhere between. It's an intellectual, academic, and professional journey. And a deeply personal one.

In many ways, this journey began in the summer of 1994. Doug Healy, whom I would marry the following year, had just graduated from pharmacy school and moved to Tampa. His trainer at work was David Holland, a man who would alter the course of our lives. Doug and David became friends almost instantly.[21]

For a couple of weeks, Doug and I had an ongoing conversation about whether David might be gay, a question David all but answered by inviting us out to Tracks, a gay nightclub in nearby Ybor City.[22] At twenty-three, neither Doug nor I had ever had an openly gay friend before. Both of us had grown up in the rural Midwest with conventional, small-town ideas about sexual orientation and sexual identity.[23]

Despite our limited exposure to gay people and cultures, we agreed to meet David at Tracks. As it turned out, this was only the beginning.

In November 1994, David mentioned to Doug that he played softball. When Doug asked if his team needed players, David told him that the team (sponsored by a bar called the Cove) and, in fact, the whole Suncoast Softball league were gay identified.[24] If that didn't bother him, David said, Doug could join under a league provision that allowed each team to field two straight players.[25]

Doug had been longing for the camaraderie he had experienced in his college fraternity and during his years of playing competitive sports. While Suncoast Softball offered the possibility of male companionship, Doug had learned to create and sustain this in largely heterosexist environments. Sure, David was helping him unlearn homophobia, but was Doug prepared to spend two days each week—most of his free time—on a field where he (a white, middle-class, Protestant heterosexual) would experience an unfamiliar status: minority; on a field where he might be an object of the male gaze; on a field where others would assume he was homosexual? Probably not, but he went anyway.

Throughout the spring and summer, Doug attended weekly practices and games. Though he enjoyed softball and liked his teammates, David continued to be the only Suncoast player we saw off the field. That changed in August, when Tim Mahn, the coach, and his partner, Brandon Nolan, began inviting us to social events.

For the next year, our journey would be an innocently personal one—a straight couple venturing outside the conventions of their small-town socializations. But in the fall of 1995, it took an unexpected turn.

Merging the Personal and the Academic

That semester, I was enrolled in a graduate seminar on qualitative methods. After a month of class, my intended study fell through. I called Carolyn Ellis, the course professor, to discuss alternative projects. For a half hour, we reviewed and rejected every topic, group, and site that came to mind. Then the line went silent.

At last, one more idea surfaced. Since January, I explained, Doug had been the Cove's "token heterosexual." Carolyn agreed the situation sounded unique, but could I gain entrée? What issues would I investigate, which methods might I use, and where in a gay community would a straight woman find a place from which to speak? Though I had no definitive responses, I told myself not to worry. After all, it was just a class project—or so I thought.

Carolyn's questions in mind, I considered my associations with the team. The Cove, at that time, had over a dozen men on its roster. Unwilling to conduct a covert study, I knew that a single objection to my proposal could end the project before it began. And why wouldn't they object? I had attended not a single team practice and only a couple of games. Why would men who knew so little about me choose to participate? Moreover, though I felt somewhat close to David and Tim, I wasn't sure they would support my research either. Why would *any* gay man allow a straight woman to investigate and write about his life? This was a question I would grapple with for the next three years.

The night before the fall season opened, I proposed the study to Tim. He was surprised but pleased by my academic interest in the group and immediately agreed to help secure the team's permission. Because many of the players concealed their gay identity in nongay contexts, I expected the Cove men to express reservations. But when Tim presented me to the team the next day and told them my request, I fielded but a single question: "So what do you want to know?"

It seemed straightforward enough. But, indeed, what *did* I want to know?

By this time, I had defined myself scholastically as a student of close relationships. So I told the team, "I want to know about friendship in the lives of gay men." It sounded like a plausible academic response, but the truth is, I had no idea what I was looking for. I had thrown myself into a fieldwork site a month into the semester. Struggling to "find my feet," I found myself making it up as I went along.[26] Much later, I would come to understand that the real learning took place not in answering a preconceived set of questions but in figuring out what the questions were in the first place.

I began attending Sunday games, weekly practices, team parties, and fund-raisers. With the Cove's consent, I often used a microcassette player to record dugout interaction. I also carried a camera and a pocket-sized notebook for jottings and verbatim quotes. While driving home from an event, I spoke additional reflections into my recorder. Then, as soon as possible, I typed field notes from the tapes and jottings, detailing my observations of the social actors and scenes I had encountered.

As much as I tried to practice the tenets of good participant observation, nothing went according to plan. When I examined and tried to code each day's field notes, I found it difficult to draw definitive conclusions about "the gay experience" or gay men's friendships. What I did find, however, were descriptions of, and passionate reflections on, my evolving relationships with the Cove men. My interactions with them moved me to question the dichotomous construction of hetero- and homosexuality. Their pain and anger associated with coming out and homophobia increasingly became my pain and anger, and their struggles with HIV deepened and personalized the way I thought and felt about AIDS.

In November 1995, I began composing narrative episodes based on my collected materials. The evolving work took readers into the possibilities for, and consequences of, being a straight woman who both studies and practices friendship in a gay male community.

The following semester, I entered the classroom with a new sensibility. For the first time, I noticed the absence of openly gay and lesbian authors on many syllabi (including my own). I also recognized, as never before, how gay and lesbian experiences can be marginalized in the classroom, through both heterosexist comments and silence. These realizations moved me to continue writing about the softball league; to examine and alter my syllabi, class exercises, and teaching stance; and to confront latent and overt homophobia in the courses I was taking.

Every aspect of my identity was becoming increasingly "queer." My use of this term is not in the traditional disparaging sense. Instead, it stems from queer theory, a system of thought that emerged from lesbian and gay studies and from the more radical strands of gay and lesbian activism in the 1980s (e.g., Queer Nation and ACT UP).[27] Queer theorists attempt to uncover, defy, and contest homophobic and heterosexist assumptions, discourse, and practices.[28]

As my professional commitments deepened and expanded, so did my personal attachments to members of my research community. When I wanted a lunch date, movie companion, or just someone to talk to, I found myself, more often than not, consulting the list of phone numbers for members of the softball team. The Cove men began calling me as well. Over coffee or dinner, we shared stories of childhood, school, work, and family. The subject of romance also rendered us confidants, and I valued the unique insights reached by comparing our perspectives on relationships with men.

Doug's connections with his teammates blossomed as well. Old assumptions about homosexuality withered, leaving him open to new ways of being and relating. Emotionally and physically, these became the closest and most expressive male friendships of his life.

Meanwhile, we noticed our marriage evolving—and not always comfortably. We were raising our consciousness about sexual orientation and identity and discovering uncharted territory in our own sexualities.

The more time we spent with these men, the more invested we became in their lives and concerns. Doug and I tried to serve as ambassadors, both to our straight associates and to our gay associates' straight associates. In dialogue and by example, we hoped to debunk myths and clear new fields for friendship.

To educate others, I first had to educate myself, so I explored lines of academic research more thoroughly. My reading prompted more talking. These men were authorities on the lived experience of being gay, and I could offer knowledge from scholarly literatures on gay identity, relationships, and cultures. Our conversations brought together these personal and academic discourses, comparing, contrasting, and critiquing them.

As I read, I became increasingly convinced that the relationships Doug and I were building with the Cove men could be not only personally fulfilling but also socially transformative. For a time, I wanted nothing more than to close the chasm between gay and straight communities.

But then something started to happen in my encounters with heterosexuals.

A slight grimace, an altered intonation, an ambiguous remark—anything that smacked, however slightly, of heterosexism or homophobia—was enough to get under my skin. And stay there. I continued to play the teacher, the mediator, the bridge, but I was growing increasingly impatient with, and frustrated by, the requirements of these roles. Perhaps I forgot who I had been less than two years before, but sometimes I needed my straight associates to "get it" on their own; sometimes I didn't care what they thought; sometimes I just wanted to run home. But where was home now?

Suddenly, I began to question what *really* brought me into this community, what kept me there, what happened to me along the way. One thing was certain: I was feeling more and more like an outsider in my old circles. The familiar had become strange, and I wasn't sure I wanted it to be familiar again. Where did I belong?

There was no turning back. By September 1996, I felt sufficiently prepared, personally and academically, to write my dissertation on this community. But what would be my focus and stance? I had been asked many times by many people, especially my professors, "What can a straight woman reveal about gay men's lives?" Though initially I had no adequate response, I felt strongly that I was witnessing—and ultimately would bear witness to—something important and meaningful. What it was, however, I couldn't yet articulate.

Turning to Narrative Ethnography

In May 1997, I had a meeting with my dissertation adviser, Art Bochner. I expressed my continued difficulty in finding my ethnographic voice. "If I take a traditional stance," I told him, "I'm supposed to be 'objective.' But I'm emotionally attached to these men and politically invested in their welfare. If I take an autoethnographic stance, I can recognize and write from my interests and sympathies, but I'll be focusing on my own experience. I value and want to feature *their* experience as well."

"You're making a false distinction," Art replied. "Even the most traditional ethnography is, in some ways, autoethnography. At the same time, all good autoethnography draws from, and teaches about, cultural life.

"Besides," he continued, "what you always have seemed most passionate about is what happens *between* you and them. Perhaps you can approach your project as what Tedlock calls 'narrative ethnography,' where the *intersubjectivity* you co-construct with your participants becomes the focus of investigation."[29]

Art gave me Tedlock's essay. Reading it, I learned that narrative ethnography is both a way of practicing fieldwork and a way of writing about fieldwork experience and relationships. As a practice, narrative ethnography occupies the middle terrain between traditional, realist ethnography and autoethnography.[30]

Traditional ethnographers engage in participant observation, usually in cultures to which they don't belong. Autoethnographers, in contrast, are participant observers of their own experience. Both aim to increase cultural understanding, traditional ethnography by studying others' experience, autoethnography by studying one's own. In narrative ethnography, researchers move from participant observation to the *observation of participation*.[31] When we make this move, cultural analysis emerges from the character and process of the ethnographic dialogue— a move from studying them or oneself to studying *us*. Narrative ethnography requires us to think in unconventional ways about the role of the researcher, the look and feel of ethnographic writing, and the position of readers.

First, because narrative ethnography centers on the mutual and reciprocal relationship between researcher and participants, a high degree of reflexivity is required. Narrative ethnographers must recognize both self and others as historically positioned and locally situated in cultural categories such as gender, race, and sexual identity.[32] Fieldwork, in turn, involves communicating about, through, and across these categories.

Because of this, narrative ethnographers try to maximize collaboration.[33] Moving toward participatory inquiry, we seek as much *co-constructed* meaning as possible.[34] Our projects, therefore, center on communicative *interaction*.[35]

Narrative ethnographers also are self-consciously political. We view objectivity and neutrality as synonyms for estrangement and find that both are unachievable and undesirable.[36] We take instead a *purposefully ethical stance* toward research and participants.[37] Ideally, suggests Denzin, our work sparks conversation and action directed toward greater social accord and justice.[38]

As writers, moreover, narrative ethnographers strive to compose texts quite unlike standard academic works. A narrative ethnography may draw from fields as diverse as communication, sociology, psychology, cultural studies, media studies, the visual arts, popular culture, and literature. This radical intertextuality renders narrative ethnography interdisciplinary, transdisciplinary, and even counterdisciplinary.[39]

A narrative ethnography also has a different "feel" from an orthodox social science text. Narrative ethnographers privilege embodied experience as both a subject of research and as a *method of inquiry*.[40] Our texts move beyond the ethnographic gaze, emphasizing what is smelled, heard, and felt as much as what is seen.[41] If successful, the text gives readers, in Stoller's words, "a *sense* of what it is like to live in other worlds, a taste of ethnographic things."[42]

To produce an evocative narrative ethnography, we employ techniques more often associated with fiction and new journalism than with social science: thick scenic description, reconstructed dialogue, dramatic tension, foreshadowing, and temporal shifts.[43] Taking shape in one or more forms, such as ethnographic short stories, ethnographic fiction, ethnographic poetry, ethnographic drama, and layered accounts, our texts invite readers inside fieldwork experience and relationships.[44]

The criteria by which we judge narrative ethnographies are different from those used to evaluate traditional social science.[45] Moving from factual truth to narrative truth, such projects can be assessed by their personal, relational, and cultural *consequences*.[46] Says Robert Coles, "There are many interpretations to a good story, and it isn't a question of which one is right or wrong but of what you do with what you've read."[47] The best stories, according to Bochner, enlarge our capacity to cope with life's challenges, deepen our ability to empathize with others, and expand our sense of community.[48]

Readers of such works are positioned differently than in traditional research. Narrative ethnographers write for those who want to be engaged on multiple levels—intellectually, emotionally, ethically, and aesthetically; to confront texts from their own experience; and to participate as coproducers of meaning. Narrative ethnographies embrace, in Denzin's terms, a "dialogical ethics of reading."[49]

Because narrative ethnographies remain open-ended, encouraging multiple interpretations, readers are invited to offer personal, analytic, and critical responses. Texts thus become sites of political empowerment and resistance.[50] Ideally, by interacting with the work, readers find something to take in and use, both for themselves and for social change.[51]

What you take away from this text largely will depend on what you bring to it. If you are a practitioner of qualitative research, you might be interested in my fieldwork practices. While maintaining a first-person narrative voice, I discuss these practices throughout the book (a thorough review of my writing procedures can be found at the end of chapter 6, and the most comprehensive examinations of methodological issues are located in chapter 7 and the epilogue). Among other issues, this book explores the ethics of studying a (marginalized) group to which one doesn't belong. In addition, I work through the strengths and challenges of conducting research in a community one has befriended. In this project, my researcher and friendship roles fused so completely that I posit friendship not only as a subject of my research but also as a primary *method*.

Briefly, friendship as a method of ethnographic inquiry involves researching with the *practices* of friendship: conversation, everyday involvement, compassion, giving, and vulnerability; conducting fieldwork at the natural *pace* of friendship—one that often is slow, gradual, and unsteady; and, most important, upholding an *ethic* of friendship—a stance of mutuality, caring, and commitment.[52]

Other readers may find the *form* of my study provocative and instructive. I offer not only detailed ethnographic stories but also metastories, in which I recount the process of transforming field materials into narrative ethnography.

Still others might be drawn to the identity, relationship, and/or cultural issues raised by this project. Some of the central ones include the possibilities for, and significance of, communication and friendship across sexual identity; the sources and consequences of heterosexism and homophobia; and the construction, usefulness, and limitations of cultural binaries (such as gay–straight). In each chapter, I have layered in reflections from literatures such as friendship, queer theory, and gender studies. More extensive treatments of the study's issues and implications can be found in chapter 7 and the epilogue.

If you are a gay or lesbian reader, perhaps you will find encouragement to continue reaching out to your straight associates and giving them a chance to know you *as gay or lesbian.* Your courage will challenge stereotypes and allow heterosexuals to see the depth and breadth of, and diversity *within* and *between,* gay and lesbian communities.

I hope that both gay and straight readers will take the story I offer not as a program that everyone must live out in the same way but as one possible path toward the more loving and just world that lies on the other side of our cultural assumptions and prejudices. If we commit ourselves to bridging our divides, our journey will be neither easy nor comfortable. But we all must keep in mind the consequences of remaining silent and separate. The cruelties visited upon Matthew Shepard, Billy Jack Gaither, Gary Matson, Winfield Mowder, Barry Winchell, Steen Fenrich, and so many others stem from our *collective* fears and anxieties about difference. The cruelties will not end until there is no "they" or "them," only *us.*

Chapter Previews

In the chapters and stories that follow, I first will offer glimpses of my life before I stumbled into a community of gay men. Then I'll show how identities and relationships were transformed as Doug and I moved from outside this community, to its periphery, to its center.

Chapter 1 spans from my childhood to June 1994. I recount memories of my hometown, where homosexuality was largely invisible to me. Despite this, I meet three people who alter my thoughts and feelings about sexual orientation and identity. My encounters with them, and my academic socialization at Marquette University and the University of South Florida, lay groundwork for the connections I later make with gay men.

Chapter 2 extends from June 1994 to September 1995. It opens with Doug meeting David and continues through our initial visits to gay spaces. Also in this chapter, Doug begins his four-year tenure with the Cove.

Chapter 3 marks the beginning of my academic journey into this community. It's the fall of 1995, and I'm taking a course on qualitative methods. Unexpectedly, the softball field emerges as a fieldwork site. As I become immersed in the Cove men's lives and stories, I begin exploring how to "work the hyphen" between gay and straight, to practice research (and friendship) *with* and *for* my participants.[53]

Chapter 4, which extends to the following September, shows how my relationships with these men alter how I position myself in graduate courses, how I practice research, how I write, and how I teach my classes. As a student, I delve into new projects on sexual orientation and identity; as an instructor, I alter course reading lists, assignments, and activities. This chapter also moves through my increasingly problematic encounters with heterosexuals. My new consciousness makes me impatient for my straight associates to raise *their* consciousness.

Chapter 5 spans the period from the fall of 1996 to January 1997. I'm taking a course on life history, and I ask the Cove's twenty-seven-year-old left fielder, Gordon Bernstein, to participate in my project. During our interviews, Gordon teaches me about the ongoing process of coming out—to oneself, to other gay men, and to coworkers, friends, and family. Later, I grapple with elements of this gay male culture that can be unsettling, especially for women. I bemoan its obsession with appearance, and I question how gay male communities might become less exclusive and sexist. Taking this stance feels risky because it adds the entanglements of the critic role to those of researcher, friend, and advocate. By now, I'm a fully "vulnerable observer."[54]

In Chapter 6, I present events that took place during the spring 1997 semester and that summer. An issue that comes to the forefront is the binary (gay–straight) construction of sexual orientation and identity. I ask what it means to say, "I'm straight," or "I'm gay" and what options and experiences such a claim opens up and closes off. By exploring an attraction between myself and one of my participants, I question the popular wisdom that friendships between straight women and gay men are free of the sexual complications often associated with straight, cross-sex friendships. Moreover, I begin to lament the lack of female companionship in my life. In contrast to the "gay" sensitivity and intuitiveness described in some literature, I find my friendships with these *particular* gay men remarkably similar to those I've had with straight men: active and stimulating but seldom as emotionally intense as female friendships.[55] This chapter also shows one way these connections affect my marriage. In a key scene, someone tells me that the group is worried that Doug has "gay tendencies." Hearing this, I realize that my husband's level of comfort with gay men sometimes had triggered anxieties in *me*. These return in full force when Doug and I talk through our friends' concern.

Chapter 7 provides a dialogic analysis of the project. It's based on a conversation Doug and I had while I was trying to compose a more conventional conclusion on friendship across sexual orientation and friendship as method. We discuss my project's academic, personal, interpersonal, and cultural implications.

In the epilogue, the project comes full circle. The setting is the oral defense of my Ph.D. dissertation. About a dozen of the men I befriended and wrote about—most of whom have read the document—are in attendance. My academic and research communities offer personal and scholarly responses to my work. We talk through the disbelief and pain surrounding Matthew Shepard's death just four days before, and we try to direct ourselves toward a future of greater harmony and justice.

I believe that such a future is possible, because I have seen and felt that harmony in my own life. But we won't look ahead just yet. To help you understand where my journey has taken me, I first must show you who I was before.

1

Before

I grew up in the conservative farming community of Lake City, Minnesota, population 4,500. Separated from the bluff-lined Wisconsin border by two miles of the Mississippi and nestled in a lush valley carved by glaciers, my hometown is a beautiful place. For its multigeneration businesses, two-stoplight downtown, and single-section weekly paper, urbanites consider Lake City a simple place. A haven from crime and grime, it's what residents call "a family place."

This "beautiful," "simple" town does provide a comfortable, nurturing environment for some families—families like mine: white, middle-class, Christian, two-parent biological. At the same time, Lake City is a place where virtually no African, Latin, or Asian Americans live, non-Christians have no place of worship, and premarital sex and divorce still raise eyebrows and lower voices.

"Homosexual," "gay," "lesbian"—they too tend to be whispered, when uttered at all. Reflecting on my childhood, I remember few instances when these words met my ears. The first I can recall happened in late November 1983.

Lesbian Thanksgiving

On parlor couches and chairs, the men of my extended family recoup from the Thanksgiving meal. They clutch full stomachs while praising the butter-creaminess of my mother's mashed potatoes, the sausage-spiced perfection of Uncle Rick's dressing, and the cooling contrast of Great-Aunt Doris's fresh cranberry salad.

"There's this man at my office," Aunt Melanie tells my mother as we finish clearing the table. "He has a picture of his *male* lover on his desk." Melanie's eyes enlarge as she continues, "And get this: he carries a *purse*. A big white purse!" Mom shakes her head.

"Oh, lay off the guy!" Rick admonishes.

"Well, it's odd!" Melanie retorts.

"Keep talking," he warns, "and one day our daughter will bring home a woman."

"Rick!" several of us shout.

"You know what I say?" he continues. "Let her be a lesbian! I would-n't care."

"A *lesbian?*" I question. "You'd have no problem with that?"

"I'd just want her to be a happy lesbian," my uncle insists.

The family chorus crescendos, "No way! Get outta here! Yeah, right!" Shouted down, Rick folds his arms defiantly across his chest, closes his eyes, and drifts into a turkey-induced slumber.

A potential source of my family's resistance to Rick is our religious socialization. Catholic doctrine on homosexuality taught us to "hate the sins" (homosexual practices, however mysterious and ill defined) but to "love the sinners" (those sad, cursed creatures who couldn't help "what they were").[1] Of course, when a sermon or Sunday school lesson asked us to damn "the doing," it wasn't difficult to damn "the being" as well.

My primary and secondary education presented an equally cropped and blurred picture. The philosophy behind the Rainbow Curriculum never reached our textbooks, assignments, and discussions. During health class, our (hetero)sex education included not a single conversation about "alternative lifestyles." In fact, when I try to remember myself thinking or talking about homosexuality at school, I only can recall instances that show its invisibility. One such occurrence took place in seventh grade.

The Rules

The bell starts to ring, sending a throng of us stampeding toward our first-period classroom. By the time we settle into our seats, the day's announcements already have begun. The voice over the PA system alerts us to the lunch menu before moving on to the main event—prom. "All students bringing a guest must register him or her in the office. Remember, if your guest gets into trouble, *you* will receive the punishment. All participants must be in at least tenth grade. And all couples must be boy–girl."

At this, the room fills with laughter. "Duh!" the guy behind me exclaims.

I chuckle and respond, "Like, what else would they be?"

As a "boy-crazy" seventh grader, either I couldn't imagine that anyone would *want* to attend prom with a same-sex date, or I thought such a person had no place there. In the next two years, however, three people significantly affected my thoughts and feelings about sexual orientation and identity.

The first was Deborah. In 1982, my mother began nursing school at Winona State. There, she met and befriended Deborah, a fellow student. The two enjoyed many of the same activities: racquetball, golf, and camping. It was on a canoe trip that Deborah confessed to being both bisexual and in love with my mom. By the time my parents told me of Deborah's disclosure, I had come to know and like her. Still, the thought of her loving (and lusting after) my mother was more than a little disconcerting. After speaking with our priest, Mom told Deborah that while she never could love her "that way," she wanted their friendship to persist, and it does to this day.

The second person was Trent, who came into my life in June 1984. I vividly recall our first encounter.

Something Different

With friends Jean and Kristin, I stroll along the pier. The late afternoon sun chaps our lips as we breathe through our mouths, avoiding the wafts of algae and rotting fish. "Hey!" someone shouts from the water below. Thinking the call for someone else, we continue on; but at the second "Hey!" we look down. From a dinghy, two guys wave.

"The blond's cute," Jean whispers.

"Come to our boat," invites his Latino companion as they motor toward the marina. "Dock 3, the *Neptune*."

An adventure-starved fourteen-year-old, I flash my eyebrows, asking, "How 'bout it, ladies?"

"Why not?" Kristin agrees.

We make our way through the park and across the long, wooden ramp. Several slips down, we find the boat. The blond appears. He *is* cute, I think, noting his tall, lean build, piercing blue eyes, and soft, boyish features. He takes my hand, saying, "All aboard."

"I'm Lisa," I tell them, "and this is Jean and Kristin."

"Trent," says the blond, pointing to himself, "and my friend Miguel." He fills plastic cups with sweet Chablis. As we sip and chat, Trent and I exchange glances.

Several minutes later, I look at my watch and gasp. "Ooh! We're late for my mom's graduation party."

Trent jumps onto the dock to help us off the boat. "Will I see you again?" he asks, staring intently into my eyes.

"I'll leave directions," I say, "in case you want to come by for sandwiches and cake."

Back at the house, I watch for Trent but think he probably won't show. Each time the doorbell rings, I hold my ground. I've almost given up when my brother rounds the corner and says, "Some guy named Trent is at the door."

"Well," I respond as nonchalantly as possible, "show him in."

With yacht-club propriety, Trent charms everyone. While mingling, we eye each other playfully.

After most of the guests leave, he and I move outside to sit under the clear night sky. We nervously share autobiographies before sealing our attraction with a deliciously slow kiss.

"I have to get back," Trent says. "But I'll be in town next weekend."

"You know where I live," I reply.

As he walks away, two figures appear. "Who was *that*?" asks my friend Peter.

"That was Trent," I answer dreamily.

"There's something . . . different about him," observes Randy, another schoolmate.

"Yeah, different," Peter agrees, and they break into laughter.

"What's so funny?" I demand.

"C'mon, Lis," Peter says. "He's a femme."

"A what?"

"A *femme*," he repeats, louder this time. "Or didn't you notice the bony legs and fluffy hair? I bet he even had a manicure!"

"You're jealous," I retort.

"Jealous?" Randy huffs. "Of a *fag*?"

That word stings. "He is *not!*" I insist, climbing the steps and slamming the door.

I fell hard for Trent that summer. But the words "different," "femme," and "fag" remained etched on my consciousness. At fourteen, I already knew that these were among the most disparaging labels for young men, yet I became angry not at the stereotypes and misogyny but at Trent's assigned position in a homophobic framework I didn't question. Why was I so defensive? Did I fear that Peter and Randy were right about Trent's gender identity and/or sexual orientation? Was I worried that, if my peers marginalized Trent (and Trent and I were together), my own status could be in jeopardy? Given these possibilities, perhaps it's no surprise that I ended this relationship just before the new school year began—just before I again would face my classmates every day.

Later that year, I came to know a guy named Dev. As with Trent, my attraction to him was immediate and visceral. One October night, I again found myself confronting questions about a love interest's sexual orientation.

Something in Common

Dev's lips press lightly against mine. Heart thumping, I fight the urge to reach across his worn front seat and pull him on top of me. We bid good night, and I watch his car turn the corner at the end of the block. I inhale deeply, riding a wave of teenage euphoria.

"I saw that," my friend Kara teases, approaching from across the street.

"Oh god," I say breathlessly, "I can't believe he kissed me!"

"Be careful," she warns. "You know what they say."

"*What* do they say?"

"About his . . . sexual preference."

I sigh. "Do you think he's . . . ?" I can't get the next word out.

"Do I think he's *gay*? I don't know."

"Well, I don't think so," I tell her, as if pleading a case. "He *kissed* me; you saw it!"

"What if he, you know, likes men?" she queries.

"Then I guess we have something in common."

That flippant response failed to convey how disturbing I found Kara's inquiry. If Dev were gay, it meant that he wouldn't return my affections, that I could encounter more hassling from my peers, and that I had established a pattern of attraction to males with "borderline" sexualities. I wondered if that made my sexuality borderline as well.

Once my interest in Dev waned, I thought little about homosexuality until I entered Marquette University in 1989. My first year, I took a course called Theory of Ethics. I remember a discussion on sexual violence in which I commented that the punishment for raping a man should be more severe than for violating a woman. Ludicrous as it now sounds, I reasoned that male rape carried the added weight of being "unnatural" (as if raping a woman were somehow "natural"). In another session of that class, I suggested that AIDS might be a punishment for behaving contrary to God's will. Not one classmate challenged my contribution; in fact, it was met with several nods and even a bit of clapping.

By my sophomore year, however, the barriers around my old consciousness were crumbling. In seminars like Gender and Communication and Women's Rhetoric, I became inspired by feminism, and in advanced philosophy courses, I was exposed to various standpoints associated with culture, religion, and socioeconomic class.

Sexual identity was the last wall to crack. Though I increasingly sensed an affinity between women's emancipation and the emancipation of gay men and lesbians, I still found it difficult to support certain causes. In a theology and values course my senior year, for example, I argued that children of gay men and lesbians face too many hardships and too much harassment to warrant custody rights for these parents. Looking back, I know that I never would have suggested that a Jewish person or an interracial couple shouldn't have children. But I now see that my argument—that progeny shouldn't suffer their parents' marginalization—would preclude any nonmajority person from parenthood.

By the time I graduated in May 1993, I considered myself a "good liberal" when it came to gay people. I was sensitive, thoughtful, and committed. At least, that's what I told myself. Never mind that I counted no gay male or lesbian among my friends, not even among my acquaintances; indeed, during my four years at Marquette, I had no sustained interpersonal contact with any openly gay person—ever.

The summer after graduation, I began dating Doug Healy. Like me, Doug grew up in a rural, insular town and attended a small, private university.

That fall, as Doug began pharmacy rotations at Drake, I entered the University of South Florida as a Ph.D. student in communication. My first year, I worked hard to establish myself as someone committed to the graduate community. At that time, all my Tampa friends were associated with the university.

In May 1994, I went to Des Moines for Doug's graduation. On that visit, we had our first conversation about "alternative" sexualities.

A Twosome at *Threesome*

After an onslaught of summer-blockbuster previews, we settle in for the feature presentation, *Threesome*. The film opens on a college campus. Two men, one a sex-crazed jock (Stuart), the other a quiet intellectual (Eddy), become roommates. A bureaucratic mistake sends Alex, a beautiful neurotic, to live in the second room of their suite until she can prove she is not male, as the university computer has her listed.

A not-so-classic love triangle forms. Alex falls for Eddy, who falls for Stuart, who falls for Alex. Undaunted, Alex sets out to prove Eddy a closet heterosexual; Eddy endeavors to unleash what he perceives as Stuart's latent homosexuality; and Stuart attempts to reinvent himself as the literatus he thinks Alex desires. Alex sleeps with each man, and Eddy once tries to seduce Stuart, but as dyads, they fall flat. As a threesome, however, they make great friends and, eventually, something else as well.

One afternoon, they lie on Alex's bed, talking and laughing. Alex begins teasing Stuart. "Fuck you," Stuart banters playfully.

"You wish," Alex responds. "Fuck you both," she then says.

"*You* wish," Eddy tells her.

His statement sparks a relational epiphany. Alex reaches over for Eddy, and they share an open-mouthed kiss. Then Alex turns to Stuart, and their tongues begin probing. The film cuts, and we find the three in the same positions but without their clothes. "Oh my," Doug and I say together as we shift in our seats.

Alex and Eddy face one another while Stuart embraces Alex from behind. Eddy hesitantly reaches across Alex to touch Stuart. He grazes Stuart's buttock, then shyly pulls away. Stuart takes Eddy's hand and returns it to his thigh. The three move together slowly, rhythmically. The film ends a few minutes later.

On the way to the car, Doug and I talk about feeling uncomfortable during the threesome scene. I express difficulty breaking the frame of intercourse as a two-person enterprise, while Doug says he finds the suggestions of anal sex distasteful. We agree that Stuart and Eddy's mutual affection was "a little too explicit."

In retrospect, that we considered *Threesome* "explicit" speaks volumes about the first twenty-three years of our lives. Stuart and Eddy don't even kiss in this film, but for unworldly viewers who had never seen two men share a passionate touch—not in life, not even in cinema—any hint of male sexual intimacy felt strange, uncomfortable, and forbidden. Ironically, upon viewing *Threesome* again in June 1997, I marveled at how mainstream it seemed.

↘↘↘

In this chapter, glimpses of my family life, my education, and my early relationship with Doug offer a sense of who I was before stumbling into a gay community. Reflecting on the encounters described, I note first how invisible homosexuality once was to me. In my mind, years pass without a single reference to anything gay. When homosexuality does flash upon my mental screen, it calls forth a deeply entrenched code linking it with Otherness, deviance, threat, and sin.

For a time, I cursed my small-town upbringing for teaching me that code and for making it seem so unconsciously right. But I could have learned a similar code in almost any hometown, and if I'd come of age someplace else, I wouldn't have known Deborah, Trent, or Dev (though I might have known others like them). Even though these associations aroused fears and anxieties, they also may have provided a foundation for the deeper, more sustained connections I later would make with gay men.

Those connections might never have been forged without Doug. In June 1994, he moved to Florida and began pharmacy training at Walgreens. There, he met a man who changed both our lives forever.

2

Contact

Is He or Isn't He?

A few weeks into his pharmacy externship, Doug arrives home and says, "I think my supervisor is gay."

"Why," I ask playfully, "did he flirt with you?"

Loosening his tie, Doug scowls a bit, saying, "Of course not."

"Is the guy effeminate?" I probe.

He reflects a moment, then answers, "Not really."

"So what makes you think he's gay?"

"Some of his body language, maybe. Or the way he says certain words. I don't know. I can't give you an example. Anyway, David's cool. You should meet him."

My curiosity piqued, I offer to bring them lunch.

The next afternoon, I wander down the Hallmark-card and feminine-products aisles before locating the pharmacy. Spotting Doug behind the patient-counseling window, I straighten my sleeveless black dress, toss my chiffon scarf over my shoulder, and remove my sunglasses. This ensemble, I now realize, is a little much for Walgreens. Did David's potential gayness heighten my fashion consciousness?

Doug grins when he sees me. "David," he calls over his shoulder, "Lisa's here."

A thirtyish man with spiky, auburn-brown hair steps forward. "I tell you *whuut*," he says, extending his hand across the counter, "this boy will not stop talkin' 'bout you." Is that an edge of femininity I hear or just a slippery southern drawl?

"Oh, he's been talking about you, too," I reply. David smiles warmly.

"Just before you walked in," he reports, "I suggested we do the town some night."

"Anytime," I say. Before we can talk further, the phone rings and three customers converge. Waving goodbye, I leave a bag of sandwiches and steal another glance at David's appearance and demeanor. His preppy haircut, crisp white oxford shirt, and conservative red tie offer no clues. His other nonverbal behaviors—erect posture, confident stride, and firm handshake—say little more than "I'm the pharmacist." Still, there *is* something unique about his presence, something magnetic, but is it gayness? I'm not sure.

When Doug returns home that night, he asks excitedly if the meeting confirmed his suspicions. "I only had time to notice that David didn't swish, wear nail polish, or have a hoop dangling from his right ear," I tell him. "But I suppose that doesn't rule out anything, except him fitting the pop culture stereotypes."[1]

Cocking his head, Doug queries, "What does your gut tell you?"

I ponder this a moment. "My gut tells me I like him."

Though I've evaded his real question, Doug brightens and says, "I knew you would." With that, the subject of David's sexual orientation closes . . . until a few weeks later.

One Thursday afternoon in July, Doug phones me from work. "David wants us to go out with him and his roommate Chris."

"Chris*topher* or Chris*tine*?" I inquire.

"Christopher, I think."

"His *roommate*, huh?"

"That's what he said. They want to grab a few cocktails at Tracks."

I smile. "What do you know about Tracks?"

"I assume it's a bar," Doug answers, "or a club."

"It's a *gay* club," I clarify.

"Aaah, mystery solved."

"Still up for it?"

"We'll find out," Doug says. "I already agreed to go. Um, you're coming, right?"

"Absolutely. Watching you at Tracks *has* to be worth the price of admission." Setting down the phone, I wonder what the evening will bring.

Inside Tracks

Doug and I arrive first. Getting in line, he asks, "Ever been to one of these?"

"A dance club?" I quip. When Doug shoots me a look of you-know-what-I-mean, I answer, "No, I've never been to 'one of these.'"

"Me neither," he says, stating the obvious. From his restless posture, I surmise that Doug's anxious. I am too, frankly, but even more, I'm curious and excited.

"Feel like a kid at the entrance to Disney World?" I ask.

"No," Doug responds.

A couple of minutes later, a familiar figure turns the corner. "You made it!" David shouts to us, as if a bit surprised. As he approaches, his form-fitting T-shirt, faded Levi's, and industrial boots come into focus.

"Oh my," I remark. "That's quite a change from your pharmacy smock." I turn to David's companion. "I'm Lisa."

"Chris," he says, offering his hand.

Striking, I think, noting Chris's steel-blue eyes, coffee hair and mustache, and broad shoulders, then David's sun-kissed complexion and muscular build. A striking *couple*, I then think, applying an old category to an unfamiliar kind of case.

"Ready to go?" asks Chris.

With a glance toward each other, Doug and I say, "Ready."

Moving through the door, I first encounter a large posted warning. The sign says, "Tracks is run by gay people, for gay people. Enter only the open minded." I hope we qualify, I muse silently, my pulse quickening.

A young woman with ebony attire, hair, lips, and nails takes my five dollars and stamps my hand. I want to ask if she's been sitting shiva, but the pained expression of teen angst on her face keeps me quiet. As we venture inside, David says to Doug, "Take a good look at Lisa. She may be the only one here you'll know for sure is a woman."

"You don't say," replies my South Dakota farm boy, wiping his palms on his jeans.

"C'mon, Doug," beckons Chris, "let's get a round of drinks." They walk away, and Doug peers over his shoulder. I give a nod of encouragement as he disappears into the crowd.

When they've gone, David says in my ear, "I was nervous 'bout bringin' y'all here."

"Why is that?"

"Because I never told Doug I'm gay." Just then, a man built like a linebacker passes by, wearing a royal-blue cocktail gown and matching feather headdress. He—or she—must be 6'2" in those pumps.

Trying to refocus, I say, "I don't think there's much need for disclosure now."

He smiles, then asks, "Know when I decided that Doug was okay?" I shake my head. "When I first saw you. As you sashayed around the pharmacy in that little dress, chewin' on th' arm of your sunglasses, I said to myself, 'This girl just might be too cool for words.'"

I'm stunned by his impression. At last, I respond, "I'll try not to disappoint you."

Doug and Chris return from the bar, and I can't tell if Doug's smirk suggests, "I'm having a good time," or, "I'm trying not to freak out."

Next, David gives us a walking tour of the establishment. "Here we have the disco room," he points out as we file past small groups and pairs of males, some absorbed in their dance moves, some putting the moves on one another. My eyes hone in on two nipple nibblers.

Having never witnessed such an overtly sexual display between two men, I wait for a jolt of embarrassment or discomfort. But no such jolt, not even a twinge, comes. To my surprise, I don't pull back at all; instead, I take in this image with a child's curiosity. I feel like I'm fourteen again, watching a steamy scene from a movie I'm too young to watch; only here, the characters are both men. My body tingles with excitement, intrigue, and . . . what else? There *must* be something else. Something should feel unsettling, strange at least. But nothing does. How is that possible?

I look down and notice that David is holding my hand. Is he the reason I'm not afraid or uneasy? Somehow, I think I could follow him anywhere. Why is that? I hardly know David.

We come through a doorway, and our guide informs us, "This is the stripper room."

"The *what?*" I query, looking up to find a long-haired surfer dude in a silver Speedo using the bar as a runway. His tanned, ripped, shaved, and oiled body catches my eye, but my mind flashes back to a recent conversation with Doug.

As soon as he walks through the door to our apartment, I greet him with, "I chased a cockroach into the utility closet today, and I found something very interesting there."

"The utility closet?" Doug asks, not sure where I mean. I cross the room to open the sliding door that conceals the water heater. "Oh," he utters guiltily, "*that* utility closet."

Retrieving a *Playboy* magazine from its once-secret hiding spot, I snap, "I thought you were going to cancel your subscription."

"I told you I wouldn't *renew* my subscription."

"I can't believe you consume this objectifying trash," I scold, flinging the evidence at him.

"Look," Doug says. "it's no substitute for your beauty—"

"Oh, spare me!"

"But that magazine helped me through lonely nights when I was living in Des Moines."

"Well, you're not living in Des Moines now!"

"Don't overreact. It's my last issue anyway."

I stare down into my vodka tonic. Focus on the lime, I tell myself, focus on the lime.

"Girl," David assures me, "it's okay to look."

"Oh, I'm looking," I say, letting him see me take a peek. Away, Speedo Man, away!

"Let's head over," Chris suggests. "The show's about to start."

"The show?" Doug queries.

"You'll see," David says.

On the opposite side of the club, we enter a room with a stage in the middle. "I'll get another round," Chris offers. "You three stay put; we'll have the best view from here."

"Best view of what?" I ask.

"You'll see," David says again.

Within minutes, the room fills with people. As Chris returns, the lights lower, and Donna Summer's "Hot Stuff" begins thundering from the speakers. The spotlight comes on; curtains part. From backstage emerges a troupe of Las Vegas–style guys-as-girls with bigger-than-mall hair and slinky evening wear. Stepping, grooving, even backflipping, they work the crowd, allowing patrons to peck their lips, nuzzle their cleavage, and feel between their legs.

"Now, *Doug*," says Chris when a strutting Barbie takes front and center, "if you didn't know that was a guy, you'd be attracted, right?"

Before he can answer, (s)he leans over, permitting a view into her enormous bosom. "Those are gen-u-ine silicone," David informs. "She got 'em for Christmas last year." After draining my third cocktail, I concentrate on keeping my mouth closed.

Following the show, we stay for more drinking and dancing. By the time Tracks closes, I feel woozy and unstable. "I guess I haven't been out much lately," I reflect.

"How many did you have tonight?" asks Chris.

"I tried to limit myself to one per hour; I think I had five."

"You drank *five* vodka tonics?" queries David. When I nod, Chris and David smile. "I forgot to warn you 'bout how they pour liquor in gay bars," David says. With one hand he simulates a glass, with the other a bottle. "Vodka," he demonstrates, tipping the "bottle" for several imaginary glugs.

"Tonic," Chris adds, mimicking a light misting.

"I haven't been this drunk since moving to Florida," I tell them.

"Me neither," says Doug.

"Don't worry, kids," David assures, "you'll get used to it. In the meantime, you'd better ride home with us."

On the way to their car, David puts his arm around me and whispers, "Chris and I decided that you're not nearly as naïve as Doug is."

Considering my first encounters with same-sex slow dancing, male strippers, and transsexuals, I reply, "I'm not?"

"Oh, you're fiiine," he tells me. "Doug, however, needs a little more exposure."

I pat him on the back and say, "I have a feeling you'll provide it."

Grinning, he responds, "I have a feelin' you're right."

A Little More Exposure

As it turns out, both of us get "a little more exposure" in the summer and fall of 1994. Another weekend, David and Chris expand our repertoire by taking us to a gay country bar to play some pool. It is there that I first watch men watch Doug. While he lines up a shot, a group lining the bar scans his body, nodding and pointing. When Chris notices me noticing them noticing my boyfriend, he explains, "They're talking about his butt." The thought takes a little getting used to, maybe because women so seldom give men this kind of overt attention, and maybe because I'm used to men looking at *me.*

I smile, pleased that Doug can experience this side of the male gaze. A subject becomes object; perhaps he'll understand how women often feel in public: exposed, scrutinized, vulnerable.

The smile falls. With all eyes on him and other men, I feel myself shrinking, fading into the background. Am I *envious* of Doug? How strange!

But something else is going on. While I miss the validation of the male gaze, its absence feels liberating. I can move and roam. Hell, *I* can gaze—unashamed, unabated.

Liberation is not something I experience in all gay spaces. Our next stop that night is a biker bar, and from the moment I step inside, I sense male suspicion. From every corner of the dark room, narrowed pairs of eyes seem to ask, "What's *she* doing here?"

Maybe I'm just paranoid, I think. After all, I've never been inside a biker bar—gay or straight. It's a (sub)culture I know little about, save the "movie-of-the-week" perceptions linking it with hypermasculinity and violence. Don't make assumptions, I tell myself.

But then David and Chris envelop me protectively. As we head toward the jukebox, David softly explains, "They don't like women here."

What does *that* mean? I wonder. They don't like women occupying *this space?* They don't like women *at all?* Well, screw them!

Then I catch myself. Why am I so defensive? I shouldn't care about the social preferences of these leathered men.

But I do.

Given gay men's marginalization, I expected their communities to be nonsexist and nonexclusionary. I suppose that was unrealistic. Still, are they no better than straight men? Turning toward him, I want to ask David, "If they don't like women here, why bring me?"

But I don't.

David has shown me the warmth and guidance of an older brother. Maybe he's testing his "kid sister" to see if she's "mature" enough to handle all corners of his community, not just the softer, "straighter" ones. I know he thinks of me as—maybe even needs me to be—"straight but not narrow." However clichéd, the attribution is one I value and am determined to live up to, even if the process requires my confusion and discomfort, which it now does.

We stay for just one beer and one chorus of "It's Raining Men (Hallelujah)." Though relieved, I exit the bar wondering how "not narrow" I'll become.

Returned Unopened

That autumn, Doug and I see more of Tampa's gay culture than just the bars. In September, David takes us to *Jeffrey*, a play about a gay man who chooses celibacy because he so fears AIDS. In the Loft Theater production, Chris makes his acting debut as Steve, the handsome love interest who moves Jeffrey toward breaking his vow but then reveals he's HIV positive. For two hours, Doug, David, and I share many laughs, a few tears, and much pride that we know one of the stars. Afterward, David introduces us to Nathan, the stage manager.

"Nice to meet you," says the bone-thin man with hollow cheeks. When I take his frail hand in mine, it feels like it could break.

As Nathan shuffles away, I wonder what impact HIV has had on David and Chris. How many of their friends are sick? How many are gone? I turn to David and ask tentatively, "Are you conscious of AIDS every day?"

"Some times are harder than others," he responds. "I almost dread sendin' Christmas letters, for example. Each year, I have to cross several people off my list, and we always get a few cards returned unopened."

He looks away, and I feel the weight of his words. What must it feel like to flip through a stack of holiday greetings only to find a few of your own marked "return to sender"? What must it require to hold a black pen above your address book and draw a line through name after name? When will I hold that pen? Could David or Chris—no, it's a question I refuse to pose, even to myself.

In contrast to this encounter, most of the moments we share with David and Chris fall on the lighter side. When we inquire about gay life, the two patiently educate us about heterosexism, politics, and AIDS, but most of the time, they seem to prefer amusing us with humorous, animated tales and taking us on new adventures, such as a gay Halloween ball, for which Chris designs and sews our Medusa and caveman costumes.

Over time, Doug and I each grow closer to David. We remain fond of Chris as well, but we connect to him mainly through his partner. Together, Doug and I continue relating to them as a younger couple to an older, more seasoned one. Though David and Chris seem to enjoy our company, Doug and I talk sometimes about why they bother with a sheltered straight couple. Don't our wide eyes and silly questions grate on their nerves? Will they decide one day that we're not worth the effort? Surely that would end these travels. After all, our contact with this community happens only via David and Chris.

Come November, however, that begins to change.

Coming Out

On a cool night at the apartment, I stop typing when I hear the bolt click. "Hey," Doug says as he crosses the threshold. "Hungry? I could grill that chicken."

Saving the file for a class project, I say, "Great. I'll find some pasta or something."

We move into the kitchen, and he begins slathering on barbecue sauce while I inspect our supply of side dishes. "Talk to David much today?" I ask, holding up a box of instant potatoes au gratin and a package of Uncle Ben's for him to choose.

Nodding toward the potatoes, Doug answers, "I did, actually."

"What's he up to this evening? Maybe we could catch a movie."

"He has softball practice, I think."

"Hmm," I say, getting out a saucepan and mixing the dehydrated spuds and powdered cheese with milk and margarine. "Didn't know he was an athlete."

"Guess so. I told him if his team needed players, I'd be interested."

"What did David say?"

"He said, 'Before you sign on, I should tell you that it's a gay team in a gay league.'"

"A whole league? How'd you respond?"

"I said I didn't care."

"You did?" I question, not quite believing it. "Do other straight guys play?"

"Not many, but David said that each team can have two straight players."

"Huh, that's interesting. When would you start?"

"Early next year," he says, pulling a spatula from the utensil drawer. A smile must form on my lips. "What's *that* look for?" he asks. "You amazed I'm doing this?"

"A little," I admit. "I just can't imagine what your old fraternity buddies would say about playboy Doug Healy joining a gay softball league."

Heading for the grill, Doug laughs a bit and remarks, "I can't either."

I all but forget about softball until 9:30 one Tuesday evening in January. As Doug enters the apartment, I'm surprised to see him dressed in sweatpants, T-shirt, and baseball cap. "Thought you were working," I say.

"I tried out tonight."

"Oh my! How'd you do?"

Joining me on the sofa, Doug reports, "Played pretty well. When I came up to bat, David was catching, and the first two pitches I hit over the fence. Don't be too impressed—it was a Little League field. But David said to me, 'I'm glaaad you're my frieeen'.'" We laugh at his mimicking of our associate's drawl.

"Was it a good time?" I ask.

"Yeah, they seem like a fun group."

"Were there any other straight guys there?"

"I don't think so."

"Did you feel out of place?"

"No. I've always been at home on the field, so I was fine. Felt good to be out playing sports again. Besides, I knew they weren't going to come up and start grabbing me." He pauses. "Still, it seemed like people were checking me out, not only as a ballplayer but also as a person. When David introduced me, he said, 'This here's Doug. He's my intern, my *straight* intern.' But from the looks on some of their faces, I could tell that a few of them thought, 'Yeah, right. Closet case.'"

"Did that bother you?" I ask.

"Nah."

Does that bother *me?* I wonder, then quickly dismiss the thought. "So, you're staying with it?"

"Oh, yeah. Maybe you can come to a game. They start in February."

"I'll try, but you'll probably go alone most of the time."

"That's okay," he says.

David Holland and Doug Healy

A few weeks later, Doug debuts in Tampa's Gasparilla Softball Classic. My courses and teaching in full swing, I'm unable to attend. In fact, I don't make it to the field until March, but when I do, I meet several people who become key players in my life and my work.

"Thanks for coming," Doug says as we pull into the lot behind the Hyde Park field.

Reading the logo on his jersey, I ask, "What is 'the Cove' anyway?"

"A bar," he tells me. "We'll go there sometime." Doug grabs his glove and cleats from the back seat, and we walk toward the crowd of spectators. When he spots a group of his teammates gathered by the home stands, his pace quickens.

Meanwhile, a few notice us and begin approaching. "Hey Douuug," greets a blue-eyed blond built like a fullback.

"Al Steel," Doug says, "this is my fiancée, Lisa." I grasp his large, strong hand.

"Oh my gosh," banters a fit, muscular man with short dark hair, "we thought she didn't exist!" He gives Doug a half embrace while saying to me, "I'm Tim Mahn."

"Our coach," Doug adds.

"And I'm just a front," I play along, then wonder if I should have.

"Please," a broad-chested guy with a northeastern accent warns, "don't give Tim any ideas. My name's Gordon Bernstein."

Pointing to the well-defined six-footer next to him, Gordon says, "This is Jack."

Tim's partner, Doug mouths. I give Jack a nod.

A pale, gaunt man moves toward me. "I'm Colin," he lets me know before being overcome by a fierce coughing spell.

Then I'm greeted by another man too thin for his height and frame. "Normally I'd remove my cap," he tells me, pulling it back a little. "But chemo hair is not so attractive."

"Michael has Kaposi's sarcoma on his lungs," Doug later explains.

I offer my right hand, but he takes my left. "Fabulous," Michael says of my new engagement ring. "I wish you a happy marriage." I smile, wondering what his future holds.

"We better get started," Tim says.

As the Cove begins its warm-up routine, I walk to the visitors' stands and sit on the second bleacher. Several men and a couple of women make eye contact and say hello. Feeling a little self-conscious amid so many strangers, I don't strike up any conversations. Instead, I concentrate on the game in progress, democratically clapping for both teams.

After the inning's last out, I look over and see Doug, David, Tim, Gordon, Al, and several other men in gray Cove shirts congregated beneath a tree. They're all talking boisterously and laughing between comments. I can't make out what they're saying, but I notice something about Doug's demeanor. Grinning widely, he looks . . . *comfortable,* like he did with his college drinking buddies. And happy. In this moment, I think, Doug looks happier than I've seen him since he moved to Florida last summer. Suddenly, I understand his desire—his *need* even—to play for the Cove. Perhaps it's not exactly the way he experienced it in his childhood baseball league or in fraternity flag football, but it *is* male companionship, something he's obviously been missing.

Though I enjoy myself that Sunday, my studies consume the spring's remaining weekends. In May, the league votes to continue playing in the summer, but I make it to the field just one more time.

During the interim between summer play and fall preseason practice, we see David a few times but hear nothing from Doug's other teammates . . . until one August afternoon.

The phone startles me out of a nap. "Hello?" I say groggily.

"Is this Lisa?" asks a male voice I don't recognize.

"Yeah, who's this?"

"Brandon Nolan. I just joined the Cove, and I've been seeing Tim Mahn, if that helps you place me."

What happened to Jack? I wonder but don't ask.

"I'm planning a birthday party for Tim," he says. "I hope you and Doug can make it."

Pleasantly surprised by the invitation, I ask, "When is it?"

"This Friday, seven o'clock, at the Red Pepper."

Glancing at my daily planner, I note that Friday night is blank. "See you there, Brandon."

"Great! I look forward to getting acquainted; Tim talks of you both all the time. Bye!"

Unsure I heard right, I hold the phone to my ear for several more seconds. Did Brandon say that Tim talks of us both *all the time*? That's interesting . . . and unexpected. He knows Doug from softball, but Tim's hardly familiar with me. I wonder what he says.

That Friday, Doug and I are excited, both to learn more about Tim's impressions of us and to expand our connections with other Cove players. But when we enter the Red Pepper, I survey the crowd and recognize only Tim. "Where are your teammates?" I whisper.

"I thought they'd be here," Doug replies.

A man in his mid-twenties who could model for *GQ* crosses the room. "Hi, Doug," he says, "thanks for coming. And Lisa, I saw you once at the field, but we've never been introduced. I'm Brandon. Let me show you to your table." When he doesn't seat us with Tim, I begin to worry about fitting in. But as soon as our host says, "This is Doug and Lisa," we get nodding and a round of "Aah!" from five men and a woman. We seem to have acquired a reputation.

"Glad you're in the league," says a balding man to Doug.

Looking at me, his companion adds, "Glad you *let* him be in the league." He then pours me a glass of champagne.

After toasting Tim's twenty-fifth, Brandon comes over and sits next to me. "Tim said you're in graduate school. Tell me about your program."

Brandon listens attentively as I talk about my classes and research. Trying not to bore my host, I keep it short and sweet, but then he asks, "What's it like, dealing with college students?" I see others listening as well, so I tentatively offer a teaching tale.

"Mostly wonderful," I tell them, "with a few notable exceptions. Last semester I had a Murphy's Law student. The night before his first speech, his grandmother died; on the way to the next one, he wrecked his Camaro; the morning of the final presentation, a dog mauled him. Of course, he could provide no documentation that any of these events actually occurred." They laugh.

"In four years of college," recalls the man across from me, "I lost eleven grandparents."

It continues around the table, each trying to outdo the last person's most egregious school excuse. "What about you, Miss Thang?" someone asks when it's my turn.

I begin the story of how the wife of my high school dean of students caught me sunbathing—topless—during school hours. Their laughter sends an energy rushing through my body. As I talk on, I become more animated, more performative, more *me*, than I've been in some time. "What could I do?" I pose. "I knew I was—"

Right there, midsentence, something clicks.

Looking to my right, I discover that Doug's no longer there. Where did he go? And when? My fiancé left, and I didn't even notice. I scan the room, finding him over by Tim. Doug and I make eye contact, and he raises his glass to me.

"Well, don't leave us hanging," Brandon goads. "You knew you were *what?*"

Members of the 1995 Cove softball team

GREG WILLIS

"I knew I was *busted*," I say, "pun intended." For this, I get a round of applause.

What just happened? Until this moment, our gay connections have seemed more Doug's than mine. Doug and David, after all, share professional knowledge and experience. When together, they tend to talk shop, which leaves me feeling peripheral. Moreover, Doug and his teammates meet twice a week for softball, a sport I've played just a few times. Though I've tried to learn the pharmacy and softball lingoes, I've still felt somewhat out of the loop. Tonight, however, I find myself not needing

Doug to bring me inside. Could this group, I wonder, become my friends—our friends—as much as my partner's?

Something else occurs to me. Here we are, carousing and laughing with a roomful of people—mostly gay, mostly strangers—without David or Chris to mediate. In other words, they brought us into a conversation; perhaps it's now becoming ours as well.

During the months that follow, I participate in the conversation in new and unexpected ways. That autumn, I have a course on qualitative methods. When my intended project falls through, I'm left without a fieldwork site. In that vacuum, it occurs to me that this group could be not only socially engaging but also ethnographically interesting.

3

Tales from the (Softball) Field

From Life to Project (and Back Again)

A few weeks after Tim's party, the fall semester begins. Since January, I've been writing about the connections between body image, eating, and identity. During the first month of my qualitative methods course, I investigate how these relationships are performed in public life. Observing how people interact with each other and with food, I take field notes at a grocery store and some restaurants, but nothing suits my ethnographic tastes. Frustrated, I call Carolyn Ellis, the course professor and a member of my doctoral committee.

"Are you sure you want to write another paper about eating?" she asks.

Gripping the phone tightly, I admit, "No."

"What else could you study?"

"I'm not sure," I reply. "That's the problem."

"Can you give me a general goal?"

"I'd like to study communication and relationships ethnographically."

"That sounds good," Carolyn affirms. "What settings come to mind?"

"A family dinner table?" I offer hesitantly.

"Hmm," she responds. "What about something totally unrelated to food? Where do you go after class or on the weekends?"

After several minutes of suggesting and rejecting site after site, group after group, Carolyn asks, "Can you think of *anything* else?"

I say nothing; she says nothing.

Suddenly, a light goes on. "Doug plays on a gay softball team."

38

A slight pause, then, "He what?"

"He's the only straight guy on his team; in fact, the whole league is for gay men and lesbians."

"That's, um, rather unique," Carolyn says. "Is there a project in it?"

"Maybe I could learn more about . . . hidden identity. No, how about gay men's friendships?"

"Could be intriguing. Are they playing together this fall?"

"I think they're starting Sunday."

"Before then," Carolyn instructs, "think about some specific issues you'd like to investigate, how, and for what reasons. Some people will question your position in a community of gay men and ask what a straight woman can bring to the study of gay male friendship. Keep your options open, and most of all, trust your instincts."

As I hang up the phone, I feel both relieved and apprehensive: relieved that I may have escaped class-project limbo, apprehensive about the concerns Carolyn raised. She's right, I think; I can't just show up and start taking notes.

I begin contemplating how to secure the team's permission to conduct a participant observation. Should I talk to David? I know him the best. Or Tim? He is the coach. I wonder who's more likely to be receptive. What will either think of a straight woman wanting to study gay softball players? It does sound a little strange. How will I frame my interest in the group? Saying "The food thing didn't pan out" isn't much of a pitch. What *is* my interest? Am I only seeking the completion of a project? What's in it *for them?* Could my study harm our relationships?

But just when fear and concern threaten to overwhelm me, something indefinably exciting begins to stir.

The phone rings, Doug calling from work to say that Brandon and Tim have invited us to a benefit concert tomorrow. I hardly can believe my luck—a face-to-face meeting I didn't have to contrive. My choice is made; I'll approach Tim.

As soon as I hear Doug's car, I rush out to greet him. But the numb expression on his face tells me his news is more pressing than mine. "You remember Michael?" he asks.

"Your teammate?"

He nods. "David called me just before I left Walgreens." With quiet tenderness, Doug says, "Michael passed away." I gasp.

Not sure how to mourn him, we embrace. He and Doug played only one season together—Michael's sickest season. I'd met him a couple of times. He was sweet, always a gentleman, but I can't say I really knew him. Doug fills me in with the few details he has: Michael's family was with him, and he seemed at peace, but he was just twenty-nine.

"I didn't know he was that ill," I remark.

Sighing, Doug changes the subject, "So what's your news?"

"Given the circumstances, it seems inappropriate—"

"Why? Is it good news? I could use some."

I muster a little excitement and tell him about the study. He kisses my cheek and says, "I'm happy you've settled on a project. It should be really interesting." Much later, however, Doug admits having some initial worry that I would "take over" this area of his life and that my study could negatively affect my, his, and our relationships with his teammates, especially if they didn't like what I wrote.

Thinking Doug is firmly in my corner, I begin preparing for tomorrow. How should I raise the issue with Tim? I mentally rehearse both a detailed explanation that anticipates his questions about what I'm seeking and a brief one that solicits his responses. After much consideration, I decide to wait for an opening. Then, as casually as possible, I'll say, "Tim, I'm interested in learning about gay men's friendships, and I'd like to study the team." I practice this line over and over, stressing different words each time.

That night, I dream it's Michael who presents me to the team. "She needs you," he tells the Cove men, "and while you don't know it yet, you need her too." With that, Michael dons his cap over a full head of hair. He then strides into the outfield and disappears.

I awaken long before the alarm goes off. Unable to focus on school-work, I spend the day scouring the kitchen and the tile floors. At last, 7:00 P.M. comes.

Getting In

Doug takes the driver's seat of my Nissan 240. The occasional grind of his awkward shifting makes me uneasy, but his boyish grin keeps me from criticizing. We follow Brandon's pickup across the Gandy Bridge, down to Madeira Beach, and into a parking lot.

"Love the sundress!" Tim praises as I walk around the car. He then whispers playfully, "Are you wearing a bra?"

"Do I need one?" I ask, half returning his flirtation, half expressing self-consciousness.

"Do you *have* one?" Tim asks.

"In the back seat," I admit, and we both laugh.

The damp air sits heavy and still as I inhale scents of salt water and smoked oysters. We move swiftly toward the waterfront pub. Its purposely weathered exterior wood, entrance path covered with sand, and mariner décor are so very Florida.

Doug walks with Brandon, whose closely cropped hair draws attention to large, long-lashed eyes, proud cheek- and jawbones, and the perfect teeth of an orthodontist's poster child.

A couple of paces behind, Tim and I stroll in silence as I work up my courage. He doesn't know me that well, I remind myself, and some of the players don't know me at all. Is this asking too much? Will Tim question why a straight woman wants to study a gay softball team? Do I have a reasonable answer?

When we reach the line, Doug turns around and queries, "Did you ask him yet?"

With a narrowed gaze, I tell him, "Not yet." So much for a graceful approach.

"Ask me what?" Tim probes.

"You're coaching again this season, right?"

"You want to play?"

"No . . . but I'd like to write about the team." Tim's haunting, mossy-green eyes widen. "In my communication program, the area I'm focusing on is personal relationships. I want to learn more about gay male friendship, and I'm hoping you'll help convince the team to let me conduct a study."

Did that sound convincing? Stupid? Will he agree? If he says no, both of us will be uncomfortable, and I'll need to come up with yet another project. My heart pounds.

"You'd just hang out at the games?" he asks.

"Pretty much; pose some questions, take some notes."

"Fine with me. I'll ask the rest of the guys tomorrow. You coming?"

"Count on it," I say, not quite believing how easily he consented. Tim takes my hand. As we sway to the thumping music coming from the bar, I anticipate an enjoyable evening, which it turns out to be, except for a single—but unforgettable—moment.

We make our way inside, ascend the stairs to the deck, and take a table overlooking the bay. A waitress in short cutoff jeans brings us drinks, fried gator tail, and jalapeño poppers.

Nearby, throngs of UF and FSU fans stake their claims to Florida's football throne. While I sip my cheap tequila margarita, their drunken banter escalates. Suddenly, something slices through the commotion.

"Faggot!" a man shouts before barking out several guffaws. "Your quarterback is a *faggot!"*

I lick the salt from my lips and swallow hard. The hairs on my neck stand on end as I dig my fingernails into my palms. Do I say something to the besotted oaf? Given the context—the bar setting, the crowd of inebriated strangers—what would I say? And our companions, what do *they* want? I feel like, I don't know, apologizing. I glance across the table. That slight smile on Brandon's face seems to cloak something. But what? Anger? Pain? Fear? He says nothing. I study Tim carefully as he rolls his eyes. What do we do, Tim? Confront him? Discuss it privately? Let it go? I'm taking my cues from you. A moment later, Tim resumes talking about his accounting program.

I try to move on but can't. *Faggot, faggot, faggot*—it won't stop echoing in my head. Slowly, I take in the word, chew on it, swallow it, and feel it move downward. For many years, I've consumed that term at the tables of insult and "humor." How many times did I absorb it without notice? How many times did I not hear it, not *feel* it, because it didn't hurt me or anyone I knew (or *knew* I knew)? Still, I met David over a year ago; since then, surely I've heard such disparaging words on many occasions. Why the outrage now? Perhaps I needed to hear it in the presence of gay men. Tim and Brandon—how their faces, their voices, redefined my experience of this term! For my whole life, "faggot" has gone down like water. Never again. From this night, it will digest like a piece of glass.

In spite of my feelings, I allow the incident to pass without comment. Why? I tell myself I'm just following my companions' leads, but what would they say about it anyway? Wasn't it my place to note, "What a jerk," or to ask, "How does that feel?" How else can I know? How will anything change if everyone sits, as I just have, in complicit silence?

I'm exhausted when we get home, but I head immediately for the computer to write my first field notes. After describing the setting and my research proposal, I spend a long time recounting the incident on the deck. I'm not sure it's relevant to the topic of gay male friendship, but the words come quickly, furiously.

Given tonight's impact on me, I crawl into bed wondering how prepared I am to undertake this project. What's around the next corner? More ignorance, more pain? Do I have the capacity to understand and respond to what I see, hear, and feel? How will I change—emotionally, politically, ethically? To gain the knowledge I need to do this project well, what comforts, what privileges, must I concede? The last time I look at the clock, it's 4:13 A.M. I'll be at the field in just a few hours, I drift off thinking, just a few hours.

Opening Day

I park my car in the street between the Kash N' Karry grocery and the field. Gathering my pen, notepad, and tape recorder, I sense a slight queasiness in my stomach. Doug works every other weekend, and this Sunday I'm here alone for the first time. Get a grip, I tell myself. If I'm going to understand these men's experiences and feelings, I need to establish and deepen relationships with them on my own. But how?

My role could be pragmatic, I guess, keeping stats or something. It also could be more personal. I don't see many women around; perhaps some of these men would like more female companionship (perhaps not!). Until I know what they need, I'll just remain open and listen well. Plunge in, Lisa, for today begins a new season.

The Cove assembles at the parking lot's edge. Most of the old players I recognize. I know David and Tim, of course, and the mid-thirties burly guy with lots of chest hair is Al. Now who has the round glasses and receding hairline? Gordon, that's right. Tim's old boyfriend Jack should be here too, but I don't see him. "Hey, coach," I call, "where's J—"

Anticipating my question, he says, "Wouldn't play with me after The Breakup." Note to self: romance and softball—a volatile mix.

This place, however, seems anything but volatile. A large rainbow flag flaps against the tall fence behind home plate. Red, orange, yellow, green, blue, and violet balloons held captive by metallic ribbons float gently above the stands, and streams of crepe paper flowers line the bleachers, where a sax, flute, and trumpet begin to play. I can't recall the name of the tune, but I think it's from *Cabaret*.

As I take in the surroundings, Tim calls the team together. "Ready?" he whispers.

Focusing on the familiar faces, I say, "Yes."

"Guys," Tim begins, "most of you know Lisa."

"Hi, Lisa!" several of them say.

Tim gets right to it. "She wants to study the team."

Ooh boy, I think, here we go.

"*Study us?*" Gordon repeats. "For what, a class?" When I nod, he asks, "So . . . what do you wanna know?" The big question.

"Well, um, okay." I clear my throat. "I'm a Ph.D. student in the communication department at USF. The team interests me from a relationship perspective." As soon as that leaves my lips, I wish I'd said something less pretentious than "relationship perspective."

"Because we're gay?" queries Gordon, cocking his head.

"Partially. I'd like to learn more about how you build friendships and what role the Suncoast league plays in that process." Silence. "Any other questions?" No one speaks. "Objections?" They shrug and smile. "Uh, thanks! I—"

"Coaches," a league officer calls into a microphone, "gather up your teams!"

David grabs my arm and insists that I stand with the players during opening ceremonies. "C'mon, girl," he drawls, "you can be our mascot."

Eight teams assemble on the infield as the officer again commands attention. "Ladies and gentlemen," he says, his voice garbled by the crackle of static, "welcome to another season of Suncoast Softball!" This is met with loud clapping and cheering.

When the crowd quiets, the man continues in a subdued tone. "Today, we are without a friend." The officer pauses, and several men and women remove their caps. "As many of you know, Michael died last week, and while we are deeply saddened by his passing, we are honored to have his mother, sister, baby niece, and brother in attendance today." Applause breaks out. "In our first game, Jake will play in his brother's honor. The red jersey he wears belonged to Michael." More applause.

"We got Wendy playin' too!" David shouts. "Fresh out of the delivery room!"

The announcer smiles. "Michael's sister Wendy, I'm told, will be joining the Cove as well." The crowd hoots and claps. "And now," he booms, "it is my pleasure to introduce the Rainbow Players. They'll open with 'I Am What I Am,' one of Michael's favorites." Throughout the minor-key rendition, heads bow, tears flow, and mourners embrace.

Standing here, I feel shamefully voyeuristic and terribly out of place. Their loss, their grief, is not mine. Part of me wants to grasp their sorrow, to make it my own. How else can I understand and write about their lives? But part of me wants to run from their sorrow, to maintain an "objective" distance. How else can I protect myself from this pain?

As the band finishes, David grasps Jake's shoulders, saying, "I'm so sorry," while Tim hugs Wendy. Al, meanwhile, pats the siblings' backs, saying something in Wendy's ear. When Gordon walks up, he shakes the sister's hand, then the brother's, with both of his.

Moments later, the Rainbow Players begin the national anthem. A few softly sing; the rest of us stand silent. The crowd roars during "the home of the brave," and Jake takes the mound for the first pitch. When the ball pops into the catcher's mitt, the crowd roars again.

The Cove hauls its equipment into the visitors' dugout. While Tim sets down the bats, Brandon playfully gropes his behind. Meanwhile, the band breaks into a spirited two-part "Macho Man."

"Batter up!" yells the plate umpire.

The opposing players, sponsored by a bar called Rascals, assume their positions while Al takes a few practice swings. Before stepping up, our lead batter runs his hand over the thick, coarse hair that would be curly if longer. Sitting next to me, David whistles at Al, who shakes his butt. At this, David yells, "Bullwhip!" I laugh with him, though I have no idea what his phrase signifies. I figure it's from a secret gay code I will learn to crack.

Their pitcher stares at the plate, then arcs one high and outside. Al's sapphire eyes narrow, estimating the pitch's worth; he wisely lets it go. Arm and back muscles tensing, Al grounds the second toss. The short-stop shuffles over and scoops it up. This will be close. "Dig, dig, dig!" David yells as Al pumps toward first. The ball nearing the baseman's glove, Al dives over the bag amid a cloud of dirt. He gags and spits.

"Safe!" we yell from our bench.

"Out!" they yell from Rascals'.

"Safe!" decides Blue, and we applaud his Cove-favorable call.

"That ump is *cute!*" I say to David, enjoying how we can compare notes on men.

"Isn't he?" David agrees. "He started callin' games for us 'bout three years ago. All our umps are straight, but at the time, this one didn't know our league was gay."

"How long before he figured it out?"

"*Too long.* You've seen how nellie some of us are."

"Was he cool about it?"

"Nooo!" David exclaims. "In fact, he walked right off the field."

"Hmm. But he came back."

"I guess he figured out that this is the nicest, theeee *live*liest, and the ab-so-lute funniest group of jocks and not-so-jocks ever to set foot on a softball field. So he stayed on, and since then, we've had no more umpire problems."

When Jake steps into the batter's box, fans of both teams applaud. He adjusts his lid, tucking in auburn bangs, then strokes the milky skin at the base of his neck; it's already turning a vibrant pink. The pitcher releases, and Jake shifts his weight onto his right leg. Swinging through, he launches the ball up, up, up and over the high fence in right field for a double. That was for you, Michael.

Tight, gray cotton shorts accent Tim's muscular legs and trim waist as he strides to the plate. After passing on two bad pitches, he cranks one over the shortstop's head. Tim reaches second with ease, batting in both Al and Jake.

As the next batter steps up, our bench chants, "Gor*don,* Gor*don,* Gor-*don!*" In response, he peers over the sunglasses shielding his baby-blue eyes and shakes his head. The Cove player readies himself. He looks at a pitch.

"Steee-rike!" calls the ump.

Second chance. Gordon's ready. He swings—plink! "Foul!"

Gordon adjusts. Here comes the third toss; it's over the plate. Another swing, and yes—contact! "Damn!" Gordon curses as the ball again drops outside the left-field line.

"Straighten it out," I encourage. But then Gordon jogs toward the bench. "What's he doing?" I ask David.

"In this league, sugar, a foul ball's your third strike."

"Harsh," I remark.

Wendy grabs her bat, and the crowd perks up. She curtsies and pulls off her cap, releasing wild, flaming-red tresses. Wendy steps up, swings, and misses—*big*—then pauses a moment to laugh at herself. "C'mon, darlin'," Al calls, "after givin' birth, softball's a walk in the park."

"You aren't kidding," she responds, changing her stance. On the following pitch, Wendy slugs a perfect single up the middle, sending Tim home. The rally ends when the next two batters make outs, but the Cove takes the field up 3-0.

As our players gather their gloves, a weathered, silver-haired man approaches. "Hi, huuuney," he says, pushing large square glasses up the bridge of his nose. "I'm Barry, bar manager of the Cove."

"I'm Lisa," I tell him. "My fiancé plays for your team."

"Your fian—oh, the straight boy! He's haaandsome." Barry then gives a scratchy, four-pack-a-day yell, "Three uuuuup!"

Teammates respond together, "Three down!"

Unsatisfied, Barry screeches, "Three uuuuuuuuuuuuuuuuuuuup!"

The players burst out laughing, each calling, "Three down!" at a different time.

"Pa*thetic*!" scolds Barry. He offers me a giant Tums bottle filled with a slightly pink liquid.

"What's that?" I ask.

"Mostly vodka, with a splash of Gatorade for the athletic supporter."

"Why a Tums jar?"

"'Cause the Blue Nazis told me I couldn't bring liquor containers to the field. Besides, I figure its previous contents might coat my stomach a bit."

"I'll pass for now."

At the top of the last inning, it's fifteen-all with Al leading off. When David again calls, "Bullwhip!" the batter cracks a smile.

"What does that mean?" I venture.

"I dunno," David answers, innocently batting his eyes. "I just like to see him giggle." Hmm, is "bullwhip" not part of "the code," or is my gay mentor not telling me something?

With his trademark wood-chopping swing, Al sends one over the second baseman's head for a double. Then, after waiting for his pitch, Jake powers one deep into left center. The Cove dugout rises as the ball rolls into the fence. Despite his less-than-lightning speed, Al should make it home, but will Jake? Yes! Five batters later, we're up 21-15 with a half inning to go.

Top of their order steps up. Tim's first pitch falls a foot behind the plate; Blue calls it deep. Strain evident on his forehead, our coach drops the next two short. With a 3-0 count, the batter judiciously holds back. The fourth pitch is right on—strike one. Tim then offers a perfect arc. Strike tw—no, it nicks the corner of the plate. Ball four.

The second batter moves inside the box. Liking the first toss, he fires a shot up the middle. On impulse, Tim raises his left arm in time, and the ball rips into his glove. He shakes out the sting and says, "One out."

Batter three tries to work Tim for another walk, but the Cove pitcher answers with two textbook tosses. At this count, both know the batter must swing. Strategically, Tim pitches him outside. Our opponent reaches and pops up to short. Two down.

But here comes their big gun, just who Rascals need to start a two-out rally. Offering no "meat," Tim sends one high, ball one. The next pitch has little arc—exactly what a power hitter wants. Swinging through, the batter whacks it up the left field line. Gordon takes off but won't get there in time. The ball drops. "Foul!" calls the ump. Whew, strike one.

Thinking it outside, the Rascal looks at the next one. "Steee-rike!" rules Blue. Yes! Two on him.

Tim again pitches him high, but the batter takes it anyway. He knocks it deep into left, sending Gordon back, back. Barry and I gasp. Striding all the way, our fielder turns to gauge it. His arm at full extension, Gordon reaches out, then collides with the fence. "Holy Mary!" exclaims Barry. "Is he all right?" Gordon turns, pulling the ball from his glove.

"Game!" shouts the plate ump as we stand to cheer. After shaking hands with Rascals, the Cove clears the dugout for the next team. Unsure what to do, I'm relieved when David suggests lunch.

We buy pasta salad and bagels at Kash N' Karry, then return to the field and climb onto the back of a shaded pickup. Before long, Tim and Gordon join our picnic. Immediately, Gordon asks, "So Lisa, why are you so interested in gay men?" I can't tell if his tone is one of curiosity or skepticism.

"I'm interested in all kinds of *relationships*," I tell him. "But I must admit, I do find myself drawn to gay men." Why is that? I wonder.

"I'm drawn to women," Tim shares.

"As in *attracted* to women?" I ask.

He smiles. "I'm attracted to some women. In fact, I was engaged a couple of years ago. Of course, I eventually told her I was gay. She wanted to stay together, to try and make it work, but I knew it wouldn't."

"I've never been engaged," Gordon offers, "but I've dated women, even since moving here from Philadelphia to *escape* the straight life. Romantically, women were easier for me to approach and relate to than were men. But after a while, I thought, 'This is ridiculous; this is *not* why you came to Tampa.' So I really tried to put a stop to that."

"Many believe that humans are naturally bisexual," I toss out. "Do any of you agree?"

"Not me, sugar," insists David. "I have tried—yes, it was *years ago*—but I have *tried* havin' sex with women. The day I gave up all that was the happiest day of my life, so please don't take it personally when I say that *I am not one bit bisexual.*"

"Not even toward *me*?" I tease.

"Oh giiirl, you are as cute as cute can be—for a *fish.*"

This is a term that I have heard used only by gay men. Women (especially straight women) in gay male circles also are called "fag hags," "fruit flies," and "faggotinas." Of these, "fag hag" is the most popular. According to the stereotypes Robert Rodi articulates in his novel *Fag Hag*, straight women who befriend gay men "aren't, or don't consider themselves attractive to heterosexual men, so they cultivate friendships with gay men, because gay men aren't threatening to them. If there's no possibility of romance, there's no possibility of rejection, either."[1] As a woman who "mothers" gay men by exchanging emotional support for the male affirmation she so craves, the fag hag lives a sad existence.[2] Describing such a woman, Rodi writes:

> She pressed herself, all hundred and seventy-odd pounds, through crowds of taut, muscular young men and, through sheer flamboyance, attracted the attention of a few of them. And as she talked to them, using every ounce of feminine wile and wit at her disposal, they laughed in delight and flattered her and sometimes even kissed her, but never, never once, not even for a moment, did they stop looking over her shoulder for something better.

All told, the fag hag is little more than "an amusing diversion," "pathetic," a "figure of fun," a "silly indulgence, of no importance—not beneath notice, but not much above it, either."[3] Curiously, as Nardi indicates, "no equivalent phrase exists for friendship between straight men and lesbians, straight men and gay men, or lesbians and straight men."[4]

Some women wear (and some gay men bestow) the label fag hag as an ironic badge of honor. The term "fish," however, is not one I've heard reclaimed in this way. In his short story "One of Us," William J. Mann offers this story and interpretation:

> "*Tish*," one friend in D.C. had said, scrunching up his face. What he was doing, really, was affirming that he could finally, after many years of secrecy, proclaim his sexual attraction to other men in public. . . . [T]he real objects of his scorn were the straight men who'd oppressed him into toeing the line. But instead of bashing the straight boys, many gay men fall into the age-old sexist trap of using women as a means for men's ends."[5]

"*Fish?*" I say to David, giving him a swat. "Don't comment on where you don't go."

"I'm just fuckin' with ya."

"You are *not*, and that's why you should withhold judgment."

"Agreed," he says. "But, Lisa, not all gay people are comfortable with the idea of bisexuality. Lot of folks use it as a steppin'-stone."

"How so?"

"Sayin' they're bisexual lets 'em act homosexual without havin' to stand with—and up for—our community."

Along these lines, Chris Shyer writes in *Not Like Other Boys*, "Bisexualism we took as a joke. Many homosexuals dip their toes into the murky waters of public opinion by claiming to be bi. It sounds less unacceptable . . . not as final."[6]

While David's and Chris Shyer's opinions may stem from experience (i.e., they know people—or *are* people—who began their coming out by calling themselves bi instead of gay), their comments reflect a binary construction of homo- and heterosexuality. Later, I will problematize the move to shore up—rather than deconstruct—these categories.

"But what is sexuality anyway?" I query.

Is it a set of genetically programmed impulses and/or environmental influences? A collection of fantasies, sensations, pleasures, and/or behaviors? A lifestyle? An "orientation"? A "preference"? A cultural affiliation? A political one? Is it an identity? Conferred by others? Adopted by oneself? Is it, as Foucault suggests, culturally and historically specific discourses that serve the interests of those in power?[7] A "continuum" of desires ranging from exclusively same sex to exclusively opposite sex?[8] A two-dimensional index that treats one's level of attraction to men separately from one's level of attraction to women?[9] Is there some truth in each of these?

The range of possibilities elucidates the difficulty in communicating about—and across—sexual orientation and identity. So how would a scientific determinist trying to map "straight" and "gay" genetic codes talk to a radical social constructivist critiquing "compulsory heterosexuality"?[10] Perhaps one way would be to sit them down, over bagels and pasta salad, and invite them to share stories.

"What is sexuality?" David repeats. "Better let me think on that one."

After lunch, we stroll over to the chain-link fence. Hanging from it is a framed picture of Michael. His smiling face, free of the ravages of AIDS, must have been photographed some months ago. Next to this, petals of white memorial flowers waft gently in the breeze. I inhale deeply, savoring the carnation perfume and wondering how my life will change during this fall season, a season born of loss but filled with the promise of eight glorious Florida Sundays.

I bid the team goodbye and return to my car. The thirty-minute drive passes quickly as I speak everything I can remember into my microcassette recorder. At home, I use this tape and jottings taken during the game to compose field notes.

Writing through my impressions of the conversation on sexuality with David, Tim, and Gordon, I note how each had dated and had sexual experiences with women, with responses ranging from discontent (David) to a level of comfort not yet found with men (Gordon). My own theory of sexuality, moreover, takes on a "both, and" quality. It occurs to me *both* that, from an early age, I have desired males in a more sexualized way than I have desired females *and* that these desires have been shaped and constrained by a heterosexist culture.

Then I write of Michael. The photograph of him won't leave my mind. Whose face will be the next to occupy that frame? Will it be one of the men I sat with today, sharing a lunch of bagels and pasta salad? "I'm afraid of AIDS," I type into my field notes, "afraid of others' suffering, afraid of being left behind."

In spite of this fear, I feel driven to know these men, to understand not only their friendships but also the larger context of their lives and struggles. I turn off my computer, wondering what more I will learn from them and who I will become.

Spinning Straw into Gold

The following Saturday, Tim and Brandon come to our place for a bar-becue. Doug and Tim head outside to fire up the grill, leaving Brandon and me to oversee the kitchen. Adding carrots to the steamer, I request, "Tell me how you met Tim."

Brandon smiles. "Last year, I went to a club with my old lover. He stayed by the dance floor while I went for beers." Blushing a little, Brandon says, "I noticed Tim right away: nice features, really attractive—even for a bartender." His voice intensifies. "When I tried to pay, Tim waved his hand, refusing to take my money. We exchanged glances, and I returned to my boyfriend. Later, I made sure I went for the second round as well. Of course, I ordered from Tim. And again, he waved his hand, not letting me pay."

The themes in Brandon's story are remarkably ordinary: an existing partnership, an intriguing stranger, a coy flirtation. I can imagine any of my girlfriends telling a similar tale. But there's nothing ordinary about the sparkle in his eyes; you'd think Brandon was pitching a Hollywood screenplay.

"Several weeks ago," he continues, "I went to a different club. And there again was Tim, handsome as ever, behind the bar. I approached. This time, I ordered one beer and handed him ten dollars. When Tim came over with change, I waved my hand, just as he had. Suddenly, Tim recognized me. After all those months! 'Just *one* beer?' he asked, want-ing to know if I was alone. 'Just one,' I told him. 'For now.'"

"You're happy with him," I observe.

"Never been happier," says Brandon. "And what about you? How did Doug come into your life?"

With that, I take my turn spinning straw into gold.

We could become close, I think, as Brandon and I stand here sharing, giggling, and tending the vegetables, *really close.*

Managing Identities

Tuesday brings softball practice. As Doug drives us to the field, hum-ming along with the radio, I test my tape recorder, double-check the bat-teries in my camera, and make sure I have three working pens. Eyeing me, Doug asks, "You nervous or something?"

"Excited," I reply as Tim's Jeep and Al's car come into view.

"Twenty minutes early," Doug remarks. "Just for you, dear."

Smiling, I settle into the dugout while Al, Tim, and Doug begin warming up. I inhale, ready to take in new knowledge. But something soon spoils the practice parade.

Plop, plop, plop, the droplets burst against the wooden roof. It escalates into drizzle, then a low-pressure shower. Within minutes, it's coming down in sheets. The guys sprint for cover.

We huddle in the cement-block-and-fencing shelter. The players shake water from their hair and wipe muddy feet on the still-hard ground next to the bench. When the pitcher's mound becomes an island, Tim says, "I think the others will assume it's a rain-out."

"Anyone for a drink?" I ask, trying to salvage this fieldwork opportunity.

"Hops is right down the street," Al suggests.

We count to three and make a collective puddle-leaping car dash.

The host shows us to a booth against the back wall. As we pat our faces with napkins, the waitress brings samples of their microbrewed beer. Setting a golden pilsner in front of Al, she asks, "What can I get you to eat?"

"Nothing," he tells her. "I have dinner plans."

"A date?" she nosily queries.

"Somethin' like that."

"She's a lucky girl!" gushes the waitress.

"*Isn't she?*" he wryly replies.

When she leaves, I say, "I suppose you always have to monitor how much to tell."

"Been doin' that about ten years now," Al reports. "Most times, I figure it's not worth gettin' into. It's almost funny, the dumb things people say when they don't know who they're talkin' to. One time, Gordon and I were at a bar in Orlando where we met this straight couple. We were havin' a real nice conversation, when all 'a the sudden, the guy spouted off, 'You're not gonna believe what I saw today—two faggots holdin' hands!' He didn' have a *clue* that Gordon and I could 'a been those two guys."

I shake my head in empathic displeasure. "How do these issues play out at work?"

"I'm a general manager for a manufacturing company. Been there over a decade. I'm not about to put my career on the line, so I don' talk about my personal life. My coworkers can draw their own conclusions."

"What about your family?" I probe.

Al falls silent a moment. "My parents, my brother," he says, "they have no idea."

"How do you—"

Checking his watch, he says, "Listen, I'm already late. I'll tell ya more some other time."

When he disappears from view, I sip my beer, pondering what a momentous project it must be for Al to manage his gay identity. The everyday irritations. Is it worth confronting this presumptuous waitress? The financial costs. Given the lack of federal, state, and local civil rights protections, can Al afford to jeopardize the career in which he's invested so much time and energy? The emotional weight. How would his straight friends react? Would his family reject him? Will he keep this to himself for *another ten years?*

In some ways, it reminds me of my experience as a woman who's struggled with bulimia. Diminishing remarks, isolating secrecy, fear of others' responses—this is everyday life for anyone who conceals a stigmatized identity. Perhaps one day I'll risk sharing my own secrets with these men.

After a second beer, Tim and I wait by the crowded, noisy entrance while Doug signs the credit card slip. "I'm in trouble," Tim predicts. "Someone won't like that I went out for drinks without checking in."

"Here," I say, handing over a stick of gum. "Your man will never know."

Tim's eyes grow large; I'm confused until he mouths part of what I just said: "Your man."

Was that a mistake? I wonder, as the once talkative couple next to us quiets and an elderly woman turns around. Did they overhear? Are they staring? Does it matter?

"Your man," I hear myself say. Should I have made no public reference to Brandon? Should I have lowered my voice? I don't want Tim to feel exposed, but I also don't want to suggest that his relationship is something to hide. Damn, I don't know the rules! *Are* there rules?

My pulse picks up as Tim motions for us to leave. We exit the restaurant quickly, and when the door closes behind us, my "I'm sorry" overlaps his "That's okay."

Touching his shoulder, I say, "I didn't mean to out you in front of all those strangers."

"Don't worry about it. I was just giving you a hard time."

"It's not my place to decide how open you'll be."

Tim stops walking. "But you know why it came out like that? Because you didn't have to think about it. You said 'your man' the same way you'd say 'your girlfriend' if I were straight. It's a good sign."

"You think?"

"Well, are you as comfortable as you seem?"

For a moment, I gaze into the clearing sky. "I think I am," I say.

But am I?

"Then how about coming to the Pride Film Festival with Brandon and me tonight?"

I turn to Doug, who just caught up with us. "Why not?" he replies.

Images and Imaginings

After picking up Brandon, we head to the Tampa Theater, a historic cinema house complete with balcony, vermilion carpet, and pipe organ. Finding David in the lobby, the five of us move into the next room.

The scent of coconut popping oil fills the air as we admire the ceiling, which sparkles with stars. The sparse audience consists of men in both couples and small groups and a few pairs of women. Scanning the program, Tim reports, "Looks like three short films tonight." The lights dim.

Stark black-and-white images flash: two smiling men holding each other, then only one with eyes glassy and forlorn, then the profile of a church. Bells ring. The unseen narrator speaks with a quiet Irish intensity. When his partner died, he tells us, the family—who didn't visit, assist, or nurse—swoop in to claim the body, whisking it away for a "proper" Catholic funeral. There, his partner, lover, and caregiver must sit in the back with distant relatives and acquaintances.

House lights flick on, and the audience begins to murmur. Tim looks over as if asking for a response. Still trying to absorb the haunting representations, I only can say, "Powerful," before darkness falls again.

The second piece opens with scenes of water: a claw-foot tub with a handsome pair of bathers, a solitary swimmer descending to a pool's cement bottom, an ominous, swallowing sea. As in the first film, two have become one, bound forever by rituals of love and AIDS. The weary survivor stumbles into solace at an unlikely place. Wandering the zoo, he finds an exotic reptile, and in its eyes the man sees himself—caged but still living.

The lights come up. "Not sure I understand the whole man–lizard connection," David quips. Dimming lights quiet our cathartic laughter.

The subject of the third film speaks directly to the camera. "This is a picture about coming out as a gay man," he says, "and about living with AIDS." We accompany him on a painful journey to the grave of his dad. The tombstone reads, "Beloved son, brother, and husband." The man, not much a father in life, we see, is not a father at all in death.

We later find ourselves in the kitchen of the mother who cried when her son told her he was gay and the stepfather who reassured her, "At least he didn't kill someone." Can our young narrator go home again? Are these the people who will comfort him as he dies? We are left to wonder.

When the theater brightens, the crowd stands and begins filing out. Making our way through the lobby, we hear a weak, throaty voice, "David?" Our companion turns to embrace a sallow man whose black suit would fit someone twenty pounds heavier.

Opening his stance, David reminds Doug and me, "Y'all met after we saw Chris in *Jeffrey*. Nathan's a stage manager at the Loft Theater."

"Oh, sure," I recall. "Such an enjoyable production." Immediately, I wonder if "enjoyable" is an appropriate description of a play about AIDS. I wish I'd said "heartwarming" or "thought-provoking."

Nathan smiles and bids us goodbye. Once his friend is out of earshot, David comments, "He looks better."

We step onto the sidewalk, and without looking at David, I ask, "How many guys on the softball team would you say are HIV positive?"

With no pause, he answers, "A third, possibly half."

"God," I gasp, "I had no idea."

"Stick around, sugar," he says, "and you'll get more than an idea."

I take a deep breath, trying to face AIDS, the abstraction, so that one day I might be strong enough to face its reality. What will happen to the Cove men? Will they become the shadows and ghosts I saw in those films? Who will *I* become? Someone who runs off to compose a paper when fieldwork gets too painful? Someone too busy tending deathbeds to write?

"Need a drink, girl?" David asks, as if reading my mind.

Laying my head on his shoulder, I reply, "Straight up."

In the months that follow, David continues to serve as a powerful presence and educator. He becomes so central to both our lives that Doug asks him to be a groomsman in our wedding, set for New Year's Eve. From the moment he accepts, David helps us create an occasion that reflects our evolving values.

Gay Etiquette

"On'y a hun'red lef'," garbles Doug as his well-worn tongue runs across yet another line of glue.

The dining room table lies somewhere beneath black markers, red felt-tip pens, and piles of wedding invitations, RSVP and thank-you cards, response envelopes, gratitude envelopes, inner envelopes, and outer envelopes. "Who invented the multienvelope invitation?" I ask, nursing my third paper cut.

"Somebody who owned a paper mill," answers David.

"You are a saint for helping with this," I tell him.

Smiling, David says, "It's a privilege."

"Fifty invitations from now," Doug responds, "you might change your mind."

When I finish writing out my cousin's address, I check the next name on my list. "Ah, David Holland. Will that be David Holland and—"

"And *guest*," interrupts David.

"Things still rocky with Chris?" Doug queries.

"As crack cocaine." Moving us along, David says, "Who's up?"

"Tim Mahn," I report. "What should we do for Tim and Brandon? One invitation with both names? They do live together. Two, each with 'and guest'? That's so formal. Or two, each with the addressee's name only? Mm, that doesn't acknowledge them as partners."

"What does Miss Manners say?" asks Doug.

"Well, 'proper' etiquette requires a separate invitation for each unmarried person," I say. "But what about gay etiquette? I don't think Miss Manners has a chapter on that."

"Our etiquette would have you treat them as a couple," David suggests.

"So one invitation," I say.

"Right."

"Now . . . Tim before Brandon because his last name is first alphabetically, or Brandon before Tim because he's older?"

David laughs. "*That* I don't think matters."

After David goes home, I sit at the computer, reflecting on my evolving relationships with the Cove men. I write about David's validation of Tim and Brandon as a couple and how he used the wedding invitation as a teachable moment for Doug and me.

I note that he called it a "privilege" to help plan our wedding, but the privilege we didn't talk through was that of marriage itself—a privilege to which David may never have access. He and Chris are reminded of this in virtually every context of their lives. They cannot legally have sex (Florida still has laws against sodomy); they have no community property rights; neither can receive health or life insurance through the other's employment. As I ponder these things, images come to mind, fragments falling down the page, like poetry.

Keys

As a little girl,
I wouldn't have seen you, believing you didn't exist.
You were an innuendo, a caricature.
a punch line, a hairdresser's flaccid
wrist.

While an adolescent,
I would have tolerated you, believing you didn't choose.
You were an accident, a sickness,
a pity, an affliction for shrinks
to muse.

In college,
I would have accepted you, believing you were oppressed.
You were a movement, a platform,
a cause, another liberal
quest.

Today,
I watch myself   watching you,
and wonder   what lies in store.
You are my informants,   my teachers,
my friends,   the keys
unlocking   my doors.

Tomorrow,
I must turn outward again,
and look beyond myself.
With our experiences, our stories, our friendships,   .
I'll be the keys for someone else.

Throughout October, I spend as much time as possible with the Cove team. I continue observing games and practices, and Tim turns over the scorebook, giving me an "official" reason to sit in the dugout.

There I develop further my dual role of friend/researcher. Much of the time, players treat me as "just a friend." They ask about my life as much as I ask about theirs; they tease me; and they solicit my participation in cheers and practical jokes. Once in a while, though, the team "remembers" my other purpose. On many such occasions, my researcher role provides a source of humor. With an eye toward my tape recorder, David will josh with his old friend (and the Cove's first baseman) Jeff Grasso. Sometimes Tim will speak surreptitiously into the recorder. Later, when I listen to the tape, I discover his humorous message or sexual innuendo. In the playful relationships we're building, the Cove men seem to accept (and even enjoy) my dual role.

One Sunday, I arrive as usual. Unpacking my camera, notepad, and tape recorder, I don't suspect that today, the people I need to conduct my research will need me as well.

Liabilities

As a stiff gust whips long bangs across my face, I take a seat on the bench. Behind me, I hear Tim shouting, "Where the hell is everyone? If we can't cover the positions, we have to forfeit!"

Entering the dugout, Jeff asks, "How many short?"

"One," Tim answers.

The wisecracking thirty-five-year-old lights his usual Sunday morning cigarette and says, "I guess Li will hafta play." Jeff always calls me Li, and I like how it rolls off his New York–Italian tongue.

"Wait a second," I defer. But the idea catches on. Jeff tosses me a glove, and I try it out as Tim adds me to the batting order. "It's really not my sport," I explain.

"Listen, Missy," Tim says, "you'll be taking notes in right field today."

I want to protest, but ethnographers Clifford Geertz and Dwight Conquergood sit in my imaginary stands. Both demand my bodily participation in this participant observation, so I jog to catch up with Brandon, who's playing center field. He waves and smiles.

As Tim warms up at the mound, I vacillate. Even though I haven't played softball since a family picnic five years ago (and I played *really badly* then), part of me wants the ball to come my way. That's the kind of athlete I am: bring it on! But most of me hopes the scent of my fear doesn't reach the visitors' bench.

During the first inning, a batter sends a pop fly to shallow right field. A "real player" would get there, but I misjudge it by several feet. Mine is not the only error, however. A few plays later, one goes high and foul beside the third base line. Ron calls it but loses the ball in the sun; it bounces off his glove and onto the dirt. An inning later, Brandon drops one as well. "Lisa," he says, "you fit in perfectly."

My last shot at softball glory is a popper that flies between Brandon and me. I race toward it, then wimp out. "Brandon?" I plead, passing the buck.

"It's all yours, honey," he calls. Thunk! Not mine.

At bat, I cause two outs, but I do hit the ball twice. On my initial attempt, I take the first pitch and send it up the right field line. The first baseman scoops up the ball and walks over to step on the bag. "Way to hit opposite field!" Tim encourages.

Batting the second time, I follow Coach's advice to "look at one." When the ump generously calls a ball, the crowd praises, "Good eye, good eye!" At the next toss, I swing, causing a pop fly that never leaves the infield. The woman playing second makes the easy catch. When I apologize, my "teammates" respond with, "Nice cut!" and, "Great contact!"

Everyone seems in good spirits, even though we're getting massacred. After our next at-bat, the mercy rule is invoked.

"Hey," Jeff says as we come off the field, "you should play."

"Oh, thanks," I tell him, "but I'd be a liability."

"We're *aaawl* liabilities, Li," he replies, and we jog to the dugout laughing.

As I gather my things, a young woman approaches. "Hello," she greets, tucking brown hair behind her ears.

"Hi," I say, wondering who she is.

"You play for the Cove?"

"Not usually, but my fiancé does."

Tilting her head and letting out a skeptical giggle, she asks, "Your *what*?"

"Fiancé," I repeat, then realize she needs more context. "We're friends with David, Brandon, and Tim."

The woman nods. "Oh, I see." She purses her rosy lips and adds, "Tim and Brandon are two of my best gay friends, too."

Best *gay* friends? I reflect. I wonder what she meant by that.

"So why can't your fiancé play for a straight team?" she queries with a note ringing somewhere between suspicion and condescension.

"He *can*," I tell her, "but his *friends* play for this team." I throw my bag over my shoulder and walk away.

What nerve, I think, hands clenched. Irritation rises within me, but just as it's about to bubble into anger, I stop myself. Why this reaction? She called Tim and Brandon "gay friends." So what? They *are* gay; I probably wouldn't know them if they weren't. And big deal, she questioned a straight man's presence here. Who wouldn't? Most Suncoast teams have no straight players. Maybe she was sizing me up, finding out who I am and what my motives are. Maybe she's a straight woman looking to connect with other straight women who connect with gay men. Here was an opportunity to know someone associated with this community—maybe even someone like me—and I walked away. Why? Did it give me pleasure to one-up her as a "sensitive straight"? That seems counterproductive. I should have been more patient, more open.

Suddenly, I stop walking. I still can be. I'll go back over, introduce myself, and try getting to know her. After all, if Tim and Brandon like this woman, there's a good chance I will too. Turning around, I scan the crowd, searching for her brown hair. I move closer to where we stood, then closer yet. But with each step, it becomes more and more evident that she's already gone. I leave the field feeling like a jerk.

That night, Doug and I drive to the Cove Lounge, site of the 1995 Miss Suncoast Softball Pageant. Ballplayers in drag, we're told, compete for the crown.

What a Drag

When I pull open the door, several patrons seated in swiveling, high-back bar stools turn to check out the latest arrivals. I wonder what they think of the tall blond who holds the hand of a woman. With the billowing smoke and dim recessed lighting, I can't make out their faces.

"Hey!" someone calls from over by the jukebox. Jeff appears, looking enchanting with his ebony hair shiny and slick, mustache impeccably groomed, and curly-lashed eyes smiling from Grand Marnier swirling about the almost empty rocks glass in his hand. When he asks, "Wanna see a party?" Doug and I follow him to the poolroom.

Rounding the corner, we come upon a statuesque figure with her back turned. She looks glamorous in a sleek, ankle-length gown, black with a sheer white sash across one shoulder. From her ears dangle long silver earrings with three stars, each stacked atop the other. Velvet-and-rhinestone pumps adorn her feet. "Look who came!" Jeff announces, and the figure pivots around. Beneath the ringlets and rouge is outfielder Terry.

"Oh my god," I gasp. "You're hot!"

"Don't sound so surprised, daaahhhling," Terry says in his best breathy voice.

I take a closer look. An upswept wig conceals his James Dean sideburns. Bronze foundation, fuchsia lipstick, coal-black eyeliner, and false lashes complete the illusion. "Did you shave your chest?" I ask him.

"Only as far down as I had to." Terry pulls out the front of his dress to show me the line.

We return to the main bar, and I spot Cove teammate Bob at a table close to the stage. I haven't had much opportunity to get acquainted with him, but I know Bob is thirty-four, a New Jersey transplant, and a right fielder somewhat new to the game. Seeing me, Bob flashes his eyebrows and waves me over. "Sorry I missed your softball debut," he says when I reach him. "Thanks for covering my position."

With a good-humored grin, I reply, "I'll thank *you* not to make me cover it again."

Just then, the announcer calls into the mike, "Are you ready for this year's Miss Suncoast Softball Pageant?" The crowd claps and whistles. "Our first performer represents Rascals. Here's Anita Dick!"

Blue and red stage lights flick on, and a large "woman" appears wearing a full-length, hoop-skirted dress in cotton-candy pink. Puffy short sleeves accent her lineman shoulders, and ringlets cascade down her back. With metallic belt and wand, (s)he looks like the Good Witch on a very bad day. "Somewhere over the rainbow," (s)he mouths to a jazzy Judy Garland recording. Her teammates howl, and a line forms to offer her tips.

"Let's hear it for Anitaaaah!" the announcer inspirits when Ms. Dick moves into the finale. "Next up, I give you Mary Contrary!"

From the speakers booms Alanis Morisette's "You Oughta Know," an anthem for the (wo)man scorned. A man clad in bad-boy boots and hat comes into view followed by his sequin-gowned partner. The cowboy sits in a chair looking cold and aloof as the man in drag mouths a tale of devastating betrayal and wrenching loss.

After the crowd applauds Mary's intense presentation, the smoke of dry ice begins blowing over the front of the stage. When Terry appears amid the fog and music by the Pretenders, the Cove men jump up with bills in hand. Some turn their cheeks for a lipsticky kiss; a few slip dollars into Terry's bodice. Not to be outdone, Doug lies on the floor and crawls beneath his teammate's dress, making him the first to discover that Terry performs au naturel. Leave it to the straight guy. Reeling from my third vodka tonic, I snap an off-center shot of Terry finishing with a parade wave—elbow, elbow, wrist, wrist, wrist.

A cheerleader troupe represents Angels. Five guys wear yarn pom-poms on their white Keds, periwinkle T-shirts with their team logo in pink tucked into raspberry pleated miniskirts, and wigs styled with little-girl bows and ribbons. Throughout "Leader of the Pack," they roll their fists, as if revving a cycle, to the "vroom" sound that follows the title line.

When the MC switches tapes, the Eurhythmics meet my ears. Roars of pleasure permeate the room as another contestant takes the stage. Sporting a body-hugging sleeveless dress in violet with gold trim, white athletic socks pulled over calves, and chunky shoes, (s)he grooves to the spooky, pulsing melody. During the refrain, (s)he tugs on the ends of a frizzy flaxen wig, head tilted and eyes opened as wide as possible, revealing long, brassy lashes. The performer's twilight-zone stare and unshaved mustache keep everyone in stitches.

A trio of Miss Americas takes its place. The middle one looks stunning in her honey-colored wig and model-perfect makeup. While the others cover the "oohs," she mouths the refrain to the Supremes' "You Keep Me Hangin' On."

The next performer is Ima Guy, whose tight, ruby tank of sequins is stretched to the limit by giant breasts shaped like construction cones. Gyrating about, Ms. Guy continually hikes these from waist to chest.

At this, I sit back, feeling conflicted. Part of me finds this pageant deliciously provocative and irreverent. I've laughed as hard as anyone tonight. On a deeper level, I sense a kinship with the male performers. Certainly they "oughta know" as well as I how wrenching it feels to be kept "hangin' on" when nothing's left.[11]

But another part of me grapples with the fact that the characters being embodied here are not gay men; they are women—grotesque versions of female torch singers, cheerleaders, and beauty contestants. The men's slathered-on makeup, ridiculously high hair, oversized breasts, and fuck-me ensembles glorify—worship even—the most oppressive aspects of feminine "beauty" (no wonder I've seen only two other women here tonight). Perhaps they also scorn and critique those aspects, but do they scorn and critique women as well? (I wonder how entertaining these men would find a parade of women competing for a Swishy Sissy title.)[12]

And yet drag can be read as an ironic and critical response to misogyny. By undermining the system of gender identification, drag reveals that gender and sexuality are not stable *things* we have but repeated yet revisable *performances* we enact.[13]

The announcer introduces the final act, a plump fellow in a straight black dress and full, Cher-style wig. (S)he performs the evening's most danceable tune, "We Are Family." As "sistas" Jeff and David start singing along, I decide to give my critical consciousness a rest.

When the song ends, I escape to the ladies' room. There I find several contestants competing for space in front of the mirror. While Anita Dick holds my stall door shut, I realize that I'm the only "lady" sitting down to pee.

I find Doug outside, and we take our seats for the moment of truth. "Before we begin," says the announcer, "we want to recognize the most photogenic performer: Terry from the Cove!" Having just kicked back shots of José Cuervo, our outfielder wobbles up the steps for his award.

"And now," the MC continues, "the 1995 Miss Suncoast Softball title goes to . . . Ima Guy!" The breast man. Ima sashays to the stage, offering some blown kisses and mock tears as (s)he is crowned and given a dozen red roses. At this, patrons begin draining the night's final drink.

Doug and I bid our goodbyes and move toward the exit. On our way out, we bump into Ron, whose ribbed T-shirt hugs the cut upper body that defies his forty years. "Feeling okay?" he asks me.

"A little tipsy perhaps," I confess.

"Careful driving home," he cautions.

When we get in the car, Doug turns to me and says, "If I were going to date someone on the team, I think I'd choose Ron." A bit taken aback, I laugh, wondering how many heterosexual men would make such an admission. "Have you ever been attracted to a woman?" Doug then asks.

"Hmm," I murmur while reclining my seat. "I've always been drawn to my friend Kara. I'm not sure I'd label my feelings sexual, but there's definitely an intensity between us. Have you ever felt that way about a man?"

"Once," Doug admits, "but I bet he'd find that perverse."

At the last word, I know exactly who he's talking about—a nice, though rather traditional and reserved, friend from home. We pull out of the parking lot, and I sleepily reply, "Life-affirming-energy 'perverse,' huh? What a drag."

The next year, at the 1996 Miss Suncoast Softball Pageant, it becomes even clearer to me how the performance of drag can move us to think— and feel—outside of our cultural boxes.

Border Crossing

Bob, Al, and I cluster together in front of the stage. The contender before us is Andy, the catcher for a team called the Wet Spot (sponsored by a bar of the same name). The long blond mane is his own; the rest, glitz and glamour: charcoal-lined, cerulean-shadowed eyes, rosy cheeks and glossy red lips, scarlet press-on nails, and low-cut blue taffeta dress.

Bob leans in to say, "Now *that* should've been a girl."

"Woman," I correct.

While a hip-hop tune begins thumping, (s)he struts about, lip-synching

the in-your-face lyrics that instruct the listener to observe a "body beautiful." With every step and groove, Andy radiates confidence.

From center stage, (s)he makes eye contact with me, pivots, and
approaches. My heart beats faster. Our gazes lock as we synchronize our
motions. I adopt the performer's hip swaying; (s)he mimics my shoulder rolling. "Body beautiful," we mouth together, nodding and smiling
each other on.

Why does (s)he focus on me? I wonder, this beautiful man. Or
woman. Or man-as-woman. In this moment, to which am I drawn? Does
it matter?

For much of the song, we peer intently into each other's eyes. The
rhythm picks up, and we match each other move for move. At the
song's finale, Andy bows in my direction, as if sharing credit for the
performance.

On my left, Al bumps me. "What was *that* all about?" he asks, his
mouth slightly agape.

"Border crossing," I say.

The Friday after our first Miss Suncoast Softball Pageant, Doug and I
again make our way to the Cove, this time to help the team raise money.

Jell-O Fellowship

At fifteen, I peddled fund-raiser candy bars for choir. Teenagers, chocolate—it wasn't a hard sell. Ten years later, I prepare myself to hawk
squares of colored gelatin made with vodka instead of water. I wonder
how friendly this crowd will be.

Inside the bar, Doug and I find Gordon, already vending strawberry-
banana and orange-mango shooters. "C'mon," he calls over the happy-
hour buzz, "let's get you started."

We find six large trays of translucent cubes in the cooler. "Can you
handle a full one?" Gordon asks.

"Please," I tell him, "these hands spent five summers serving cocktails."

"Haven't been in the back yet," Gordon reports. Say no more.

On our way to the poolroom, we pass a Rastafarian with scraggly
braids and round John Lennon sunglasses. "Gelatin?" I offer. With a too-
cool glance, he waves "no."

We then approach a pair of grunge guys standing with their backs
against the wall. One has streaked hair bleached platinum and a ring in
his nostril; the other, a shaved head and baggy thrift-store jeans. "Cove

softball shooter?" I propose, waving the tray to jiggle the Jell-O.

"Later," says the shorn.

I start to feel discouraged, but then some PR comes over the PA. "Suncoast Softball shooters," says the announcer, "as fruity as you are!"

Looking a bit juiced himself, Terry approaches. I hold the tray up to his nose and ask, "Orange-mango or strawberry-banana?"

"I jus' bought sssix from Gor'on," he slurs.

"C'mere, huuuney," someone calls from across the room.

"I think he means you," I tell Doug as we make our way over. Suddenly, a man in a white dress shirt and linen pants turns around. The perfectly poufed sandy hair and wide beryl eyes belong to Dennis, our wedding coordinator.

"Oh my," he says.

"D-dennis," I stammer. Of course, I'm not nearly as surprised to see him here as he is to see us.

"Never expected to find *you* at the Cove," Dennis remarks.

"Doug plays for their softball team," I say, feeling the need to justify our presence.

"We're, um, raising funds," adds Doug.

"No kidding?"

In one sense, I feel a new connection to Dennis. Even though wedding coordination is a rather "gay" profession, I suspect he still feels guarded at the conservative social club that employs him. Perhaps Dennis now will see us as allies, and he'll feel more at ease than he did when we were "regular" clients. In another sense, though, I feel like Doug and I walked into his private party. Surely Dennis came here to escape, to be himself, to feel safe. I worry that we violated his sense of security.

I can't do anything else, so I smile at Dennis. A moment later, he smiles back and says, "Give me a shooter for everybody at the table."

"Wow!" I exclaim, handing over eight Dixie cups. "Thanks!"

He slips me a ten. "Take one for yourself," Dennis tells me, "and one for Doug."

In the next month, Doug and I have a few business meetings with Dennis. Though he never mentions the Cove encounter, I notice that he smiles more, and there's a deeper warmth in his tone. It may be just my imagination, but I like to think that "our moment" had something to do with it.

Out of shooters, Doug returns to the cooler while I check out the main bar. There I find a crowd of men moaning, shrieking, and laughing. At first, I can't see the target of their vigor. Moving closer, though, I behold the man at work.

Men at Work

He fills the small, black stage, his white T-shirt and cutoff overalls hugging rippling abs, pecs, bis, and tris. Atop his head sits a hard hat, slightly askew. The music, teasingly slow, sets the pace for his swaying, shaking, and strutting. The hat goes first; he flings it, Frisbee-style, into the corner. Howls of approval follow as he unhooks one strap, then the other. Tongue circling his lips, he wiggles the denim over his abdomen, down his hips, then past his knees. With a brown Caterpillar boot, he kicks the overalls into the crowd.

A man with feathered auburn hair and long mustache approaches, ten-dollar bill between his index and middle fingers. Spectator whispers into performer's ear. With a nod from the stripper, the tipper pulls the T over Construction Boy's head. Down to clinging Calvin's, he bows and exits stage left.

Bruce Springsteen's "Born in the USA" begins blaring from the sound system. The second act flexes and poses his too-tanned, too-tattooed body. Save the Stars and Stripes boxers, his routine bears no relation to the Boss's post-Vietnam, working-man anthem. At the refrain, the brown-haired beauty brushes back the long, wispy bangs of his bowl cut. In a snap, the boxers fly off, revealing a silver-sequined G-string. At this, a man twice his age steps before him, trying to keep pace with his gyrations. Admirer tucks a five into the desired pouch. The dancer smiles a teeth-only smile, thanking the man but sending a "don't-linger-too-long" gaze.

Behind me, someone asks, "Still with us?"

I spin around and find Doug, Gordon, and Terry. "Gosh, I've never seen so many—"

"Steroid users?" Doug questions.

Gordon and Terry laugh. "You've been going to the wrong bars," Terry says to me.

"Apparently," I respond. Looking over at my partner, I'm unable to decipher the expression on his face.

Most times, Doug is good humored about my new opportunities to watch men. Two months from now, we'll have the following encounter at Impulse, a club where Brandon tends bar. We go there with Alexandra and Christopher, a straight couple who mixes well with our gay associates.

A Gay Gaze

As we approach the door, Christopher asks, "Will I know anyone?"

"Brandon should be working," Doug tells him.

"Aah," Alexandra sighs, "Braaandon." Her husband turns to fan her.

The bulky bouncer wears a thick silver-link chain, a size-too-small T-shirt with rolled sleeves, and baggy black jeans. While checking our IDs, he gives each of us a twice-over. "Are we that obvious?" Doug whispers.

Looking at his plaid polo and golf shorts, I reply, "We are."

Inside, I survey the room. Behind a small bar between the pool table and stage, Brandon busily mixes and uncaps. Before turning toward the cooler, he makes eye contact and tips back his head, indicating that we should come his way.

When we reach him, I say, "You remember Alexandra and Christopher."

"Great to see you," he tells us, flashing a smile. "What can I get you?" We order beers and step off to the side, making room for several new patrons.

"He may be the best-looking man in Tampa," Alexandra says in my ear. She may be right, I think, as we watch Brandon work the crowd. Alexandra notes his chiseled features; I comment on his sculpted body. We both approve of the Gasparilla Fest pirate attire: red bandanna, gold hoop earrings, and eye patch.

Our husbands watch us watch him, shaking their heads at the intensity of our stares. "I know what your name will be tonight," Doug tells Christopher, loud enough for us to hear.

Laughing, Alexandra responds, "Straight men look at women all the time."

"No one's criticizing," Christopher replies.

"I never used to look at men like this," I say.

"Like how?" Doug asks.

I mull it over, then respond, "In this prolonged, objectifying gaze."

"But gay men look at each other like that," Alexandra remarks.

"That they do," I concur. "So maybe I'm learning a gay gaze."[14]

"Me too," she says, glancing over at the pirate pouring Perrier. "He is beautiful."

"Mmm hmm," I agree.

On the way home from selling shooters at the Cove, I ask Doug how he feels about watching (and watching me watch) strippers and other attractive men. "A little weird," he admits. "Straight men aren't exactly encouraged to check out male bodies. I'm also envious. I've always wanted larger arms, a bigger chest, more definition, and when I see you admiring them, I assume that you wish I had that kind of physique."

"That's interesting," I tell him, "because when I look at them, I'm not comparing the perfection of their bodies to your body, but to *mine*. Seeing them, *I* feel soft and unfit."

"Me too!"

"When we first associated with gay men, I thought I'd feel more at ease about my appearance. I assumed they wouldn't be looking at me, so I wouldn't be worrying about myself."

"But many of the gay men we know are obsessed with age, hair, skin, body."

"And it makes me even *more* self-conscious than I was before! Really, they're worse than most women."

"Most *straight* women," Doug says. "Lesbians seem to be less superficial."

"Touché. We haven't really interacted with the lesbians who play Suncoast Softball, but they do seem to create their own kind of beauty, one that, in many ways, contests our culture's oppressive standards."

"You should get to know Anna," he suggests. A few weeks earlier, Tim had introduced us to the Cove's only female recruit. Doug and I also met her "friend" that day.

"I really should," I decide.

Two days later, I get my chance. While the Cove concentrates on defeating Angels, I concentrate on Anna.

Watching Assumptions

Just to her left of third, she snags a solid shot that could have cost two bags, easily. The base coach drops to his knees and bows before her, chanting, "Not worthy!" She laughs.

When Anna returns to the dugout, I wave her and Al into a pose. He holds one hand in front of her, as if about to grope her breast; both offer open-mouthed smiles. Click! I put down the camera and watch her a moment. She has the build of a softball player, I note: athletic, a little stocky perhaps. Her no-fuss sienna mane is held back by a simple rubber band. No makeup, no nail polish. I wonder if she thinks I'm too much of a "girly girl," a (not always complimentary) reference to the femme role.

As I scan the stands for her companion, Tim teases, "Are you staring at Anna?"

"Maybe," I confess.

"She wouldn't be interested in you anyway," he says.

"And why not?" I ask, a bit defensively. Doesn't she like girly girls?

"She's *straight*," Tim says, offering a wry grin.

"Huh?"

He rephrases, articulating each syllable. "An-na is *not* a les-bi-an."

"Oops," I utter, to myself as much as to him. "Watch those assumptions."

Doug, meanwhile, spends the day struggling at the plate. Hitting one for four, he descends into a slump that rolls into December. Two Sundays from now, his on-field demeanor becomes an issue. While every Cove player experiences bouts of poor hitting, no one seems to respond quite the way he does.

Watching Them, Watching Us

We sit under a tarp, shivering through the final inning and clapping as much for the heat it generates as for team spirit. Down by three with two outs, Doug steps up. Squinting, he gives the ball a look. Our batter thinks it junk and steps back. "Steee-rike!" yells the lanky, mustached ump.

The pitcher fires again. Doug waits . . . waits . . . swings! His cut, slicing nothing but air, brings shouts of "Whoa!" and "Whoo!" from the crowd. He rolls his eyes, embarrassed.

Last chance. Eyes following the high arc, Doug pivots through, scooping the ball from underneath. The instant it leaves his bat, he knows the path—right to the fielder in left center. His opponent won't even have to move.

Doug hurls the aluminum culprit into the dirt; it bounces with the sound of a distant gong. Grinding his teeth, he curses, "*Dam*mit!"

His teammates emerge from the dugout, patting him on the back and shoulder. "Don't worry, Doug," they say. "Nice swing, buddy."

He shrugs them off. "*Dam*mit!"

Watching Doug kick the fence, David shakes his head, saying, "Such a het'ro."

For a moment, his comment surprises me. I've seen many aggressive, competitive gay players. Tim, for example, attacks the ball, both defensively and offensively, and Gordon chases down and dives after even the most remote pop fly.

Still, I've never seen either throw a bat or kick the fence. By his account, Doug only reacts negatively to his own performance, but do his teammates know that? Some participants here, like David, came of age never playing sports; some grew up rejected by those who did; many others competed but silently struggled with a sexuality still marginalized by sports.[15] Will Doug's behavior remind them of the homophobic jock culture Suncoast Softball tries to counter? In this moment, I'm reminded of our outsider status.

"When you're on their turf," I tell him as we clear the dugout, "remember that they watch you." As I say this, I reflect not only on Doug's tantrum but also on the following interaction, which took place just before today's game.

"Hey, Lisa!" Brandon shouts. "Come see."

I make my way down the bleachers and meet him by the scoring table. He points to a corkboard where tacks hold rows of pictures in place. "What's up?" I ask, slipping my arm through his. Taking a closer look, I realize why Brandon called me over. In the right corner hangs a photograph of me. As I enjoy my image's slight, close-mouthed smile, I remember the camera's click when I walked by a spectator last week.

"What a star!" Brandon says. "Shades on, hair blowing, you could be Demi Moore."

"Ha!" I say, giving him a mock punch. I lean toward the board for further scrutiny.

"What's the matter?" he asks. "Don't you like the shot?"

"It's not that," I tell him. "I guess I've been observing all of you so carefully that I haven't thought much about *being observed*." As I say this, other teammates begin congregating around us, watching me watch myself being watched.

That Sunday brings the fall season to a close. With all practices and games behind us, it's now time to write.

Writing "Tales"

When I return home, I print out a copy of my field notes and read through it several times. I then begin writing comments in the margins and highlighting themes in different-colored markers. I also listen to my field tapes and study the dozens of photographs I've taken since September.

Though I try to be thorough and methodical, the more I pore over these sources, the more difficult and uncomfortable it becomes to draw definitive conclusions about "them." I scour my materials for insights into gay male friendship, but I find that my deepest and most passionate insights are not into "their" relationships but into *our* relationships.

Because of this, I decide to use my field materials to compose ethnographic short stories about my evolving relationships with the Cove team. For the next month, I write about how these men have changed the ways I think and feel about sexuality, coming out, heterosexism, and AIDS. Throughout the episodes, I layer in reflections from some of the literatures I've been reading on identity, friendship, gay cultures, and representing one's fieldwork community. I work hard to move seamlessly between scenic description and more analytic reflection.

The project consumes me. On several occasions, I awaken in the middle of the night to scribble notes or return to my computer.

When I read over the final draft, I feel an intoxicating rush. My qualitative methods class meets for the last time this week. It will be my first opportunity to share this journey with colleagues.

Presenting Self, Presenting Fieldwork

My spirits are high when my turn comes. I've decided to perform a couple of the narratives, hoping my voice can convey the significance of what I encountered and the emotionality of the bonds I formed and solidified.

As I speak of the Cove players, I realize that I've probably "fallen in love" with my informants a little too deeply; surely someone will question my lack of critical distance. At the same time, I expect a generally positive reception to my ethnographic project and writing.

When I finish, the first hand in the air belongs to a graduate student in sociology. I wait excitedly for her question or comment. After a bit of reflection, she asks, "Do you ever wonder why?"

Confused, I query, "Why *what?*"

"Why they're, you know, *gay?*"

I pause, feeling my body tighten a bit. "I don't," I tell my classmate.

"Do you think it's a biological aberration?" the woman then asks.

"Aberration?"

"Abnormality, then," she says.

"I wouldn't use that word either," I tell her.

"From the available evidence and from your experience with gay men, do you think it's biological, psychological, or environmental?" she asks.

↖↖↖

Importantly, as Stein indicates, "almost every investigation into the causes of homosexuality has aimed at its elimination."[16] The consequences for gay men and lesbians have ranged from psychoanalysis and electroshock treatment to genital mutilation and brain surgery.

"I don't think bodies, minds, and contexts are separable," I reply. "I've met gay men who say they knew their sexual orientation early in childhood; others believed they were straight until their teens or twenties. Some say that they choose to be with men; others say the 'choice' was made for them. It seems highly unlikely that a single factor or path leads one to a particular set of fantasies, desires, and behaviors. Besides, my own interests lie more in what it *means* to be gay—emotionally, relationally, and politically—than in *why* someone's gay."

"You never wonder about it?" presses a male student.

I let out a sigh, then retort, "Not any more than I wonder why I'm straight. We always seem to assume that *heterosexuality* needs no explaining."

Cupping his chin, he says, "Your project does lack a theory of sexual orientation."

I stare at him a moment, disbelieving where the conversation's going. "I don't claim to advance a theory of sexual orientation. I claim to show narratively the possibilities for, and consequences of, studying and befriending members of a gay male community." My voice rises in pitch. "Frankly, I'm surprised and disappointed by this exchange. After all the characters and situations I offered, *this* is how you want to spend the discussion period, focusing on why my participants are gay?"

Many people—gay, bisexual, and straight—share an interest in the origin(s) of sexual orientation. It is widely believed that discovering biological bases for homosexuality will improve the cultural climate for nonheterosexuals (because such bases would suggest that one does not choose homosexuality, just as one does not choose the color of her or his skin—a frequently invoked analogy). On one hand, people who believe in biological bases for sexual orientation tend to be more supportive of gay and lesbian rights than people who do not hold this belief; on the other, we might question how solid a foundation for gay and lesbian rights can be provided by *lack* of choice or agency.[17]

"I wish we had more time," Carolyn says apologetically. "I know others had comments and questions. But we have many more presentations scheduled for tonight."

I stand there a moment, immobile, and study the faces of my classmates. Do I know you people? Reluctantly, I gather my notes and relinquish the floor.

My mind races throughout the last hours of class. What about my performance moved them to focus on causes of homosexuality? Did the narratives not evoke the power of my journey? Was it somehow safer to intellectualize about sexual orientation than to examine my fieldwork experiences and relationships? *Would* a theory of sexual orientation have helped me frame those?

Regardless, their remarks struck me not only as professional inquiry but also as personal attack. Given my growing identification with the Cove men, perhaps that's to be expected. But a reactionary stance will do little to promote dialogue. I need to prepare myself for these kinds of responses. When taken by surprise, I move too quickly to defensiveness. It's possible that I heard homophobia when it didn't speak; and even if it did, wasn't it my call to answer?

Nine o'clock comes, and I leave the room feeling disappointed about the presentation. The class is finished, but as I will discover, the project is just beginning.

Negotiating Academic and Personal Selves

Christmas Charade

I'm as decked as the halls. The midnight-blue slip dress and pumps are new. The hair is by Omar; the lips, Ultima II.

I park across from the Columbia Restaurant in Ybor City. After the final touches—drop earrings on, engagement ring off—I make my way to the bar. Inside, I find Bob waiting at a table illuminated by a single votive. We kiss each other's cheeks. With a slight New Jersey nasality, he says, "You look wondahful."

"And you too," I tell him, admiringly stroking his soft beige sweater.

"Wine?" he offers.

"Red, please." When Bob returns with a house Merlot, I say, "Perhaps we should get a few details straight—so to speak."

He smiles. "Like how we met?"

"Exactly. People always ask about that."

"How about the truth?" he proposes. "Through a softball league."

"Are we dating or just friends?"

Bob ponders this a moment. "Dating."

"For how long?"

"Um, a couple of months?"

"Since September," I clarify.

Suddenly, his dimples recede, and his brown eyes focus. "You okay with this?"

I pause. "I'm happy to be here, Bob. And I can appreciate your predicament."

"I *am* an untenured high school teacher," he reminds me.

"Not the most secure position," I say.

Under both Florida and federal law, an employer may refuse to hire and may take adverse employment action—including termination—on the sole basis of sexual identity. Perhaps no profession has felt the effects of this more than education. In 1985 the Supreme Court refused to hear the case of an Ohio guidance counselor fired for disclosing her bisexuality, letting stand a lower court's ruling that this did not violate her rights to equal protection.[1]

Still, even in a context prone to the misguided association of homosexuality with pedophilia, there's a difference between electing not to come out and actively constructing a false front. In my mind, the latter tactic seems regressive, but in Bob's it seems *necessary,* and right now, I'm not about to question his definition of the situation.

Checking his watch, he says, "It's time."

We cross the Spanish tile floor leading into the restaurant, where mariachis play "Feliz Navidad" and the air smells of saffron and fresh Cuban bread. "Look just beyond the stage," Bob instructs, pointing at two tables, each with about fifteen people in their finest sparkling attire.

When the group spots us, they greet with a round of, "Bob! Hey! You made it!"

"Everyone," he says, "I'd like to present Lisa. Lisa, these are my colleagues."

Several women and men rise to shake my hand. Taking the seat Bob pulls out for me, I struggle to keep up with the barrage of names.

"It's so nice you came," says a woman with long, pulled-back hair. "Bob is a great guy."

"He certainly is," I agree.

She then begins the anticipated interrogation. "How long have you two—"

"Since September," I reply before she can finish.

With that remark, I take on what Warren calls the "functional" role of a woman in a gay man's life, helping him keep a "straight face" for heterosexual associates.[2]

\\\

The sangria-sipping woman next to her adds, "I'm glad Bob *finally* found someone."

Ten years ago, I silently correct.

"That guy is too sweet to be alone," she continues.

He had a partner for ten years.

"I must say," the woman tells us, "you two make an attractive couple."

"Thank you," Bob and I chorus. We lean in, holding back a laugh.

My evening with Bob opens an unforgettable holiday season. Doug and I spend Christmas with both our families, who come early to help organize the big event.

Wedding Bells

Walking down the aisle, I find a delightful mix: family from Minnesota, Wisconsin, Missouri, Texas, and Washington, high school friends, college roommates, USF people, Walgreens people, and softball people.

Doug and I take our places on the veranda, and the minister offers a meditation on the scripture reading, a passage from 1 Corinthians 13. In his reflections, he praises our best friendship, our balance of independence and interconnection, and our engagement with diversity.

At that, I look to David, who wipes away a tear before coming forward to deliver the passage.

We had to coax David into this role; he's not fond of public speaking. "Why me, baby?" David implored.

"Because you're the most upstanding, church-going person in our wedding party," Doug told him.

A delectable pause followed, then David, right on cue, replied, "Well, ain't that a switch!"

"Love is patient," reads our groomsman. "Love is kind. . . . Love does not delight in evil but rejoices with the truth. It always protects, always trusts, always hopes, always perseveres."

When the ceremony ends, we direct everyone inside for the reception. Tim catches me on the way to the receiving line and says, "I saw the program: 'Tim Mahn and Brandon Nolan—host couple.'" Studying me a bit, he grins.

"I was happy you consented to that. It doesn't make you uncomfortable I hope."

Tim pauses. "I just wonder what your other guests will say."

"What *can* they say?" I reply. "It's *my* night."

And a fabulous one at that. Seventy guests spend the dinner hour sipping sweet Asti and feasting on Caesar salad, pecan-crusted chicken, and chocolate-raspberry cake.

Afterward, we celebrate our new life (and the approaching new year) by dancing each other into a frenzy. When groupings form for a twirl with the bride or groom, I try not to take personally the fact that Brandon, Tim, and David join Doug's line.

Years later, Tim and I reminisce about that night. "It was a turning point for me," he says. "The whole experience of being out—up front and at a wedding. I remember that you encouraged Brandon and me to dance together. I'd danced with men before, of course, but never 'couples dancing,' and *never* in straight context."

By 11:00 P.M., I can't take another hokey-pokey, electric slide, or boot-scootin' boogie. My ivory satin bustle now feels like a fifty-pound dumbbell. Stretching my lower back, I decide to do a little meet-and-greet. I stop by a table of Doug's college friends to ask if they enjoyed the bachelor party.

"It was an eye-opener," Bruce says, and the group shares a knowing snicker. "Your friend David gave us a real tour."

"Where did you go?" I ask.

"We started at Fat Tuesday."

Thinking of my last visit there, I recall, "Mm, yuppie crowd, syrupy frozen concoctions. Not a beer joint like you're used to but still up your alley."

Bruce's brown eyes expand. "Then we went to the Cherokee."

"The Cherokee?" I repeat, laughing. "Why would you take Doug to a lesbian bar?"

Blushing a bit, he explains, "We wanted some exotic dancing, but David only knew where to find strippers who are, well, *men*. He figured lesbians would know where the hot chicks were."

"And did they?"

"They sent us to Seventh Heaven."

"I'll bet. Did my husband enjoy the scenery?"

"Doug 'suffered through' his table dance," says Bruce.

"What a trouper," I reply.

"Then he bought one for David, who slipped the girl twenty bucks, saying, 'Puh-*leaze* do not dance on my lap.'" When I laugh, Bruce queries, "By the way, who's the guy with the purse?"

"Oh, Barry. He manages the bar that sponsors Doug's softball team. He's a stitch."

"He's *somethin'* all right." Bruce swills his Bud, then says, "We ended up at the Cove."

"That I heard," I reply. "Your first such establishment?"

"What do *you* think?" he fires, eyes narrowing.

"Well, how was it?"

"Uh!" Bruce exclaims in exasperation. "These men, they *gawked* at me!"

I give him a once-over, noting his pudgy face and the gut that spills over his Sunday trousers. Sure they did, I think.

"One of 'em followed me into the bathroom," he continues. "I said, 'Hey man, I'm straight. I just wanna take a piss!'"

"Sweetheart," I instruct with an edge of condescension, "when you're in a gay bar, people tend to assume that you're gay."

"You wouldn't understand," Bruce insists, dismissing me with a wave of his hand.

"Right," I snap sarcastically, "I have no idea how men behave in bars. And I'm sure you've never made a woman feel the way you claim that man made you feel."

"Whatever," he scoffs.

Time to move on, I think. Just then, the DJ begins spinning a lively polka. "Ah, perfect," I remark, "I believe they're starting the chicken dance."

I walk away, reflecting. On one hand, Bruce's encounter in the men's room could be instructive if he reframes it. He could view the experience as a window into another culture or as a source of insight into an apprehension women often feel.

On the other, the sources of apprehension are gendered. As a woman in that situation (alone with a propositioning man in an enclosed space), I fear for my physical safety, while Bruce probably does not. For a (homophobic) straight man, this encounter arouses fears about the security of his sexual identity; for a straight woman, such an interaction seems more likely to reinforce than to challenge hers.

During the bathroom encounter, Bruce may have sensed—perhaps for the first time—just how precarious and questionable a (hetero)sexual identity is. Given the context, the gay man in that scene probably assumed that he was meeting a social equal (privileged by sex, marginalized by sexual identity). Perhaps Bruce's hostility was a strategy to reassert his sexual-identity-based privilege. But unless he recognizes this and wants to move beyond defensiveness, the only thing Bruce will glean is reinforcement for his homophobic framework.

And what about my role in his negotiation of identity? Given Bruce's limited exposure to gay culture(s), could he have responded in any other way?[3]

Was *I* too defensive? Too confrontational? I make a mental note to keep working on my approach.

In the next room, I find my father standing at the bar. Straightening his bow tie, I ask, "What's new?"

A smirk forms on his full lips, making round cheeks even rounder. "I was just talking with David."

Anxiety pinches my neck. I've been afraid to ask what my father thinks of our groomsman and host couple. When I was growing up, Dad was no queer basher, but he tended to treat the subject of homosexuality with about as much consideration as he treated an underemployed, overstepping in-law with his hand out for yet another loan.

Two nights ago, my father opted out of Doug's bachelor party, claiming he didn't feel "up to it." I've been wondering what that meant but haven't wanted to risk being disappointed by the answer. He knew, after all, that David was gay and in charge of the festivities. I love my dad intensely, but we don't always agree, and tonight I would rather not be on opposing sides.

"David's funny," he says at last.

Funny ha-ha, I wonder, or funny, y'know . . . ?

"And nice," Dad continues.

Nice, huh? That's the first time I've heard him use that word to describe a gay man.

"A great guy," adds my dad. For just a moment, his large brown eyes—the ones I inherited—drift away. He's pondering something. But what? What's going on here? I almost reply, "You don't have to tell me," but I bite my tongue when I realize that my father probably is telling all of this to himself as much as to me.

"David's a good friend to you," he observes.

I want to shout, "Eureka, Dad! That's just how it happened to me! I had accumulated a set of scripts about sexual orientation and identity. Then one day, I encountered this human being named David—this 'funny,' 'nice,' 'great guy'—and suddenly, the old associations didn't work anymore, so I made new ones. And they've changed everything."

But I don't shout. Instead, I smile at the man who assembled my first bike, taught me long division, and clumsily danced through Campfire father–daughter banquets, and I say, "I love you, Dad."

Back to School

The honeymoon's over one day, second semester starts the next. It takes almost no time to discover that the impact of my fieldwork will continue to reverberate throughout my personal and professional lives.

"What a Waste"

As I grab my attaché from the backseat of my car, a familiar voice finds my ears. "How was Jamaica?"

I turn to find Tami, a graduate student in humanities. We took a class together a year ago. "Hey, Tami! It was nice, really nice."

We begin the hike to our buildings, and she says, "Heard your wedding was magical."

"It was!" I beam.

Her lips purse. "I also heard that—aside from your husband, of course—the two best-looking men present were there with each other."

I laugh. "You must mean Brandon and Tim."

"God," Tami says, "what a *waste!*"

"Waste" hits like a dart, and emotions flood my body: first surprise (Did I hear right?), then confusion (What did Tami mean?), then disappointment (She's supposed to be educated!), then anger (Who does Tami think she's talking to?) I flash back to my disappointing conversation with Bruce. Here we go again! How do I respond this time?

Silence falls between us. Another woman's voice resounds in my mind. "What a waste!" she said of gay men. Then another's. "What a waste!" she too insisted after meeting our host couple. With incisors gnawing at the tip of my tongue, I shake my head.

"What's *that* look for?" asks Tami.

Without unfurling my brow, I bite back, "How exactly is Tim and Brandon's relationship 'a waste'?"

She pauses, unsure how to answer. "I, um, only meant that they must be handsome."

Gazing into her espresso eyes, I know that at her core, Tami is a good person, a visit-the-sick, care-for-the-animals humanitarian sensitive to others' experiences and feelings. She's well intentioned. She probably *did* mean only that Tim and Brandon must be handsome, and I suspect she now recognizes the heterosexism in her comment. All that in mind, now would be a good time to step back and be understanding. Isn't that stance more likely to promote learning than a hostile one? Besides, *I've* said worse things than "What a waste."

But in this moment, I can't get past the anger.

I release another arrow, "So it's fine for unattractive men to be gay, but—"

"I didn't say that," she replies.

We near the crosswalk, and Tami steps away, allowing a mass of book-baggers to file between us. What now? Should I push further? With what kind of approach? Adversarial, cooperative, educative? Part of me wants to shout, "Your comment was stupid!" But what would that do besides raise my blood pressure and alienate a colleague? Another part feels obligated to mediate between gay and straight communities. If I don't play this role, who will? But part of me is *exhausted*. Heterosexual ignorance is so assaulting and pervasive that many of my recent interactions with straight people have left me feeling angry, hurt, or empty. How do gay people stand it? I now think I understand why so many enclose themselves in their own communities. It's about self-preservation. Sometimes *I* would like to feel enclosed again. Can I renegotiate such a position in my straight worlds, or must I leave them behind? This gay community seems to have a place for me, but can it ever be *my* community?

When Tami and I reconnect at the other side of the street, I say nothing more about her remark. My silence doesn't reveal how much I understand where she is; I was there not so long ago. It doesn't promote dialogue on this issue and doesn't teach her to react differently. For those things, I feel regret. Still, I know that right here, right now, my silence is what keeps me from screaming.

New Courses

I return to my classes and teaching with a new consciousness. I see, as never before, how gay and lesbian experience can be distorted and silenced in readings, discussions, and assignments. As a result, I reexamine my own syllabi and course materials. When I notice my complicity in marginalizing gay and lesbian life, I decide to make some changes.

In Family Communication, I show *The Wedding Banquet*, a film about a gay man struggling to tell his traditional Chinese parents he's gay. Instead of framing this as a text about nontraditional family forms, I use it the week we happen to be talking about family secrets. Though I would have liked to address issues related to sexual orientation and identity more directly, this backdoor approach allows me to test the waters as a facilitator of such discussions. The results are encouraging. Weighing the merits and consequences of secrecy and disclosure, many students invoke their own experiences with concealment and revelation, demonstrating an ability to identify with the gay male protagonist.

When I later teach Gender and Communication, I show the HBO documentary based on Vito Russo's book *The Celluloid Closet*. It's my first direct classroom engagement with sexual orientation and identity. I schedule the film late in the semester, giving me time to lay some groundwork. In scenarios and activities I've used before, I change gender-identifying names to gender-ambiguous ones. In lectures and discussions, I consciously speak in terms of "partners" instead of "spouses" and "commitment" instead of "marriage." By the time we watch *The Celluloid Closet*, my students seem prepared to respond thoughtfully, and our conversation ends up almost totally devoid of the kind of reactions I had to *Threesome* in 1994.

But not every classroom interaction is quite so inspiring.

Family Communication 1

It's the last meeting of the spring 1996 semester for sixty Family Communication students. From their final presentations, we'll learn what sank in and what washed over.

The second group sets up. One student turns off the lights while another presses "play" on the VCR. Elbows propped on the desk, I rest my chin on folded hands.

The scene opens in a middle-class living room, where a young man argues with his sister. The student-scripted dialogue sounds too contrived, and the acting is overdone; still, I'm impressed by the extra effort that went into producing the video. I begin writing in my notes, "Nice use of—"

It is a thought I never finish.

"You're such a faggot!" screams out from the monitor.

My spine straightens. What? No. No way did she say that. I couldn't have heard right, could I? The character puts any doubt to rest. "You little faggot!" she jabs again.

After fifteen weeks of talking about diversity, multiple definitions of family, and deconstructing canonical stories, how can this be? Haven't I seen that woman every Monday and Wednesday since January? Didn't she get it? Didn't *anybody* in that group get it? I slump against the backrest, covering my face with my hands. The tape rolls for several more minutes, but I don't hear another word.

The lights come on and the room clears for a ten-minute break. Art

Bochner, the professor I'm assisting, approaches. "You okay?" he asks.

Images flash in my mind, images of David, Chris, Tim, Brandon, Al, Gordon, Bob, and so many others. I look up at my adviser and query, "What should we do?"

"I'll handle it," Art assures me.

While students retrieve Cokes and snacks, I ponder the options for dealing with this. Option one: let it go. The moment has passed, and perhaps ignorance doesn't always merit a response. On the other hand, wouldn't our silence make us complicit in the denigration? If university instructors don't address this issue, who will? What changes if we say nothing? Wouldn't we be telling our gay and lesbian students that it's acceptable for them to be verbally assaulted in our presence and suggesting to our straight students that "faggot" is an appropriate term for the classroom when it's not an appropriate term *at all* (except, arguably, between gay men)?

Option two: get angry. Believe me, I'm already there. Anger conveys the seriousness of an offense. In this case, it would advise students in no uncertain terms that the word "faggot" is as inflammatory as "nigger" or "spic." But is the classroom the proper context in which to communicate anger? In any situation, I find it troubling to express this toward a student, who's already in a one-down position. Besides, offering a diatribe might do little more than publicly shame the offending parties. It also could foster pervasive defensiveness, moving other students to wonder if their ideas are welcome only if they align with the (often left-of-center) politics of the faculty.

Option three: build a bridge. This comment could be used as a teachable moment about heterosexist assumptions. We could talk about audience analysis, reminding students that 10 percent of the population—meaning at least five or six people *in this room*—identifies as gay, lesbian, or bisexual, and that many others are offended by terms such as faggot. "After all," we could tell students, "we shouldn't alienate those we're trying to influence."

My thoughts are interrupted when Art directs everyone inside. "Let's have group three," he says, and with that, we continue moving through the presentations.

After the final skit, Art takes a chair at the head of the class and offers some parting comments. "Your performances today illustrated both the strengths and the weaknesses of our semester. Many of you demonstrated an understanding that family stories function to connect generations, to shape personal identity, and to define the family's hopes and expectations. At the same time, there were some lessons your instructors must not have conveyed clearly enough. Had we done so, I doubt we would've seen, for example, a final presentation in which the word 'faggot' was used so flippantly and derogatorily. I assume responsibility for that failure and will rethink my approach the next time I teach this class." Art then moves on to other issues, saying nothing more about the incident.

My adviser's handling of the situation gave me an option I hadn't thought of: take the blame. In the moment, I worried that Art too quickly absolved the student group. In retrospect, however, I find his approach rhetorically savvy. He conveyed the message "What was said was not appropriate" while allowing everyone in class (except perhaps the instructors) to save face. Assuming responsibility seems particularly effective at the end of a term, when all material has been presented and all lessons (supposedly) learned.

Family Communication 2

In the summer of 1996, I teach my own section of Family Communication. Near the end of class one afternoon, I look out at my students and say, "To review, if Tim believes that his partner Brandon needs too much 'we,' whereas Brandon thinks Tim is overly 'me'-focused, then the couple is grappling with which relationship dialectic?"

"Stability–change," one student answers.

"No," corrects another, "independence–dependence."

"That's the one," I say. When I turn to write the words on the board, mumbling breaks out in the back corner of the room. "What's that?" I ask over my shoulder.

Trying not to grin, a guy with Sigma Chi on his T-shirt and cap replies, "She said you give us a lot of *gay* examples." From across the aisle, the ponytailed woman I assume made the comment swats her classmate on the shoulder.

She clears her throat. "Do you have a lot of gay friends?"

"Yes," I tell them. "My husband plays on a gay softball team." Muffled laughter and whispering crescendo into a dull roar. A bit rankled, I ask, "Something funny?"

"How did *that* happen?" inquires a wide-eyed male.

I smile at his surprise and explain, "Doug's trainer at work recruited him."

"*Recruited* him, huh?" he retorts.

Ignoring his classmate, another guy probes, "His trainer's gay?"

"Yep."

"Is your husband the only straight guy?" the woman next to him queries.

"On his team, yes."

"He *is* straight, right?" quips the man of (Greek) letters.

Unsure whether he aims to tease or annoy, I reply, "As far as I can tell."

The ball keeps rolling. "What if he did, ah, come out of the closet?"

"Ohkaaay," I redirect, "unless there are questions related to *the material* . . ." The class groans. "We're adjourned. Read chapter 7 for Wednesday."

They file out, some giggling, some smiling, some eyeing me. When I bid him goodbye, Sigma Chi warns, "If I were you, I'd keep a close watch on my husband."

I spend the walk to my car grumbling about how "small-minded" my students were. But as I drive home, I try to imagine our situation from a nineteen-year-old undergraduate's perspective. At that stage of my life, I surmise, *I* would have thought it odd. Still, some—particularly the men—didn't just find Doug's participation in Suncoast Softball "strange"; they found it *suspicious.*

Doug once told me that some of his teammates thought him a "closet case" when he first joined. I wonder what they think now. Should I be concerned that my husband is so comfortable around gay men? Is more than friendship on his mind? As I park next to his Grand Am, I scold myself for asking that. Besides, even if he is curious, is that really something to worry about? Whatever his fantasies, he's married to *me*; he's sleeping with *me*. Just then, a little voice in my head whispers, "For now." I shout down the voice, head inside, and throw my arms around my husband.

Endings and Beginnings

In the classroom, I continue grappling with how best to incorporate issues related to sexual orientation and identity. It remains a bumpy ride of trial and error, but my generally receptive students help keep my chin up.

Outside the classroom, however, as my encounter ("What a Waste") with Tami illustrates, many of my professional relationships are withering. I once devoted myself to the departmental community by hosting parties, organizing outings, and championing graduate student causes. But more and more, I find myself on the periphery, making fewer phone calls to colleagues, arranging fewer meetings, even turning down invitations. Am I "going native"? I wonder. What happens then?

\ \ \

The last two years, I spent my birthday with many fellow graduate students. This year, when Doug asks whom he should invite out to dinner, I name only Brandon and Tim.

"You sure?" he asks.

"I'm sure," I say, concealing the ball of alienation and confusion thrown by this neither-here-nor-there social position.

Birthday Blues

Outside Castaways, the gulf folds into the rocky shore. Inside, candles flicker, and a baby grand softly serenades as couples lean in, trading spoonfuls of conch chowder for a taste of coconut shrimp. Our waiter stops by a third time. "Why don't we order?" Doug suggests. "We've been here forty-five minutes."

"All right," I reluctantly agree. "I just hope nothing's happened." Doug grins when I request seafood pasta in a very naughty cream sauce.

Taking a sip of water, I feel a hand on my shoulder. We look up to find Tim. He kisses my cheek and says, "Hey, birthday girl."

Scanning the lobby, Doug asks, "Brandon's parking the car?"

"Brandon's . . . at the apartment," Tim reports. "Long story."

"You aren't going to leave it at that," I protest.

He begins rubbing his forehead. "We broke up," Tim says. When I gasp, he adds, "And now we're half together again."

"Half?" I probe.

"It's complicated."

"You didn't have my permission to break up," I say to lighten the mood. He smiles. "You can always come to me, to us."

"I know." Eyes fixed on a still-fanned napkin, he asks, "Have you eaten?"

"Just ordered," Doug tells him.

"Great," he says, "I'll go track down a menu."

When Tim is several paces away, Doug fires a stern glance. "Be careful," he warns.

"He's hurting," I demur.

"And how can *you* help? You don't know what it's like to be in a gay relationship."

"I know what it's like to fall in love with a man, to hurt and be hurt, to leave and be left. What else do I need to know?"

Tim reappears, and Doug shakes his head. "I have no idea," he tells me, lowering his voice, "but since you never leave anything alone, I'm sure you'll find out."

I crinkle my nose at him. If it were your breakup, I silently retort, you'd run to the nearest woman willing to hear your sorry-ass tale.

As it turns out, I hear nothing more of the conflict tonight. Tim asks that we spend dinner talking about "anything else."

Later this week, however, I gain another perspective on their problems.

"I Want to Be with Him . . . Regardless"

"Yeah?" I say into the phone.

"Lisa, it's Brandon."

"How *are* you?"

He pauses before admitting, "Not great." As I settle into the couch, Brandon begins, "Tim said you wanted to know if things were falling apart again."

"I only meant that I'm here for both of you. Do you want to tell me what's going on?"

"Well," he says, straining to get the words out, "Tim's not sure what he wants."

"Meaning . . . ?"

"I don't know. I fell for him so hard and so fast. We moved in together right away. Now he thinks maybe it's all too much."

"What do *you* think?"

"I love him," he says, his voice cracking. "I want to be with him . . . regardless."

"Regardless of what?"

Silence, then, "He, um, he cheated on me."

I exhale my disappointment, saying, "That must be very painful for you." As soon as the words leave my lips, I wonder about my involvement here. Maybe Doug's right; maybe I *am* too nosy! And maybe my relationships with men are not comparable. After all, my understanding is that gay male couples tend to be less monogamous than lesbian or heterosexual ones, more tolerant of outside sexual involvements, fraught with power struggles, and (because both partners are socialized into masculinity) lowest of all romantic relationships in expressiveness and nurturance.[4] Bottom line: I don't want to impose a (heterosexist) set of standards not applicable to Brandon and Tim's relationship. Just listen, I tell myself, let him guide you.

"When I first found out," Brandon reports, "oh!" Unable to go there, he changes gears, "But I can forgive that." Shifting again, he says, "Anyway, I thought you could come over, maybe help us talk it out."

Doug's don't-meddle gaze appears in my mind. "What does Tim

think of this idea?"

"He just walked in. Hold on." Brandon puts down the receiver and crosses the room. In the background, I first hear soft pleadings, then low, muffled arguing, then footsteps.

"Lisa?" The voice is now Tim's. He stumbles through what sounds like embarrassment and betrayal, "I, I don't know what to say. I didn't think Brandon would . . . god, I can't believe he told you! I never wanted . . . I'm not proud of—"

"Tim," I interject, "it doesn't change how I feel about you."

"Sure it does."

"Tim—"

"I should go," he says, slipping away. "Brandon and I need to talk."

The click startles me, and I listen to a few seconds of silence before hanging up. Strings of sadness and dread knot in my stomach. I wonder what they're saying to each other. What should I do? On one hand, I feel honored that Brandon thought enough of our friendship to solicit my help; on the other, Tim seemed really upset that his partner tried pulling me in as a mediator, a role I probably would accept but a risky one for all the relationships involved.

Soon after, Tim and Brandon separate. Doug and I try to maintain relationships with both friends, a feat I've never managed successfully with any straight former couple. Still, we try our best. Doug and I visit Brandon at Impulse, where he tends bar, and we meet Tim for movies and meals. Despite their relational turmoil, our encounters with each remain light and pleasant . . . until one February Sunday, when Doug and I find out what else has been going on.

"I Have Something to Tell You"

Seated at our dining room table, I push away the remains of our postgame dinner.

"The chicken cacciatore was great," Tim praises, smiling yet clenching his jaw tight. Tension lines his brow.

"Glad you could come," Doug tells him.

We sit without talking for a few moments. Doug's fork scrapes and clanks against the bottom of his pasta bowl. I take small sips of a mild Cabernet that gently warms my throat. Tim watches as hot wax flows like tears down the sides of cream tapered candles, their vanilla scent perfuming the air. "Listen," Tim says at last, "I have something to tell you."

"About Brandon?" I inquire, wondering if the separation is now divorce.

"Well, that's a whole other mess." He clears his throat. "A few months ago, I went to the doctor." My pulse quickens. "I got tested."

"For HIV?" I ask, just to make sure.

"Yes." I swallow hard. Tim peers into Doug's eyes, then stares at me, then looks down at the table. "I tested positive," he says, exhaling audibly.

My god, how did this—oh, I don't care how it happened! Pasta, vegetables, and chicken slosh in my stomach. When I close my eyes, droplets spill onto my cheeks.

At some level, I knew this day would come. This is part of the deal, I suppose, part of being invested in the lives of gay men. But I'm not ready, Tim. I'm not ready to watch you waste away. I'm not ready to sing dirges at your funeral.

But I'm here. Biting my lower lip, I reach across the table for his hand. I lock gazes with my friend and say the only thing that comes to mind, "Whatever you need . . . "

"I know," he replies.

"Come live with us," I offer. Tim laughs. "I'm serious. Our housemate Jennifer is moving home in May."

"Jennifer has cancer, right?" Tim queries. When I nod, he quips, "What are you running here, a hospice?"

"Will you think about it?" Doug asks.

"Sure," Tim promises. "Look, I'm sorry to lay all this on you. I haven't talked much about the HIV—to anyone. I mean, Brandon knows, of course." My lips part, but I say nothing. "He tested negative," Tim reports, "in case you're wondering. Anyway, I know you won't, but please don't tell anyone about this."

"You're the boss," Doug assures him.

"What about Brandon?" I inquire. "Will you tell him that we know? We could be here for both of you."

"May I think it over?"

"Of course," Doug replies. "How are you handling everything?"

"Better now. At first, Brandon completely lost it."

"He must have been so afraid," I say, "for you, and for himself."

"Mostly for me. In fact, a couple times, Brandon wanted to be unsafe."

"So he could share this experience with you," I surmise.

Nodding, Tim rises from the table. "I've given you enough to think about for one night."

"Don't go," I plead.

"Really, I need to. I haven't studied at all this weekend."

Reluctantly, Doug and I follow him to the front door. Tim opens his arms for a farewell embrace, and I grip him extra tightly. He then turns to Doug, who draws him close. Thanking us again for dinner, Tim takes his leave. From the front steps, we listen as soft, damp mulch squishes beneath his feet, then watch as our friend climbs into his Jeep, pulls away, and disappears.

Unable to sleep that night, I try writing field notes. The scene in our dining room is fresh and vivid, but no words come. These friendships, the "objects" of my study, have become my life, and I'm not sure I'm prepared to deal with the consequences. An hour later, I shut down my computer, still staring at a blank screen.

I return to bed feeling pained and terribly naïve. All this time, I presumed that I grasped what was happening between Brandon and Tim. Perhaps I understood the infidelity, but HIV adds a dimension quite foreign to me—until this evening. Was Tim's diagnosis an unrelated, contributing, or causal factor in their dissolution? Nothing Tim said provided a clue. Whatever role HIV played, the advice and support I offered now seem embarrassingly inadequate.

All week, I imagine their fear and despair. I so want to call Brandon, but I can't break my promise to Tim. I must wait.

"It Reminds Me of . . . Happier Times"

On Sunday, I sit in the dugout, pretending it's softball as usual. When he arrives, Brandon greets me warmly. How I wish I could reach out to him! Throughout the game, he and Tim avoid even eye contact with each other.

Afterward, as I'm walking to my car, Brandon yells, "Hey!" across the parking lot.

"Hey yourself!" I shout back as we move toward one another.

In the midst of an embrace, he tells me, "I read your paper." My heart skips a beat.

I had been inspired by Fine's notion of "working the hyphens."[5] The hyphen refers to the punctuation between terms culturally constructed as binaries (e.g., gay–straight). When we work the hyphen, we promote equitable relationships in the field and dialogue about and across our differences. This in mind, I gave copies of my qualitative methods paper to Brandon, Tim, David, and Gordon.

But as a novice fieldworker and a straight woman only beginning to understand gay men's experiences, relationships, and cultures, I had no idea how these men would respond to my portrayals. After a deep breath, I ask, "What did you think?"

"I loved it," Brandon says. "Since it was for a class, I expected it to be somewhat dry. But you wrote the report as a story. It was like reading a novel where I was one of the characters." He pauses. "What you said about Tim and me—about us being beautiful together—made me cry."

"Oh, Brandon," I sigh. "I had no idea things were so complicated."

"Tim said he told you about the HIV." I exhale my relief. "I wanted to tell you weeks ago," he says, "but Tim thought we should keep it between us. I understood why, but then he shut down. I felt so isolated." His blue eyes fill with tears. "After we found out, I wanted to get sick too. I did some crazy things."

His willingness to be so vulnerable stuns me. Both Tim and Brandon have opened themselves to me in ways unprecedented in my experiences with men. I take his hands in mine. "I know, Brandon. Tim told me."

Brandon looks down and away. "He did?"

"Your intentions were noble; you didn't want Tim to be alone."

He nods. "I thought we could cope with it together."

"But Tim would *never* want that for you. He's got enough to absorb without feeling responsible for you contracting the virus."

"And if we get back together, Tim will need me to be healthy . . . down the road." When I touch his cheek, he says, "Listen, I should go. May I keep the paper?"

"Of course."

"It reminds me of . . . " His voice trails off. Then, in almost a whisper, Brandon says, "happier times." We smile for each other before returning to our cars.

In the coming weeks, I leave several messages on Brandon's machine, some just to check in, some suggesting meetings. I keep thinking he'll need to talk, to reach out to someone trying to understand his pain, but perhaps Brandon feels he already reached out too far. Maybe his openness to me now makes him uncomfortable. He doesn't return my calls.

Rewind

One Sunday morning, I speak onto the familiar tape. "I'm thinking of you; I hope—"

Suddenly, the recorder beeps. "Hey, Lisa," Brandon says.

"It's great to hear your voice," I tell him.

"Sorry I've been so distant."

"Make it up to me by coming over for dinner and a movie."

Given the unanswered calls, I await his refusal. After a pause, he asks, "What time?"

I smile. "Six o'clock, Blockbuster. The three of us can pick out something together."

"Okay. Meet you there."

Throughout the day, I half expect Brandon to call with an excuse not to come. I know I get reclusive after a breakup, reaching the point where even supportive comments from close confidants open wounds and grate my nerves. But by 5:45, no such message has arrived.

At the video store, Doug and I find a surprisingly upbeat Brandon already perusing the new releases. A case ahead of me, Brandon stops in front of the Js. "Let's rent this," he suggests, pulling the film version of Paul Rudnick's *Jeffrey* from the shelf.

Remembering the plot, Doug and I exchange a panicked glance. "You sure?" Doug asks. Brandon nods, tucks the box under his arm, and heads for the register.

Back at our place, Doug and I settle into the sofa. We make room for Brandon, but he chooses the empty love seat instead.

Like the play, the film centers on Jeffrey, a gay New Yorker who swears off sex only to meet Steve, a dashing bartender. Jeffrey's intrigued but backs off. Friends intervene, convincing him to give Steve a chance, but when Jeffrey finally agrees to see him, Steve discloses he's HIV positive.

At this, I turn to Brandon and ask, "Did you know what this movie was about?"

"Yes," he says, meeting my gaze and nodding reassuringly.

"We can turn it off," Doug offers.

"No," Brandon insists, "I'd like to see how it turns out."

A second time, the title character takes flight. After breaking his date with Steve, Jeffrey rages, "I hate the world for giving me everything and then taking it all back!"

I again look over at Brandon. His body is rigid, his face frozen, his unmoving eyes filled with yearning and grief.

In the end, the death of a close friend convinces Jeffrey that he cannot be merely a spectator of AIDS. Jeffrey seeks out Steve, making him promise that he will never get sick, never die. They embrace, and the credits roll.

Jeffrey and Steve: beautiful, healthy, and together at this fairy-tale ending. Were their tale to continue, however, either might find loving too painful in the face of AIDS. And Steve's promises would prove impossible to keep. He *will* suffer, he *will* die—and die young. Biting my tongue, I reach for the remote and press "rewind."

That evening is the last time we see Brandon for a while, though he remains present in my mind. At the next game, Tim informs the team that Brandon has decided to quit Suncoast Softball.

Tim, Doug, and I continue batting around the idea of becoming room-mates. Though Tim decides to remain living downtown, twenty miles south of us, we stay in contact with frequent phone calls, none more dramatic than this one.

"It Gets Better"

"Lisa?" says the low, smooth voice.

"Tim," I say back, "what's up?"

"Are you sitting down?" he asks.

Man problem, I silently predict. Easing into my desk chair, I tell him, "I am now."

"I just got back from the clinic," Tim reports.

Oh god. HIV problem.

"Are you there?" he queries.

"I'm here." Here shifting in my seat, drowning in the blue of my computer screen, dreading what comes next.

"Nothing's final yet," Tim says.

With my trembling left hand, I begin tracing the spaces around my function keys.

"I had some more tests run."

Keep it together, Lisa. He doesn't need you freaking out. As I drag and sweep, specks of white and gray collect at my index fingertip.

"My T-cell count . . . "

Offer reassurance, comfort, support. With a puff, the particles scatter into the air, settling into and atop the camel carpeting.

Then he tells me, almost in a whisper, "It's normal."

Not sure I heard correctly, I spit out, "Wh—what?"

"*Above* normal, actually," Tim says, releasing a blissful sigh.

"W—wonderful," I respond, joining him in laughter. "That's wonderful."

"It gets better," he continues.

"What do you mean?"

"They tested me again for HIV."

Against my better judgment, I allow myself to consider the inconceivable. Could it all have been a terrible mistake? Oh please, please let it have been a mistake. "And?" I probe.

"And it came out negative."

We exhale together. "Oh my god, Tim."

"Not too ecstatic," he warns. "I don't get the final results for another ten days. But for now, everything looks good."

"Oh my god, Tim."

He laughs. "You said that already."

"We're here for you either way."

"I know," he responds. "Listen, I need to get to class."

"Thanks for the update. You take care." Hanging up the phone, I lay my head on the desk and mouth, "Yes!"

The verdict is rendered. After months of fear, anxiety, and dread, followed by ten days of fear, anxiety, and dread, we hear the words "false positive." Nothing ever sounded so sweet.

Early in the summer, Doug and I bump into Brandon at a club. I smile as our friend speaks dreamily of a new love interest. When I invite them to dinner, he lights up, exclaiming, "I can't wait for you to meet Beau!"

That night, Brandon walks through our door with his companion, an almost alarmingly handsome man with ebony hair and eyes, smooth, dark skin, and perfect white teeth. These two went to the same orthodontist, I predict. Doug must be equally struck by the pair, because as we ready dinner, he whispers, "What a shame they can't produce children together."

It proves an enjoyable evening of wine, pasta, and conversation. Beau seems confident and caring, and Brandon looks wonderfully content. We bid them good night thinking another friendship has begun. But, for whatever reason, we don't see this couple again for months.

Around this time, practice for the fall season starts. Stewart, a relief pitcher tall enough to play basketball, has returned from a brief hiatus, and new to the Cove are Joe, an auburn-haired right fielder with an infectious laugh; and Pat Martinez, a strong-hitting, half-French, half-Latin pitcher who looks closer to twenty-five than to his thirty-five years. Pat also agrees to take the coaching reins from Tim, who continues to play and recruit. One night, he brings a twenty-nine-year-old blue-eyed blond to the field.

"Meet Rob Ryan," Tim says.

Comparing the two men's stature, build, handsome features, cropped hair, and midear sideburns, I observe, "You two could be brothers."

When Tim replies, "Well, we're *not*," I assume that they're dating.

Later that night, when Tim and I are alone, I tease, "What's the deal? First you and Jack play ball together, then you and Brandon. Bringing Rob to the field could be dangerous."

"Rob's got a boyfriend," Tim assures me. "We're just friends."

The "just friends" stage of their relationship barely lasts through the weekend. At first, I'm a bit skeptical. Tim's dating history leads me to wonder if he's ready for another commitment. Still, Rob strikes me as someone worth hanging on to.

Watching them together is a lot like watching Doug and me. Rob mirrors my husband's kindness, stability, and quiet ambition, while Tim reflects my independence, emotionality, and occasional volatility. One night, I tell Doug that I hope Tim doesn't "mess things up with Rob."

"Why would Tim be the one to mess things up?" Doug asks.

"Just a hunch," I say, the real answer being, "Because *I'd* be the one."

Rob and Tim soon are inseparable. For a time, I remain uncertain about their future, but one Saturday morning, Tim makes evident both the depth of their partnership and the link between *our* partnerships.

Two Grooms and a Maid

I'm revising a conference paper when the phone rings. "Hello?"

"Lisa," Tim says, "Rob and I are lying in bed discussing you and Doug."

"Discussing us in bed?" I banter. "What have you been saying?"

"I was telling Rob that Brandon and I were the host couple at your wedding. Rob said that was very cool."

"Maybe someday we can be the host couple at *your* wedding," I hint.

"Actually, I was thinking you'd stand up for us."

"Really? So what, like groomsman and *groomsmaid*?" Tim laughs then shares my new word with Rob. "This is pretty serious," I reflect.

"Yeah," Tim replies with a bit of shyness.

"Well, know this: we honor your relationship with Rob and will do anything to support you."

With great tenderness, Tim says, "I love you."

"I love you too," I reply. "Now get back to bed."

\\\

I spend a lot of time processing how my interactions with Tim and other members of this community affect my personal and professional lives. I increasingly notice, for example, that my relationships with the Cove men alter my interpretations of other cross-sex encounters, both past and present, with both straight and gay men.

Dancing Dialectics

On this crisp March night in Memphis, the crowded Beale Street pub smells of Jack Daniels, lager, and sweat. Smoothing back wiry blond curls, the blues singer entices the crowd with "Proud Mary" à la Tina Turner.

From behind, an arm slips around my waist. I glance over my shoulder and find the attractive young professor my colleague Chuck recently introduced. We're all in town for the same regional conference. Hesitantly, I begin rocking back and forth, and he moves with my rhythm. I shake my head, trying to clear the cloud of Michelob. As he undulates against me, I remember the last time I danced like this with a man not my husband.

I'm two drinks past sober when Tim yanks me out of my chair, the sudden motion sending three vodka tonics rushing to my head. Navigating the dance floor, we find our space. As Brandon and Doug look on, we begin singing Sister Sledge in each other's ears.

The beat to "Proud Mary" picks up, and so does the young professor's urgency. He pulls me closer, swinging, grinding. Reaching under my leather vest, he spins me around. When our brown eyes meet, he says, "You're a great dancer."

I run my hands over Tim's well-defined chest and stomach as he holds onto my swaying hips. When I begin sliding my body up and down his, he stares at me with those soulful green eyes and says, "You are so sexy."

His comment surprises me a little. Am I sexy to him, I wonder, and if I am, does that change the meaning of our dance? Oh Lisa, don't spoil this moment. For once, just live it. "We Are Family" plays on.

"Rollin'. . ."

A familiar tape clicks on in my head: who is this man; what does he want from me; what messages am I sending; is this dance too much, too close; what comes after? Heeding my internal warnings, I decide to sit the next one out.

I study Tim's face, his shoulders, his arms. He's sexy, I think, and tell him so. Adrenaline surges through me, and I wonder: what is this rush; how can I feel so uninhibited yet so safe? Fighting the urge to intellectualize it, I throw back my head and laugh.

Why was it that I could "live in the moment" with Tim but not with the young professor? Why did the latter case feel so much more forbidden and troubling?

I have two answers, one more immediate, the other more retrospective. Within hours of the Memphis encounter, I reflected on my dance with Tim. At the time, the contrast felt striking, and I attributed nearly all of that to my dance partners' different sexual identities. In the former case, I was locked into the assumption "He's a straight man; therefore, he may want something beyond this." In the latter, I found freedom in the notion that "He's gay, so this dance is just this dance." I decided that Tim's gay identity allowed me to explore attraction in the comfortable context of an encounter where sex (though not sexuality) was taken out of the equation, while my colleague's straight identity kept both in the equation.

Since that time, my assessment has become more complex. Perhaps Tim and/or I found safety not in our sexual identities but in our trusting friendship or in our relationships with Brandon and Doug, who sat watching. The young professor and I, on the other hand, came together as strangers and outside the presence of our significant others. It's also possible that Tim was just "playing it straight," portraying an attraction he didn't feel. Perhaps the young professor was doing the same.

Looking back on my dance with Tim, I also have to ask what it *could* have meant for him, me, and/or us. Was he stepping outside the boundaries of his sexual identity? To what possible consequences? Did I risk developing a lingering attraction to him? After all, *I'm* not gay. Mutual or not, such an attachment could have disrupted our friendship and/or our primary relationships. I must therefore conclude that my immediate assessment, though experientially true, was fraught with false (or at least incomplete) assumptions.

However, none of that changes the fact that I continue to feel more at ease being close and affectionate with gay male associates than with straight male associates. Why? Is it because I feel more equal to gay men in terms of social power?

A gay man is privileged by sex but marginalized by sexual identity, while a straight woman is privileged by sexual identity but marginalized by sex. When they come together, their privilege and marginalization may offset one another, rendering them more like peers than might be possible in straight cross-sex friendships or in friendships between lesbians and men. As Malone suggests:

> A gay man who is arriving at a more positive feeling about his homosexuality and a straight woman who is discovering a heightened sense of her own independence are traveling in the same direction, even if along different paths. Both, in essence, are reaching out toward an enhanced certainty of their own worth, and in many cases they are able to assist one another in taking new steps forward.[6]

In "Dancing Dialectics," I show how an encounter with a straight man moves me to reflect on an interaction with a gay man. But the process works the other way as well. That is, sometimes encounters with gay men move me to reflect on interactions with straight men. Such is the case in "A Tale of Two Proms."

A Tale of Two Proms

"I had such fun at the Christmas party," Bob tells me, "that I agreed to chaperone my high school's prom. I would be so honored if you would accompany me."

Immediately, my eyes dampen. Why? I am touched by his sweet, if old-fashioned, invitation: "I would be so honored." Did he really say that?

But there's more here. For me, there's a hunger for a world where, without fear, Bob could bring a tuxedoed date and hold *him* beneath the cardboard-and-glitter stars. And, deep down, there's also an old ache rooted in a prom long past.

Staring into his locker, Ken says, "I was thinking maybe we might, y'know, go to, ah, prom." At that last word, my heart dissolves into underset Jell-O.

All but ensuring a prom night of Charles Dickens or MTV, I turned down two really nice boys on the off chance that this one (whom I've had a crush on for nearly a year) might, just might, ask me.

The four blocks home become a blissful dreamscape.

Short, sexy, flirty, fun, and best of all, *black*. My dress might not measure up to the elegant ensembles high schoolers are wearing today, but it seems pretty fine for an old married woman. Stand back, Bob!

A real trouper, my mom keeps handing gowns over the dressing room door: floor length, ballerina, and above the knee; long-sleeved and strapless; jewel tones and neutrals. All get the same response: "This makes me look fat!" I settle on a ho-hum number of loose-fitting ivory lace. Gazing into the boutique mirror, I think to myself, "If I were beautiful, Ken would love me."

Pulling out my chair, Bob insists, "Get whatever you want."

I open the menu and gasp. "My god, I can't let you pay for this!"

"You can, and you will."

Flipping to the back, I say, "Maybe they'll let me order from the Kiddie Kitchen."

He takes the binder from me and reopens it at the center. "I asked if you liked lobster, and you said yes. You are *not* getting 'chicken chunks' at the Lobster Pot." The waiter arrives with our sodas, and I guiltily order the lobster dijon.

Bob grins all through dinner as he watches me devour what may be the best seafood I've ever put in my mouth. "You're worth every penny." he says.

Zack dashes around the car to open Rebecca's door. Our double-daters then look on in disbelief as my escort scoffs, "Lisa's liberated." Ken's halfway inside the restaurant by the time I retrieve my purse from the trunk.

I order lobster that night—twin tails, market price. After dinner, my date's eyes pop at the sight of the check. "How much money did you bring?" he asks angrily.

"None," I sheepishly reply.

"I think we're keeping up," Bob observes, spinning me around the dance floor.

"I *know* we are," I say. "We'll be the talk of the school."

Just then, the relentless, deafening beat gives way to an easy sway. "A slow song already?" Bob jokes. "They just played one *an hour ago*." He puts his arms around my waist, and I rest my head on his shoulder as several of his students eye us closely, smiling and giggling. We finish with a dramatic dip.

Ken reluctantly agrees to go through grand march. In return, I'm not to bother him for too many dances. I spend this beautiful May evening standing by the rented fountain, sometimes with him, more often alone, watching the happy couples whirl about the cafeteria floor, wishing that I too had someone to sing corny Bon Jovi ballads in my ear.

On the ride back to Tampa, Bob and I merrily recall the lobster sauces that spilled onto our plastic bibs, the faces of boys who looked twelve as they tried to keep pace with girls who looked thirty, and the now-circulating speculation about the computer teacher's date. At a stoplight, he slides across the front seat and sweetly pecks my cheek.

Ken takes me home three hours before the curfew I begged and bargained for. When we pull up to my house, he leaves the engine running. I sit still a moment; he makes no move. I grab my handbag from the floor and pause; he makes no move. I place my fingers on the door handle and wait; he makes no move. I turn from him and say quietly, "Thank you for dinner. I'm sorry it was so expensive." In my mind, Ken spins me around and pulls me close for a cardiac-arrest-inducing kiss. In his car, he says and does nothing. My door still closing, he drives away.

"Lisa," Bob tells me, "you were the queen of the prom."

"Bob ," I reply, *"so were you."* We laugh so hard I nearly fall out of his truck.

When I read over these pages, I see that my prom experiences hardly could have been more different. Then again, *I* hardly could have been more different. With Ken, I was self-doubting, lonely, and desperate for some kind of completion. With Bob, I wasn't chasing a dream of romantic love but fulfilling a promise to a friend. For him, the evening provided a bit of cover and some pleasant moments. For me, it was nothing short of redemption for the painful memories associated with my only high school prom.

Going Home

"A Tale of Two Proms" is an example of how my gay encounters move me to reflect on my straight ones. But not all reflection involves delving into my past. Because I take my new consciousness into straight circles, the impact often is felt in the moment.

Revelation

I'm gazing into a nearly empty bottle of Amstel Light when the chair beside me swings away from the onyx Formica table. My eyes meet tan thighs then pan upward: cutoff jeans, tight and faded; black leather belt; and white stretch tank. I smile. Even before seeing the long, sun-lightened mane, I know this figure. We survived Bluffview Elementary through Lincoln High School together, from sports to sleepovers, from choir to crushes, from dreams to detention. Rising for an embrace, I ask, "How are you Kara?" Her perfume is faint yet deep and alluring. Obsession maybe. Or Lauren.

"Fabulous," she says.

As we did in fifth grade, we pull our seats close together. Leaning in, I inquire about her lover and her impending return to college. In turn, Kara asks of my teaching and Ph.D. program. Then she says, "I heard your wedding was beautiful."

"Had you been there," I tell her, "it would've been perfect."

An awkward silence falls. Her smile recedes as Kara peels the label from a Genuine Draft. "My brother said he ran into you at the Old Bank Bar." I let out a sigh. "He said it was nice to see you after all this time."

"Three years," I reply.

"Tony's getting his life together," Kara lets me know.

"I'm really happy for him," I remark, pulling a piece of lint from her hair.

After a pause, she queries, "So what else is new?"

"I've been hanging with a lot of gay men," I tell her, though I'm not sure why.

"They can be great friends," Kara says.

I clear my throat and stare into her intense emerald eyes. "I just realized why my mind went from your brother to these men." She leans in, tilting her head with curiosity. "I think if I'd grown up with less stifling ideas about sexuality, I would've had the affair . . . with you." She lays her hand atop mine and smiles.

This encounter with Kara expanded the horizons of my sexual orientation. Talking with her about Tony moved me to see that falling for her brother years before may have stemmed from feelings I had for her. After all, she was the one I grew up with, the one to whom I told my most intimate secrets, the one I ran to when feeling pained or self-destructive. Tony was several years older and lived away from home during most of my formative years. At twenty-two, I had a brief affair with him that sent me on an emotional roller-coaster. I never understood why my feelings deepened so much in such a short period. Now I think I may have been projecting. Tony was a male Kara, a "proper" object for my abiding love for his sister. My revelation of this to her and her supportive response provided a moment of profound connection between us. I hadn't felt so close to Kara in years.

Much later, Tim and I have a conversation about this story. "I never knew you had thoughts about women," he says. "I was kind of shocked, actually, but at the same time, I felt closer to you. That you not only felt those feelings but also were willing to share them so publicly, it was like we were the same somehow."

Unfortunately, not all my hometown interactions help me move forward.

Regression

The summer air smells of exhausted charcoal and the pine of Deep Woods Off. Always the good hostess, Cindy asks, "Does anyone need anything?"

"Sit down!" someone orders. "We're all stuffed!"

Her husband, Stan, meticulously scrapes the grill as I walk over to thank him. Doug and I first connected here three years ago. "No problem," he says. "I love to cook out."

"Not just for the barbecue," I say, looking over at Doug. Stan follows my gaze and smiles. "Without you, I wouldn't know him."

He laughs. "Bet you never thought you'd meet your husband in Lake City."

"Bet *you* never thought I'd marry your college roommate."

"Hell, I never thought that old playboy would *marry*."

"Stan!" Cindy calls from inside.

"Better go," he says.

I glance across the second-floor deck. Most of the dinner guests puff on three-dollar cigars, some for the acquired taste, others to discourage the swarming mosquitoes. As I listen to the voices of old friends and new acquaintances, the arms of my small, rural hometown enclose me in a warm, familiar embrace.

Doug sits talking with a college buddy. The pair giddily reminisces about intramural sports and fraternity escapades. "And remember those guys?" his friend asks.

"Which guys?"

"Those, those faggots," Wyatt says. "I don't remember their names." Doug's eyes narrow and his lips part, but no words come. "Who were those fags?"

"I'm not sure who you mean," is Doug's only reply. I look over at my husband, impatient for him to respond. We stare at each other, not knowing who should make an issue of it. Tensing my neck, grinding my teeth, I wait. Unable to stand it, I open my mouth to speak. Just then, Doug says to Wyatt, "You make it to Drake Relays this year?" I simmer.

Later, as we drive home, I scream out my anger. "How could we have let that slide by? We just sat there! We're disgusting, pathetic hypocrites!"

Now, I feel the hands of my small, rural hometown close around my throat, choking me into silence.

The incident at Stan's leaves me disappointed, both in a friend and, even more, in Doug and myself. It proved that despite all our experiences, we remain capable of letting overt homophobia pass. That it was a pleasant evening and a meeting of old (straight) friends seems a weak excuse for choosing passivity over protest.

Doug, however, is slower to anger than I, less politically charged, and more accepting of others' shortcomings. After hearing me rant for a few minutes in the car, he asks, "Can't you just move on?" The differences in our approaches to such issues put a momentary strain on our relationship. This isn't the only time.

A Foiled French Kiss

Throughout the night, Impulse echoes with sounds of pool balls smacking, darts popping, rocks glasses clanking, and men flirting. Set on "mute," the TV mounted above the stage plays a stripper video. I'm trying not to stare at the G-stringed Swedish meatball moving to the groove only he can hear. "How's Brandon?" I ask as Doug returns from the bar.

"Busy," he replies, holding out a bottled water. I reach for the container, but Doug maintains his grip. My fingers playfully caress his hand, now cool and damp from condensation. Slipping his other arm around my waist, he pulls me close. I peck his lips and turn my cheek, but Doug moves in for another kiss. Our mouths meet, first briefly, then for a prolonged conference. When I feel his tongue prying, I push him away.

"*Enough*," I say, a little too forcefully.

With a wounded look, he steps back. "What's your problem? You've never seemed to mind a public display of affection."

"That isn't what that was," I tell him.

"What *was* it then?"

I look up, staring into his azure eyes, and say, "A public display of heterosexuality."

"*What* are you talking about?" he asks indignantly.

"You *never* kiss me like that in front of people. Maybe you were trying to prove something to the men in this bar."

"Whatever," Doug snaps, taking a few soothing gulps of Michelob Light.

"Regardless, I'm trying to show a little respect."

"For whom?"

"For them! In straight spaces, how often does a gay man feel that he can stick his tongue in his boyfriend's mouth?" Flicking his wrist, Doug brushes me off. "We're on their turf," I say. "We don't need to flaunt the privileged access we have to one another's bodies."

He downs the rest of his beer.

Intelligent retort, I think. I then try to read the strained expression on his face. Beneath the anger, is Doug embarrassed or hurt by my political reaction to his (perhaps innocent) affection? However he feels, that foiled French kiss will be this evening's final passionate gesture.

Late that night, questions reel through my mind. Was Doug using me as a badge of heterosexuality, or did he just want a kiss? Does he feel he must prove his sexual identity—to gay men, to me, to himself—or has my consciousness about these issues been raised out of the stratosphere? Am I experiencing "straight guilt"? How *did* the men at Impulse perceive our affection? As I feared? As a *positive* sign of our comfort there? Did any of them even notice? Surely they have more important things to watch than a straight couple. Then I look over at Doug and wonder, did I harm *us* by that reaction?

Still, if he hadn't met me, if Doug were straight and *single*, would he have the same kinds of friendships with gay men? It's an unanswerable question. To establish and deepen these bonds, each of us needed the other. Without me, Doug wouldn't live in Tampa; without Doug, I wouldn't know David; and without each other, we might never have had the courage to enter and explore David's world. But now that we have, what are the consequences?

When he opens his eyes the next morning, I smile at him. "I'm sorry about last night," I say. "If I overreacted, it's because our place in this community still seems precarious, and I'm sensitive to anything that might jeopardize it. But I want you to know that I'm really happy with who we're becoming together." Doug leans over, and I offer him a belated kiss.

5

Life Projects

He Said/She Wrote

In September 1996, I enroll in an anthropology class on life history. I decide to use the course as an opportunity to become closer to someone in my research community. Though I feel confident that David or Tim would consent, a siblinglike rapport has emerged in my relationship with Gordon. I decide to see what that sparks.

My finger quivers a bit when dialing his number. I'll get course credit from this project, but what will *he* gain by sharing his story? When Gordon picks up, I immediately blurt out, "I have another class assignment."

"Oh gawd!" he says, playing up his northeastern Jewish accent. "What now?"

"I only need one thing—your life story."

"Is that all?" Gordon quips. "Hey, it's no problem, Lis. Just tell me what to do."

After determining that Wednesdays work best, we schedule three meetings for October.

Behind the Mask

I'm preoccupied for most of the trip to Gordon's. Will my questions make him uncomfortable? Might he share experiences I'm not prepared to confront? How emotional will he get? In what ways could the revelations affect our relationship or his relationship with Doug?

Before I know it, I'm pulling up to his apartment. I gather my equipment, take a deep breath, and make my way to the entrance. My knock is met with a shout, "Come in!"

I open the door and take in my surroundings. Gold-framed prints and original art hang from the paneled walls painted white. The room bears the scent of his new leather couch, and a wall-unit air conditioner hums, loudly offering its chill. Gordon greets me with a hug. "How's it goin'?" he asks. "Something to drink?"

"Soda, please," I request.

He moves to the white-on-white kitchen, returning a moment later with beverages. Gordon hands me a can before sinking into his forest-green sofa. He props his feet upon the wooden trunk that doubles as a coffee table for his Snapple. I sip Diet Sprite as we spend several minutes chatting about his hair-replacement company. At a pause in the conversation, Gordon asks, "Should we get started?"

"Okay," I respond, turning on the tape recorder. "Tell me about your mom."

"My mom, Marilyn, is fifty-five. Born and raised in Philadelphia. Her mother came from Russia; she had twelve sisters and one gay brother."

The last reference grabs my attention. "Really?"

"Yeah. My great-uncle, Gene, has had a girlfriend, Donald, for about sixty years." Noting Gordon's choice of "girlfriend" as opposed to "lover" or "partner," I wonder if he means this affectionately or demeaningly.

"Gene is superfeminine," Gordon continues. "He could pass for a woman in a heartbeat. He lives on the other coast of Florida, but I really don't know him."

"Do you believe he had any role in the development of your sexual orientation?"

"No," Gordon insists, "none.

"Anyway, my parents met in Atlantic City. My mom was seeing somebody else at the time, but I guess Dad got her to the altar first. They dated eight or nine months and were married in '61.

"Quite a good mother," he says. "Always there if you need her. She's a friend, someone I can talk to about a lot of things, *but not everything.*" Gordon shoots me a look of "get my drift?"

"What about your father?"

"My dad is sixty-six. The name he goes by is Tex. Born and raised in South Philly, finished high school, joined the Coast Guard, and went to college. He was a teacher.

"I enjoy doing things with my dad. Watching a ball game, walking the beach."

"And siblings?" I query.

"I have an older brother who was born in '64; I came around in '69, and I have a younger sister who was born in '75. My mom also had a number of miscarriages."

"Has she talked about that?"

"No," Gordon answers, adjusting his round, silver-framed glasses.

"That must have been painful for her," I push.

"In my family, we've never had any real outpouring of emotion. My mom has watched two of her best friends die and both her parents, but I've never seen her cry."

Later, I wonder if this unemotional family environment discourages Gordon from disclosing his sexual orientation. Is he afraid this will crack the armor? Or might Gordon be seeking an affective response that, given his family history, he knows he's unlikely to get?

"Anyway," Gordon resumes, "my brother's name is Steven. Always the top of everything: high school, college, the military, his business. He and his wife Tobi have a three-year-old son, Harris—great kid, love seein' him—and a newborn baby, Jacquelyn."

"And your sister," I prompt, "tell me about her."

"Liz has been a gymnast since I can remember. I'm probably one of her biggest fans. My parents put their little girl on a pedestal. She's 'the golden child.'"

"What child are *you*?"

"I was always the nice one, the one who balanced everything out, the easy one. And I'm probably the one who most needs my parents' approval and support."

Approval/support, I write in my interview notes, *two resources risked by disclosure*. Not wanting to push too hard too soon, I request, "Tell me about your childhood."

"I grew up in northeast Philadelphia, where the majority of people have college degrees and are middle to upper-middle class, white, and Jewish. Not very representative of the world.

"Started school at Bustleton Elementary. I was the best math student, bar none. My comprehension in reading? Pathetic! My attention span was *the worst*. I always remember this on the back of my report cards: 'Gordon seems to find his neighbors' work more interesting than his own.' Thank god I was sorta cute." We both laugh.

"I remember playing handball in the schoolyard. I was into soldiers and superheroes. Rode my bike a lot, was on the swim team. Started baseball when I was seven or eight."

A boyhood not unlike my brothers', I scrawl in my notes.

"Thirteen was a big year. Being Jewish, I went to a bar mitzvah every weekend."

Since we've never talked about his Judaism, I ask, "What role does religion play in your life?"

"I go to synagogue maybe once or twice a year. Do I believe in a higher being? I can pretty much say no."

"I was raised Catholic," I tell him. "I'm not sure I believe in sin as it is traditionally constructed, though sometimes I wonder if I'm living a moral life."

Gordon processes what I have said. "Guilt has been big in my life. It's always looming over me, over 'the gay thing.' When I'm with a man, I have a sense like, 'This is not right.' *That* I still have not been able to block out."

As I read them now, his words move me to reflect on my socialization's sexual scripts. "Good girls," I was told, wait until marriage. It took me years to realize that goodness and chastity weren't necessarily related, so I can understand why Gordon still struggles to sever an even more powerful cultural linkage—that between "right" and straight.

We return to junior high. "I was an average student," he says. "That was sheer laziness. Outside class, I golfed and started playing tennis. Oh, and I had a girlfriend."

"What kind of sexual relationship did you have?"

He grins. "*Never* intercourse. Lots of playing, lots of kissing. My hands up and down her chest. That would be about the extent. I don't think she ever hit below the belt."

"And then high school?"

"Ah, puberty! The bad skin, the really nasty hair!" I laugh. "Dated a couple girls, nothing serious. Had my first sexual experience. I was a junior. One night, I went over to watch a movie at my girlfriend's house. It was ready to happen. Wasn't good sex by any stretch, wasn't passionate, but I scored the big one.

"As for friends, most were from the neighborhood—very homogeneous social scene.

"Senior year," he continues, "I was prepping for college." Gordon pulls off his cap and rubs his scalp. "Freshman year at Pitt was *tough*. I was pretty homesick, very close to dropping out. I think things were going to my head about the sexuality."

"Had you thought about your sexual orientation before college?"

"It was always there. I remember I must have been eight or nine and playing football. A dream that went off in my head was that the quarterback would get hurt, and I would get hurt too just to hang out with him on the sidelines."

"Any sexual experimentation?"

"Not with a guy," he says. "Not until twenty-five."

"Was there a moment when you knew for sure that you were gay?"

Gordon inhales deeply. We've hit something. "I read a book called *Behind the Mask*.[1] It's by a baseball umpire who's gay. I was in the middle of reading it the day of my college graduation. This hit me harder than anything ever in my life. The next week was *awful*. I would look at myself in the mirror and break down. No one knew what was wrong with me."

His eyes fix on the ceiling, as though envisioning a scene. "I remember, my dad and I went out to dinner. He said, 'Gordon, if anything's the matter—if you got a girl pregnant—I'm there for you.' And that shattered me because I thought, 'If only it were that easy.'

"This book ran my life for more than a year. I wrote the author, almost obsessively. He wrote me once, and I still have the letter. I'll get it." Gordon strides to the dining room, opens his briefcase, and shuffles through the top pocket. He grabs an envelope and hands it to me, saying, "You're the only one who's ever seen this."

He leaves the room, and I open the letter. It reads, "Just a note to tell you to hang in there. Things do work out. Stay well and always be proud, Dave Pallone."

Gordon returns with a well-worn paperback. "Here's the book."

Gazing at the handsome, athletic man on the cover, I ask, "Why do you think *Behind the Mask* spoke to you that strongly?"

"Pallone was the first gay man I could look at and say, 'He's a lot like me.' If he'd written about how he dressed up in his mom's clothes and pranced around in heels, it probably wouldn't have had such an impact."

Gordon's tone becomes more insistent, "You've been torn up inside for so many years, knowing something's there. This opened the floodgates, and I was a mess." He pauses, then quietly continues, "I always think of myself as my dad's boy, and being gay is not what he would envision for his son. It's probably one of my biggest hangups. There are certain songs, certain sayings that relate to your father . . ." Gordon struggles to find the words, "they hit a soft spot."

Not sure how to approach this, I paraphrase his statement, "You feel like you're not living the life he would want you to?"

"Well, they always say the apple falls close to the tree. And in so many ways, I have, but in one very important way, I haven't."

I gently press for specifics, "Can you give me an example of something that would, as you said, 'hit a soft spot'?"

Gordon picks up his Snapple and takes a long swig. "One is a song
you probably know. It's called 'Cat's in the Cradle.'"

"Why does that affect you?"

"Because it says, 'I'm gonna grow up and be just like you, Dad.'"

I sense he's ready to move on, so I ask, "What happened after graduation?"

"Moved to San Francisco for five months. That was a true running
away. Came back to Philly and got a job selling hairpieces. This was '93."

"I was bouncing off the walls, still doing the straight scene and going
home with nothing but a void. I don't know where I came up with the
money, but I went to a gay dating service. Met this guy, Sal. He seemed
'normal' to me. He was professional, a nice guy. We played around a bit,
but I did *nothing*. I was *not* comfortable. I never even kissed him. I was-
n't ready. It's still a little awkward, kissing a guy."

"Does that apply to all sexual things?"

He sits back. "That would apply to a lot of sexual things, actually. In
the past, I've had problems reaching orgasm with guys. There are times
I can't even get it going. I guess it just depends on the person, the comfort level."

Moved by the depth of his candor, I ask, "Have you ever been in
love?"

"No," he says. "I've cared for people, but you're always holding back
something. You're not really letting yourself go."

In my field journal, I note his shift to second person. Gordon seems to
do this at times when he might need some emotional distance from the
subject at hand.

The chronology resumes. "Anyway, back in Philly, I picked up the
gay newspaper a couple times. Watching me had to be a joke. It literally took me an hour to go down and grab it. And there were times I
couldn't; I wouldn't open that mailbox. I thought the whole world was
watching me.

"November of '93, I get a call out of the blue. It's Pallone, the author,
on my phone. He's in Philadelphia. He asks if I want to have dinner. I
couldn't believe it! I expected our meeting to be this total catharsis for
me, but it was nothing like that. It was just a meal.

"Soon after, I got an offer from another hair place down here. I knew
I had to take it. I had to get away. I was exploding, to say the least."

Just then, the phone rings. When Gordon returns from answering it,
he says, "I don't know how far you want me to go."

"Would you like to stop?"

"Yeah," he answers. "I've had enough. All this talking about myself—please!" I gather my tape recorder and notepad, and Gordon hugs me goodbye.

On the drive home, I reflect on what he shared. In some ways, I'm struck by how closely his narrative matches those of most boys with whom I came of age: middle-class upbringing, boyhood superheroes and baseball, awkward sexual experiments with girls. In other ways, I'm touched by the particular details of his struggles: the stereotypes that prevented him from associating his experience with that of other gay men, including his own great-uncle, the epiphany of reading about a baseball umpire, the "shattering" when confronted by his father, the lingering guilt associated with male intimacy.

He shared so much, I marvel. If we can maintain this openness to one another, I suspect that both my project and our relationship will blossom.

Saying the Words

The following Wednesday, we pick up the chronology where we left off. "I came to Tampa for a weekend," Gordon tells me. "Met Steve Hornsby, who'd placed an ad for a roommate. He told me he was gay; I told him I was. That was the first time I said those words. Went home to Philly, packed up my car, and drove down, basically with nothing.

"A week later, Steve took me to Tracks, my first gay bar."

Mine too, I think.

"My eyes must have been like a little kid's. I was staring at everybody. I'd never seen a transsexual or drag queen. The butterflies in my chest were so intense that I don't remember the night that well. For almost a year, I had those same feelings every time I walked into a gay bar.

"July of '94, Steve took me and his boyfriend to Atlanta. Did an AIDS walk there. Steve had told me, probably about a month earlier, that his boyfriend was HIV positive. You see the concern on a good friend's face. Even though his lover is still healthy, you know what could happen."

As Gordon talks on, I again note the shift away from first person.

"Soon after, I met Terry, who introduced me to the softball league."

"What does it mean to you," I ask, "participating in the league?"

"Coming into a gay softball league was a little odd for me. I don't fit a lot of the gay stereotypes. I'm very competitive, and even though we're playing in a competitive league, I don't classify it as such. But I've gotten a lot more patient with people who don't understand the game, people who can't hit, people who can't catch. I've learned that the league is, yes, for sport, but it's equally important as a social setting. It gives people who've never felt comfortable playing a forum to do that. Suncoast

Softball probably has been my best experience as far as meeting people. Some of my closest friends are from the softball team."

I see an opening to ask something I've wanted to know for a long time: "Were there any thoughts about Doug being on the team?"

He smiles. "There were definitely some kicks and jabs about the 'straight guy,' but not that often. I never even *thought* about it as a problem."

"Do you have a sense of where Doug and I fit into this community?"

"I give you a lot of credit, because I don't think I would be as comfortable as you are. *I'm* still not totally comfortable with a lot of people in the gay life. But I'm learning.

"I think Doug genuinely likes playing," Gordon continues. "I feel that when we socialize, he doesn't see us as 'gay Gordon,' 'gay Pat,' 'gay Al.' He sees me as Gordon, who likes sports but happens to be gay. And I don't look at him as Doug, my *straight* friend. I see a good guy with a nice wife who plays on my gay team but happens to be straight."

While transcribing, I wonder if it's truly possible to see someone's sexual identity in "happens to be" terms. After all, I probably wouldn't know Gordon if he were straight. I can't say he's my friend *because* he's gay. I've met lots of gay men with whom I haven't become friends. But neither would I say that Gordon is my friend *in spite of* his gay identity.

He then looks at me and observes, "You're friendly with everybody on the team. You know people better than some of us know each other."

I smile, then ask, "What else happened after you joined the Cove?"

"Went to my first gay softball tournament. We played a team of lesbians, and they beat the shit out of us."

His playful tone fades. "We had one guy there who passed away a couple months later, Michael, whom you knew. He was sick as a dog from AIDS, right near death, but out there to play hard and have his last hurrah." Gordon's voice softens. "When he did die, they had a memorial for him. Michael was always attractive, a very outgoing, athletic person. You see somebody—one day he's alive; the next, you're sitting with your friends who also are HIV positive. It makes you more compassionate."

He quickly changes the subject. "As far as relationships, I dated a couple people here and there, but nothing more than a month. That was usually my doing. There were times when it was very lonely.

"Then, in March of this year, I went to Vegas with my friend Hope. She was the first person from Philly I told. Hope kept pushing the questions: 'You go out much? You seein' anybody?' So finally I said, 'Listen,

I'm gay.' I didn't bounce around too much. It was like, 'This is it; deal with it.' Hope sat back, and she goes, 'I'm shocked.' And I said, 'Bullshit.' I know my old friends, and my gut feeling is that they all know. Still, it threw Hope a little, because now she was confronted with it. She asked questions like, 'How long have you known? Why are you gay?' I told her, 'This is not a phase; it's something that's been in my head since I was a kid.' Then she wanted to know about the sex, but I wasn't willing to tell her about that. I basically copped out. 'I haven't done that much, so I'm not the best person to ask.' I didn't want to get too personal; besides, I'd never ask Hope what position she takes in the bedroom."

"How did it feel to tell her?" I ask.

"I had a little rush," he recalls. "It felt good."

"How has the disclosure affected your relationship?"

"I went to see her a couple weeks ago. Nothing's changed, except now we can talk about it. I still don't want to discuss it too much. I don't like throwing it in people's faces."

Later, while reading the transcript, I write in the margin, "What's the assumption here? That any statement is somehow 'throwing it in people's faces'? We don't think of references to heterosexuality (e.g., mentioning one's wife or husband) in this way."

"Memorial Day," Gordon continues, "we went to a softball tournament in Atlanta. The Friday night I got there, I saw this guy and could not catch his attention for the life of me. Oddly enough, I got an introduction to him the next day. We had dinner that night and went back to his house. As usual, nothing happened. Sex is one thing that I do hold in some regard. I don't give myself up to a lot of people. I'm a big flirt; I have no problem admitting that. But as far as what I do in my bedroom—with others anyway—it's fairly minimal. Still, it's nice having someone next to you in bed. This Atlanta guy was my 'type': strong personality, well built, a little older, probably in his early forties. But nothing came of that.

"Around that time, I also was in the midst of opening Progressive Hair Designs."

"Everybody at your office knows, right?"

"Now they know, yes. There was a gay night at Busch Gardens, and my receptionist got free passes. So I went, and she saw me there. From that moment on, it was understood.

"Then my sister was down a couple weeks ago. We're pretty close; we talk a couple times a month, usually about what's going on in her life. But this time, she had to listen. I'd waited until I thought she was mature enough to handle it, but when she got here, I still saw my sister as a kid. That was probably why I held off.

"I was hemming and hawing," Gordon remembers. "Finally, I sat her down in my office. I said, 'Liz, we need to have a talk.' I asked her, 'Do you have any idea what this might be about?' And her, her, her words were, '*Are* you?' And I said, 'Yeah, I am.' So she knew." He then adds, "She had a look of disappointment on her face."

"Mmm," I utter, nodding my head and thinking, *I'm sorry for that.*

He must read my nonverbals, because Gordon reassures me, "It didn't really bother me, because I love my sister, but we're not on equal levels. She's still a kid. You know, the disappointment didn't really bother me. And really, she didn't say anything else." As Gordon removes his cream Nike cap to rub his scalp, I note the repetition in his statement and wonder if he found his sister's response more painful than he's letting on.

"How did all of this feel?" I query.

"When I told her, there wasn't much anguish; afterward, there was no big relief."

Then he says, "I took her to a gay bar that night—not to throw it in her face."

That phrase again, I note. Does Gordon believe *I* would think that?

"Liz already knew a lot of my gay friends; she just didn't know they were gay—until I said so. She was shocked about Al and Pat. Taking her to the Cove, I wanted Liz to see that my life was nothing to freak out over."

As Gordon speaks, I remember meeting Liz at that bar. By their presence there, I knew he'd told her. When Gordon and Doug struck up a conversation, I went over and said in her ear, "You and Gordon must have a very special relationship. It's nice he has family he can trust." She nodded and smiled, seeming to appreciate the compliment.

"I'm glad you were there," Gordon says. "You guys helped out a lot. Liz could see that people who aren't gay can be totally comfortable around us."[2]

This gets me thinking. For some time, I've wondered about the roles Doug and I play in this community. In addition to teammate and friends, perhaps we also serve as confidence builders and ambassadors. That is, our friendship can give these men hope that other straight associates will be supportive. Moreover, by showing our acceptance and support to their family and friends, we might help cultivate such feelings and behaviors in them.

Gordon then says, "I was very open with Liz, but I did ask her to keep things between us. When it's time, and I need to tell other people, I'll handle that on my own."

When he pauses, I nod, sensing that he's completed his chronology.

On the drive home, I think about Gordon's coming out. I wonder why he told his friend Hope first, and why then? I next consider his conversation with Liz. Was he really so unaffected by her look of disappointment? Are there no other emotions there? Finally, I wonder about the nondisclosure to his parents. Why hasn't he told them? What's at stake? What does he fear? Maybe I'll learn next time.

"There's No Looking Back"

To make our final session more interactive, I bring along my photo albums and high school yearbook and ask Gordon to dig out his.[3] In our first half hour, he shares pictures of his family, his old house, girls he used to date, the street he lived on in San Francisco, and softball teammates. We pause longest on a photo of Michael at a tournament in Boston.

In the next half hour, I give him a visual history. I share my parents' courtship story, my birth story, and tales of growing up in rural Minnesota, going to college, meeting Doug, and coming to graduate school in Florida. During this time, Gordon becomes my interviewer, asking about, for example, what it's like to live in a small town, what separated me from my last boyfriend, and how Doug and I handled our once long-distance relationship.

When I close the album, he asks, "So where are we?"

"I'd like to talk more about disclosure, how you decide whom to tell and when."

Gordon exhales. "One problem is that I tend to see my family on special occasions: Thanksgiving, my sister's graduation. A conversation like that isn't meant for a time of celebration. It wouldn't be fair to them."

What's fair to *you?* I silently query.

"If I'm going to have 'the talk' with somebody, it has to be the right time, one-on-one, and preferably in the privacy of my home or that person's home. I don't know if it's necessary to tell everybody. My sister was 'cause we're close, but my brother doesn't need to know. My parents, in due time. When they want to hear it, I'll tell them."

I wonder how Gordon will know that they "want to hear it."

As if reading my thoughts, he says, "I don't think they'll ask, 'Gordon, are you gay?' But someday, my mom will give me an opening. If she's ready for the answer, I'll give it. She asks questions now, like, 'Do you want to get married?' But she does it in a way that ensures we can't have a conversation. She'll ask when she knows I'm walkin' out the door."

"What about your dad?"

"He's clueless."

"Would you tell both your parents at the same time?"

"I've talked to people about that, and some say, 'Tell them together,' but then I've heard, 'Tell them separately.' I probably would tell Mom first. I talk to her a lot more often."

"That conversation won't be very emotional," he predicts. "I'm not gonna spill my guts and cry. I've done that a thousand times by myself, going over it in my head."

There's the emotion, I reflect, perhaps already exhausted from those "thousand" private moments. I then ask, "Is there anybody you hope never finds out?"

"No," Gordon answers.

"Who would be the most difficult for you to tell?"

"I don't think 'difficult' is the right word."

I decide to push, "It doesn't scare you to think about talking to your dad about this?"

"No. It won't be like a conversation about a ball game, all smiling and laughing. It'll be a pain in the ass. Will it help him know who I really am? I don't think so."

Gordon Bernstein and Lisa Tillmann-Healy

Will it help *you?* I wonder.

"He's not gonna ask me a thousand questions. My father wants to know that the weather's nice and the car's driving well. My fear is not rejection but that he'll look at me differently. Like I said, this isn't a life my father would envision for his son."

"Do your parents have any gay friends?" I ask.

He laughs. "How many married couples have gay friends?" I raise my hand, and Gordon shakes his head, saying, "Would you classify yourself as *anywhere* near the norm?"

"What would your life be like if you still lived close to your family and your old friends?"

"If I hadn't come to Florida, I would be

living the straight life today, I can guarantee it. I'd be miserable, probably suicidal, because I wouldn't have anyone to talk to. Eventually, you're going to bust. So I'm glad I did what I did; there's no looking back."

I finish with, "Do you want to say anything about the process of being interviewed?"

"I don't talk about myself that often," he reflects. "I'm much quicker to listen. Most people know me as always pleasant, always happy. I'm definitely good at putting on a show. I'm actually very sensitive, very affectionate, very caring. But I don't give that up to everybody." Laughing, Gordon observes, "You probably know more about me than just about anybody else does." I smile, and Gordon says, "I enjoyed this."

Returning to the Field

The life history interviews inspire me to invest even more of my personal and professional selves in this community. On occasion, however, I'm reminded of my old straight(er) self.

Fund-Raiser Feelings

The Cove begins to bustle this Friday night. The place has filled rapidly in the last half hour, making it difficult to navigate with my tray of shooters. I've already made three passes around the establishment and am not looking forward to another. I suck a pineapple square from its plastic cup, hoping for some sticky courage.

I approach a group of African American males, put my hand on the tallest one's forehead (as if checking his temperature), and say, "Mmm, gelatin deficiency."

Smiling, he asks, "Is it serious?"

"Well, it has been known to cause boring conversation, bad dancing, and [lowering my voice] *impotence.*"

"Quite a sales pitch," he replies, pulling out a five. "Is one enough?"

"Better have two," I suggest.

I move on to a couple standing at the edge of the dance floor. "Jell-O?" I offer. "Like your mother used to make."

"How's that?" one asks.

"With vodka!"

"Ah," he plays along, "you've met my mother."

After this sale, it's time to take inventory. I've eyeballed a dozen remaining shooters when I feel a hand on my backside. I turn, expecting to find my husband or maybe a guy from the team. Instead, I meet the chocolate eyes of a stranger—muscular, well oiled, with bare, shaved chest. Must be a stripper. He winks, then turns away.

I'm speechless. I feel a bit flattered, a bit more violated, but mostly surprised. Has it been that long since I set foot in a straight bar? In here, I realize, my guard goes down, *way* down, wonderfully down. Too far perhaps.

As I continue learning about my research community, I continue learning about myself. Each day, I'm reminded that my connections with the Cove men shape, maintain, and transform my identities. But sometimes, I wish a self that is maintained could be one transformed.

Fussing over Me

"Lisaaa?" Doug calls from the living room. "It's 10:37."

"I know," I say, changing my shorts for the third time. "I'll just be a second."

"You said that ten minutes ago," he replies with more than an edge of impatience.

Rushing into the bathroom, I take another glance in the mirror. I blot my lipstick and tuck unruly bangs behind my ears. When I reach for a pink bottle of perfumed lotion, Doug appears in the doorway. "What are you doing?" he asks. I put down the container and begin a search for my dangling gold earrings. "Lisa," Doug pleads, grabbing me by the arm and catching my gaze, "we're going to the *softball field*." I nod. "Why are you fussing then?"

I freeze. "I, I don't know."

"Besides, they're all *gay*; if anyone should be worried about looks, it's *me*."

I know he's right, but at some level, being attractive to them *does* matter to me. Why? Do I so need male validation?

As a feminist, I should be able to release myself from our culture's impossible ideals. If I can't do that in the company of these men, where can I? Then again, some of them can be equally fixated on appearance. How did we get this way? Are straight women and gay men predisposed to obsess about physique or complexion? Is there a gene named Maybelline?

What about the economics and politics of appearance? Don't entire industries flourish by manufacturing discontent over so-called problems (from thin hair to wide hips) whose solutions always are product based? Is it a coincidence that the more women and gay men advance socially, the more unattainable our standards of attractiveness become? At the same time, are we still so disempowered—personally and politically—that we cling to appearance because it offers at least the illusion of control? Isn't it true that the more emotional, physical, and economic resources we can be convinced to expend on our own bodies, the fewer we have left for the social body? Whose interests are served by keeping straight women and gay men in a perpetual state of anxiety?

I look at myself. I look at these men. I look at our culture(s). And I wonder how we can learn to accept ourselves, and each other, as we are.

Confessions

Al and I take adjacent seats and begin studying the café's menu. When the waitress comes, he orders lobster bisque and pasta marinara, and I request lemon linguini.

I ask my companion about his parents' recent visit. With his index finger, Al traces the rim of his water glass and reports, "They reminded me that they're not getting any younger." Then, in his mother's genteel drawl, he says, "Nothin' would make us happier than to see you settle down."

"With a woman," I add.

"What else?"

His folks' wish stirs my compassion. Sensing Al's vulnerability, I decide to share my own most stigmatized identity. I swallow my trepidation, then say, "I know how difficult it can be to reveal a secret part of yourself to your parents. When I was fifteen, I began binging and purging. To varying degrees, bulimia has been part of my life since that time."

Silence. I hold my breath, waiting. With expansive eyes, he at last remarks, "You *do* that?"

Al's tone of surprise, tinged with an older brother's disappointment, gives me pause, but I decide to continue. "This is something I've only begun to tell my family. Out of shame, I avoided the possibility of their hurt or disgust by keeping my struggles to myself."

"Well," he says, waving his hand dismissively, "I'd have *no* problem telling my parents something like *that*." My heart drops.

I flash back to my third interview with Gordon. At the end of the previous session, I gave him a piece I wrote about my conflicted relationships with my body and with food.[4] I shared it because he had shared so much, and I wanted to show him that I was willing to take risks too. But when I ask if he has anything to say about my paper, he replies, "Which?"

The question catches me off guard. "The, ah, bulimia paper."

He stumbles into a response. "Oh, right. Um, it was very short and sweet and to the point. I don't know what to say, really."

I drive home that night second-guessing my decision to share my secret life. Was it too much? Too graphic? Too shocking?

Sitting here, I similarly question myself. Obviously, Al thinks that my experience with "coming out" as a bulimic woman is trivial when compared to coming out as a gay man. Emotion rises in my chest. I consider the attention, empathy, even love I've tried to show these men. Is this what I get in return? Fuck you, Al, I think. Fuck your ignorant, self-absorbed response.

But then the anger dissolves into pain, a pain of reaching across difference and falling into a lonely abyss.

The fiery-maned server returns with our food. Picking up my fork, I stare into the oily layer sitting at the bottom of my dish. "I'm sorry, Al," I say quietly and without looking up, "I didn't mean to suggest it was the same."

For some time, I've been asking myself, "Why aren't there more women in this community?" At first, it seemed obvious: many straight women are heterosexist, and gay men retreat from that. But the picture keeps taking on new dimensions. It now occurs to me that, as in straight cross-sex friendships, women involved with gay men may not receive the kind of emotional support female friends tend to offer. My interaction with Al serves as an example. For lesbians and (other) feminists, moreover, the misogyny alone could keep them away. If I hear the term "fish" one more time, I'll scream!

In spite of my budding critical consciousness, I sometimes wonder how I'd react if another woman came on the scene. Anna, who played for the Cove in the fall of 1995, hasn't been around much since. I've been to dinner and movies with Tim and his friend Linda, and I've met some of Jeff's female coworkers out at the clubs. Still, for better or worse, I'm currently the only woman who's well integrated into this group.

Doug, on the other hand, must now share his "token" position. Hank, an old friend of Rob's, has moved to Tampa and agreed to join Suncoast Softball. This stocky, jovial character proves so aggressive, so competitive, so *straight* that I wonder if his visit to this community will be brief. Still, I extend him credit for responding supportively to Rob's coming out and for giving the league a try.

A few of the Cove men express skepticism, wondering if Hank is "a Doug." Occasionally, they push the envelope to see if the new token will take it.

Tokens

Savoring an 11-0 mercy-rule victory, the team gathers on the concrete slab outside the park's storage shed. While their teammates rehash the day's solid fielding and unusually strong batting, Rob and Hank engage in a private conversation about to go public.

"Can't someone else do it?" Hank loudly complains. "Have Doug be the nun."

"Doug is in South Dakota," I tell him.

"We always make the new people do Miss Suncoast Softball," Jeff fibs.

"C'mon, coach," Hank whines to Pat, his coffee eyes pleading.

"I had to be *auctioned off* at a fund-raiser," he retorts, "you're getting off easy with *Sister Act*."

"Tim and I will be up there too," Rob reminds Hank, "looking just as stupid."

His every utterance rejected, Hank finally concedes. With that, Pat adjourns the meeting.

As we leave the group, Al tells me, "We pushed that boy too hard. A *drag pageant?* Please! Is that really the best place to break him in?"

I shake my head. "Five bucks says we don't see his face tonight."

"No bet," Al replies.

That evening, Al and I arrive at the Cove and discover that, sure enough, Hank has dropped out of the routine. Jeff takes his place, and for the rest of the season, he'll refer to his teammate as Sister Mary No-Show.

Our trio doesn't win the pageant, but I have a boisterously good time watching our nuns doff their habits. Still, that Hank agreed to participate (however reluctantly), then backed out, then failed to attend at all is a point of contention.

It isn't long before Hank's status with the team becomes even more precarious.

Heads hanging from a 13-17 loss, the Cove players get in line to shake the hands of their opponents. Players from both sides praise one another with the obligatory, "Good game."

Suddenly, a commotion erupts. Hank stands chest-to-chest with a player from the Wet Spot. Glaring, they shout angry words I can't decipher from the bench. "Back off, Hank!" I yell as someone steps in to pry the two apart. Hank stomps off the field, grabs his bag from the dugout, and darts for his car.

Meanwhile, the rest of the Cove team congregates. Everyone's animated, most laughing, a few shaking their heads. "What happened?" I ask.

"Their guy called Hank a pussy," Tim answers. I shake my head. "And then Hank called him a faggot."

My mouth falls open. Of all the stupid things to say! This is a gay league, you dolt!

"Caaalm your liberal self down," Gordon instructs before I can speak. "I found it rather entertaining. For a moment, I thought we might have a fag brawl!"

Seeing I'm unconvinced, Pat attempts, "It's just trash talk. Part of the game."

"Insulting gay people is part of the game?" I protest, looking at Gordon, then at Pat. Unfortunately, I then think, *it is.* After all, what context has been more homophobic than competitive sports?

"C'mon," Gordon nudges, "let's go to Beef O'Brady's and forget about it."

I go to the bar, but I don't forget, and I don't allow Gordon, Pat, or Al to forget either. "How could Hank say something that idiotic?" I ask as we gather around the table.

"He was provoked," Pat points out. "The guy called him a pussy."

"Besides," Gordon explains, "gay men call each other 'faggot' all the time. The guy's probably heard it a hundred times this month."

"It's not the same," I insist. "Just because two black guys call each other 'nigga' doesn't mean it's okay for us to use the same word. There's a big difference between insider and outsider usage."

"I must say," Al agrees, "I'd be much more offended if Doug called me a sissy than if Pat or Gordon did."

"Oh, have a beer," Gordon offers, pouring me a glass.

Still annoyed, I settle in for the football game blaring from the nearest big screen.

On the way home, it strikes me that all my attention has been focused on Hank's comment. It almost didn't faze me that the other player called him a pussy, a term that assaults my feminist consciousness. Anger rises within me. Why did the gay player say that? For him, is a woman's genitalia as "low" as it goes?

I don't understand gay men's sexism. Hegemonic masculinity is as oppressive to them as it is to women. Yet so many seem to embrace it, spending hours at the gym, even using steroids, to construct a muscular, hypermasculine body. Many take pride in being (and desiring the) "straight looking" and "straight acting." I hate those terms! What do they mean anyway? That straight men are the standards by which gay men are to be judged, even by themselves? That gay men who look or act "gay"—read "feminine"—are not "real" men and therefore not as desirable and valuable?

The chapter on Hank doesn't close tonight. When Rudy, the Wet Spot coach, files a grievance, Doug suggests we attend the hearing. "Few straight men play in the league," he says. "How many are there—three? What if someone questions whether *any* of us should participate?"

At the meeting, Rudy talks first. "I have a real problem with the Cove player's use of the term 'faggot.' One purpose of this league is to provide an environment where gay people can feel safe, physically and mentally. Anything that diminishes that sense of safety should raise a red flag for us." Scanning the crowd for Hank, I exhale nervously.

The commissioner then recognizes David. "The word 'faggot' is as insulting to me as anythaang," says our friend. "But the Wet Spot player—"

"Who also happens to be straight," another man adds.

My eyes widen. "I didn't know that," I whisper to Doug, wondering if that makes the situation better or worse.

David continues, "He began the verbiage by callin' our player a pussy. Our league has players and spectators who find that term equally offensive."

"The Cove player *at least* should get a written warning," Rudy suggests, "and another violation should result in expulsion from the league."

"That's fine," David responds, "but your player needs the same warning." A vote is taken and the decision passed.

As we file out of the meeting, I overhear David say, "Would have been nice to see Hank." I'd been thinking the same thing. Why didn't he come? Was he afraid, ashamed, indifferent? Will he stay with the team? More important, will the incident affect relationships between the league's gay and straight (or male and female) participants; and how might it affect Suncoast Softball's openness to heterosexuals? My unease lingers.

Thanksgiving weekend, Doug and I drive to Fort Lauderdale for our first out-of-town softball tournament. The only player who doesn't attend is Hank. The first day, the team has just two games, leaving plenty of time to hit the town. Our initial stop is a place I'll never forget.

The Vice Squad

Stewart parks his new Explorer one lot over from the bar. "Guys," Gordon pleads, "let's go someplace else."

"What's your problem?" asks Al.

"The Vice is not appropriate for . . . mixed company," Gordon suggests, directing his eyes toward me.

"We're already here," says Joe, slamming his door. Al and Pat hop out as well.

"I'm okay," I tell Gordon.

"I know," he replies, "but this might be a little much, even for you."

As we stride to the entrance, a car pulls up. Hands out their windows, Rob, Tim, and Doug wave. They find a space while Gordon and I approach the line. Just then, a man jogs over. "Excuse me, miss," he says, grabbing my arm. "Do you, uh, know where you are?"

"She's with us," Al tells him.

The man narrows his gaze, responding, "It's your call, but there are some places in the establishment she does *not* want to visit."

"We'll take care of her," Pat assures him.

A bouncer wearing a denim jacket and black biker cap sits at a table. I hear him tell those near the door that although there's no cover charge, they are collecting for a local AIDS coalition. When I reach the front of the line, his jaw drops. "If I were you," he says intently, "I'd stay out of the backyard and the dark room."

"Why? What's—"

"She will," Gordon promises.

I make my donation and push open the door. A few feet ahead, I note an iron cage, about the size of an oven, suspended from the ceiling. To its left is a small shop selling plastic-wrapped magazines, silver-studded collars and harnesses, and various flavors of lubricant, everything from lemon to leather. Gordon takes my hand and leads me into the bar. "Drink?" he offers.

Taking in my surroundings, I reply, "I think I should be sober for this."

As we approach, the sleek-haired bartender abruptly stops pouring a shot of Jagermeister. "Lady, you'll want to stay out—"

"Of the backyard and the dark room," I finish. "Sir, if I may ask, is that for my protection or for theirs?"

"It's definitely for yours," replies the Vice rep.

Turning away from him, I wonder what the fuss is about. What is there to see: mutual masturbation, oral sex, anal sex, group encounters, sadomasochism? At one time, these practices—especially among men— would have been outside the boundaries of my consciousness. Now they seem rather ordinary terrain on the landscape of human desire.

Still, something keeps me from asking for a tour of the dark room and backyard. It's not disgust; I don't even think it's fear. Maybe it's respect. Respect for my friends. Respect for pleasures I may not fully understand, but perhaps only because I haven't experienced them—pleasures that could be associated with anonymity, which my presence as a heterosexual, a woman, and a researcher would violate. My explorations, I decide, will be confined to this room.

Orange-red lights cast a hazy glow, and the air smells of suede and cigarettes. Around the bar sit nine men, three pairs and three loners. Two televisions mounted in the corners drown their conversations. On one screen, a man performs oral sex on another. I wonder if I should be noting his technique. A second video shows a live Prince Albert, where a hoop is pierced through the urethra at the base of the penis head. Gordon looks just as the ring comes through. "Uh!" he gasps. "*What* are you watching?"

Suddenly, a man approaches Doug. Licking his lips, he moves his hand across my husband's pectoral. Doug stares back at the man, his mouth a bit agape. I think he just experienced how truly invasive men can be.

"That's it!" Gordon proclaims, rounding up the group. "We're out 'a here!"

"We're fine," I tell him, trying not to laugh.

"No straight woman needs to see any more of the Vice," he replies. Maybe so.

In spite of Gordon's protectiveness (or embarrassment), the night doesn't get any less interesting. Our next stop is the Stud.

Stud Suds

"Sign here," orders the pretty-boy bouncer.

"What for?" I ask.

"It certifies that you enter the foam at your own risk."

"The foam?" Realizing I'm holding up the Stud line, I dutifully take the pen from his hand. I loop a large 'L,' print the 'isa,' offer my middle initial, and follow with the full, hyphenated last name. Before handing back his clipboard, I glance at the other signatures—all indecipherable scratches and scribbles. Either everyone inside is a doctor, I think, or I'm the only one with nothing to lose by being here.

A shorter, bulkier bouncer smiles when he says, "I don't believe we've ever had a woman in here before."

"First time for everything," I reply.

I follow Pat and Joe into the bar. Turning the corner, we stop to marvel. The dance floor has been walled up like a hockey rink. Inside, waist-high ivory suds provide a bubble bath's cover. A few couples kiss intently, running their hands down one another's slippery chests. Small groups circle dance or form trains, grinding one another from behind. I watch for a few moments, then, feeling too voyeuristic, turn away. "Goin' in?" asks Joe.

In my mind, Carolyn Ellis tells me (half-jokingly), "A *real* fieldworker would."

"I don't know," Pat says. "In there, pretty much anything goes."

What might go for me? I wonder. Am I prepared to confront (and perhaps transgress) the boundaries between women and men, gay and straight, friendship and marriage, mystery and experience? What would happen to my identity and my relationship with Doug? Could we "cross over" together? Would such an attempt reinforce rather than challenge the binaries?

Carolyn's voice again meets my ears. This time, however, she speaks as a mentor and friend. In words I've heard before, she encourages, "Trust your instincts."

I turn to the guys and say, "Think I'll skip the foam."

For all our evening explorations, the Cove plays just as hard during the daytime. Everyone gives his all, none more than Pat in this game, the team's third on Sunday.

Blood on My Hands

Thwack!

"Ah shit!" Pat exclaims. His veteran eyes can map the line drive's path, but his weekend-wearied body lags a half second behind. The ball sneaks under his glove and rolls into left. Pat's right forearm and tricep skid across the infield. "Fuck!" he curses, spitting out dirt.

"Get up, old man," teases Al from third.

"Not much older than *you*," Pat reminds him. The inning closes when the next batter sends an easy grounder to Rob, who steps on second for the fielder's choice.

Our injured shortstop jogs to the bench. With blood dripping from a scrape the size of an egg, Pat asks for the first aid kit. He pours a bottle of Evian over the wound, cringing as crimson grime washes down his arm. "Peroxide?" Pat then requests.

He nods when I ask, "Want me to do it?" Cradling his elbow, I uncap the container. "This will sting," I say, then dump a few ounces onto his arm. The liquid bubbles as I blow on it. I then tear open an alcohol wipe and pat the affected area. We finish wrapping the gauze just as he's called on deck.

Recapping the peroxide, I stride to the tackle box that holds the medical supplies. As I glance over the Ace bandages, ice packs, and athletic tape, it occurs to me that we have no latex gloves. I look down at my bare, bloodstained hands.

AIDS. It echoes in my mind. AIDS. An intensified pulse thumps in my neck. AIDS.

Calm down! an inner voice orders. *You have no reason to believe he's HIV positive.*

I'm just being cautious, I silently reply.

You're being a homophobe! the voice corrects.

Am I? I reach for the peroxide bottle, pouring the liquid into my cupped left hand. I set down the container and close my eyes. As my palms rub together, a tear of shame moves down my cheek and off my jaw. AIDS, I tell the voice.

Homophobe, it responds.

In the end, the Cove loses that game but takes second in the tournament. The team leaves Fort Lauderdale exhausted but proud.

Doug and I ride back to Tampa with Gordon, whose sister, Liz, is coming for a visit. We're picking her up at their brother's place, where we also meet Gordon's parents. It proves an important but anxious encounter.

Don't Say the Wrong Thing

Gordon winds his Acura through the curvy, middle-class subdivision. Whipping over to the curb, he says, "Here we go."

"Any advice on meeting your parents?" Doug queries.

"Just try not to out me," Gordon says with a smile. His statement rings of lightness and good humor but falls upon my ears with solemnity. The tournament's open, celebratory atmosphere quickly recedes as we approach the house.

Gordon knocks on the door. Footsteps clonk; the bolt clicks. "Come in!" greets a woman I recognize from photographs as Marilyn, Gordon's mother. "Can you stay a while?"

"A little while," says her son.

"Nice to see you again, Liz," I tell Gordon's sister.

She points to the living room, saying, "That's my uncle." He waves without looking up from the TV. Liz gestures toward the kitchen, "My brother Steven; his wife, Tobi; and their kids." Tobi, holding baby Jacquelyn, gives a grin while Steven chases Harris, their toddler son.

Gordon goes off to visit with his uncle and siblings, leaving Doug and me in the dining area with his folks. Tex pulls out the piano bench and motions for us to sit. "How are you feeling?" I ask Marilyn, remembering her recent tumble down a flight of stairs. Doug and I laugh as Marilyn offers the step-by-step replay.

Not to be outdone, Tex recounts the clumsy fall he took while strolling along Tampa Bay. "My face was one big scab," he says.

Marilyn shifts gears. Leaning forward, she asks, "How was your weekend?"

Wringing my hands, I reply, "A lot of fun."

Tex turns to Doug, "You play on Gordon's softball team?" I swallow hard.

"For almost two years," Doug says.

An awkward pause follows, and a single thought turns over in my mind: *don't say the wrong thing; don't say the wrong thing.* When Marilyn asks, "What kind of league do you play in?" Gordon eyes us from the other room. *Don't say the wrong thing.*

Doug initiates, "It's a—"

"City league," I finish, a little too eagerly. "A city league."

Marilyn follows up with, "And who sponsors the team?"

"The Cove," Doug responds.

"What's that?" she asks.

"A bar," we say together. I stare down at my braided-leather sandals, waiting for the next question: what kind of bar?

"Like a . . . sports bar?" Marilyn inquires. I glance up to answer but am startled by her sudden change in appearance. Marilyn's red-framed glasses, each lens the size of a small yam, had been atop her head; they now cover most of her face.

Don't say the wrong thing. "I'm sorry," I reply, trying to focus, "what did you ask?"

"It's a pub with a poolroom and dance floor," Doug answers.

"Our son never wants us to watch him play," Marilyn muses. At this, Gordon rises from the couch.

"Performance anxiety?" I suggest.

"I can't understand—"

Gordon cuts her off, "We really need to go."

In unison, Doug and I rise from the hard, wooden bench. "It was so nice meeting you," I tell them. We bid goodbye to the rest of the family as Marilyn and Tex see us out.

"Drive safely," they tell their son.

Gordon and Liz take the front seat, Doug and I the back. When the fourth door slams shut, we breathe a collective sigh.

6

Homeward

Since September 1995, I've been taking field notes, conducting interviews, and writing class and conference papers on the Cove men. It's now December 1996, time to start pulling everything together for my dissertation. I recognize that my position in this community as a straight, married, female researcher is both unique and potentially problematic. I'm still struggling to find a voice that speaks not just *about* these men but *with* and *for* them as well.[1] At an advising meeting, I learn that I'm not the only one feeling conflicted about my project.

Project-ing

Art leans forward in his chair and says, "I've heard from several readers of *Composing Ethnography*. Many of them singled out your piece on bulimia, calling it 'sensual' and 'poetic.'[2] Do you think you can be as present in your writings about this gay culture?"

"I'm striving for that," I tell him. "I think it would be dishonest to write from a traditional 'objective' stance. I'm studying these men closely by getting close. I'm not emotionally or politically neutral; I'm their friend, their advocate."

"Still, aren't there limits to your access?"

Remembering my recent experiences at the Vice and the Stud, I say, "I can't imagine a straight woman could have more access than I."

"That's exactly my point," he presses. "Maybe there's only so much a gay man *can* share with a straight woman. What about the spaces you *can't* enter, the experiences you *can't* share, the conversations to which you're *not* privy?"

"Are you suggesting that we only study and write about groups to which we belong?"

"No." In a gentle tone, Art says, "You've been in the field over a year. It's time to take heed of where you are in this community and to determine what others—gay and straight—can learn from you. Give it some thought."

I spend the next few days considering Art's advice. That weekend, a conversation with Rob deepens my understanding of who I am to my research community, who they are to me, and how our friendships might offer me a position from which to speak.

In Both Worlds

After brunch, nine softball guys and a fieldworker leave the restaurant and decide to meet at Gordon's apartment. I catch a ride with Rob, who doesn't know the way. Directing him south, I ask how he's spending the holidays. He smiles. "I'm meeting Tim's parents."

"Marvelous! How are you feeling about that?"

"Nervous," Rob admits.

"How accepting is Tim's family?"

"Well, their first impulse was to 'fix' him. As devout Mormons, they feared for his salvation. Not wanting to be separated from him in the afterlife, they tried to help him 'find his way back to God.' Since then, I think they've realized that he's unlikely to 'convert' to heterosexuality. Overall, they're supportive of Tim, though I wouldn't say they're supportive of this 'lifestyle.'"

"What about your folks?" I probe.

"They know nothing." I nod but don't push. "Tell me," Rob then requests, "how did *you* get here?"

I smile and ask playfully, "Here in your truck?"

"*Here*," he responds, "among us."

When I tell him of "coming out" with David, Rob says, "I don't know if anyone's ever said this to you, but Tim and I have talked about how comforting it is to be around you and Doug. We all were raised to be straight; for part of our lives, many of us thought we *were* straight. Sometimes being gay means giving up that familiar life. You and Doug give us a chance to live in both worlds."

The profundity jolts me. Smiling, I say, "You give us that chance too."

The Dynamic Duo

I point out Gordon's place, and we pull over. Inside, Rob plops between Tim and Pat on the couch. I nestle into the recliner as our host flips to the Cowboys game. When someone raps on the door, I rise to answer it. "Hey, Steve," I say to Gordon's old roommate, a handsome Atlantan of thirty-nine with salt-and-pepper hair; long-lashed, steel-blue eyes; and wonderfully deep dimples.

"Heeey!" he responds. "I read that paper you wrote about Gordon."

A wave of anxiety ripples through me as I recall the references to Steve's old boyfriend being HIV positive. "Were you . . . surprised by some of the things Gordon told me?" I ask. When he pauses, my fingernails dig into my palms.

"Well!" Steve exclaims. "I can't believe he said I took him to that gay beach!"

"C'mon, Steve," Gordon interjects, "I edited a *lot* where you're concerned."

"She can interview me next," Steve suggests. "I'm sure you left out a few choice details about yourself."

"May I see the paper?" Rob asks.

"Yeah," Gordon says, "I'll get it." When he heads for the bedroom, I take in a soothing breath. A few moments later, Gordon returns. "Here you go," he tells Rob, handing over the document. "And I brought the first paper Lisa wrote about us."

"I'd like to read that again," Tim says. Pat looks on as he flips through "Tales from the (Softball) Field" and Rob starts examining the pages of Gordon's life history. I nervously twirl my hair, waiting for them to comment on the writing, the issues raised, or the personal disclosures, including my bulimia, which I briefly discuss in the paper on Gordon.

"I didn't know you had a gay relative," Rob says, reacting to Gordon's discussion of Great-Uncle Gene. "My sister's a lesbian."

"When I read that paper," Steve shares, "I related to lots of things—like the gay newspaper. Gordon said he couldn't bring himself to pick it up; he thought everybody was watching. Before I came out, I was just as desperate for information—and just as terrified."

Having my work passed around so casually feels odd. But it's nice to see it sparking connections and discussion. Watching them read, I marvel at how easily my fieldwork and my friendships with them intertwine, each seeming to extend and deepen the other.

In many ways, friendship has become my methodology. I study these men with the same practices I use to build and sustain relationships with them: conversation, empathy, support, and shared activities.

The writing adds another layer. On paper, I show my understanding and compassion in scenes and dialogue they can enter. In response, these men tell additional stories, to each other and to me. The cycle continues: we talk, I write, we talk.

For them, my researcher role seems to move from periphery to center and back again. Much of the time, our interactions feel like ordinary friendship encounters. They might even "forget" sometimes that I go home and write field notes. But my ethnographer self never fades completely into the background. After a telling disclosure, someone may ask, "Did you get that?" or, "Are you writing this down?" and once in a while, someone says, "Please don't put that in your paper"—a request I always honor.

Overall, my scholarly interest in the group seems to open more conversations than it closes. Since my investments in their lives are both personal and academic, they can assume that I want to see, hear, and feel this community from the inside. I've never even thought "I didn't need to know that," and I suspect they sense this about me. David once told me that he'd never seen a straight person work so hard to understand gay men's experiences, feelings, and concerns. Perhaps my dual role invites them to be more candid than they might be with someone either "just a friend" or "just a researcher."

When they reveal something private, I often wonder if they're telling Lisa-the-friend, Lisa-the-researcher, or Lisa-the-dynamic-duo. At least once a day, Lisa-the-researcher wallows in ethnographic guilt for turning these men into objects of study. If they reach out to Lisa-the-friend, I ask myself, does "the other Lisa" have a place in the encounter? I struggle, therefore, not only with writing "right" but also with writing "rightfully."

Just One Example

The night air lacks a Midwest winter's bite, but those gathered at Impulse for the league's holiday party appreciate its teasing nibble. Bar and patio sport faux greenery, white lights, and bowls of anise and peppermint candy. Over the sound system blare spoofs of Christmas tunes, lending new meaning to seasonal phrases like "don we now our gay apparel."

From a bench, Rob and I watch Tim greet someone neither of us recognizes. The two embrace, then laugh at a whispered inside joke. Tugging at the collar of his polo, Rob shakes his head. At this, I take the candy cane from my mouth and ask, "How are things?"

"There's been some tension," he admits, eyes still fixed on his partner. "He's quite the party boy. You should see him at work."

"He *is* a bartender," I say. "Kind of goes with the job."

Rob looks at me, his blue eyes large and intense. "Does *kissing* go with the job?"

Oh, Tim. "I don't know. What sort of kissing?"

"I'll give you just one example," he says. "Last week, Tim's working at the club. I go down there and hang around his bar awhile. This guy comes up, orders a drink, and in exchange for his tip, Tim kisses him— on the mouth, with tongue!" Rob exhales, then lowers his voice, "I'm sorry, but I'm standing *right there.* Everyone's asking me, 'What's up with you guys? Why's Tim acting like this?' That doesn't reflect well on me, you know? And then I wonder what he does when I'm *not* around."

"Did you talk with him about it?"

"Matter of fact, I used you and Doug as an example. Tim and I had gone around and around, but he just wasn't getting it. So finally I said, 'Tim, how would Doug feel if Lisa went around kissing other guys? Think he'd tolerate that?' A light went on. He could imagine how Doug might react. I then said, 'Guess what? That's exactly how I feel.'"

Why use us as an example? I wonder. Even in a conversation between gay lovers, does a reference to a gay couple not carry the symbolic weight of a straight, married one? Or might Rob's choice have been less general and more particular? Perhaps he perceives, as I do, that our primary relationships have some parallels.

"It's interesting that you cast Doug and me in the roles you did," I tell him, "because ever since you began dating Tim, I've seen connections between our connections. I may be projecting my own issues, but it seems to me that Tim has been caught in emotional and relational storms for some time—with coming out, with Jack, with Brandon, with the HIV scare. Your goodness and stability give him shelter, but they also frighten him because he somehow feels unworthy. So, perhaps unwittingly, he engages in sabotaging behaviors. They're his defense against vulnerability." Looking a bit stunned, Rob nods. I put my hand atop his. "You're the brightest sun I've seen shine on Tim since I've known him. But when you don't feel deserving, facing the light of happiness requires courage. I hope Tim finds that."

Kissing my cheek, Rob says, "Me too."

\\\

So I wonder: should Lisa-the-friend have kept this episode out of her field notes? Do you really need to know about Rob and Tim's latest fight? Am I exploiting Rob's pain because it shows an "interesting" connection between our relationships? Should I delete this section?

In the coming days, I continue debating the ethics of my dual role. Meanwhile, a Cove player suffers a penetrating loss. The news comes just after Christmas.

Speaking of Loss

"Hello?" I call into the cordless phone.

"Hey darlin'," answers a quiet voice.

"Al!" I respond, gripping the sofa cushion. At dinner the other night, David told us that Al's father is "covered in cancer" and that he will live only about six weeks.

"Just callin' to wish you happy holidays." His drawl is low and scratchy but cheerful.

"Happy holidays to you too," I say, thinking maybe the prognosis has improved. "How's your dad feeling?"

His silence foreshadows his words. "He died Christmas Eve."

"Oh, Al!" I gasp.

"Yah," he sighs, "his doctors led us to expect more time."

Biting the inside of my mouth, I ask, "Were you with him?"

"We all were, Mom holding his feet, me holding one hand, my brother holding the other."

"Did he go peacefully?"

"They had him pumped full of morphine." Then, with an exhausted half chuckle, he adds, "Funny thing. At one point, my brother whispered, 'This might be a good time to tell Dad you're gay.'"

We share a little laugh before I note, "I thought your brother didn't know."

"Well *I've* never said anything."

"So, um, did you tell him?"

"My dad? No, no."

We sit through several moments of silence. At last, he says, "Anyway, expect me at your New Year's party."

"I'll see you then. Take care, Al. You'll be in my prayers."

Closing my eyes, I shake my head, hurting for a son grieving for a father. Who was he, I wonder, this man whose disdain or rejection Al must have feared? Did he know his boy had loved and been loved? Did he want to know? How does Al feel, now that he never can share that part of himself with his father?

Comp-lications

I spend the next month in comprehensive-exam exile. Each of my committee members—Eric Eisenberg, Marsha Vanderford, Carolyn Ellis, and Art Bochner—asks me to reflect on one area of study in my academic program and to explore that area's applicability to my dissertation.[3] Writing my responses, I realize that I'm still trying to find an ethnographic voice that is both eloquent and ethical.

At my oral examination, my committee is supportive but cautionary. "Given that you are not male and not homosexual," says Carolyn, "how can you understand and write about this subculture from the inside?"

"All research involves communicating about and across experiential, relational, and cultural similarities and differences," I reply. "Myerhoff, for example, in *Number Our Days* is a Jewish woman studying a Jewish culture, but her respondents are considerably older than she.[4] In her study, Austin interviews Annie, a woman both like (black and educated) and unlike herself (Austin is from the rural South; Annie grew up in Africa).[5] Cherry, a straight and healthy researcher, becomes immersed in the lives of a predominantly gay community of people with AIDS.[6] These ethnographers understood and wrote from the inside by observing members of their research communities closely, by listening empathically to their stories, by participating in their lived experiences, and by committing themselves to their welfare."

"Have you thought about who this study is for?" asks Art. "If you're writing for straight readers, how will you find a tone that's not preachy or self-congratulatory? If it's for gay readers, won't some ask, 'What can a straight woman teach *us* about being gay?'"

"As I move from writing field notes to writing the text, those issues will be in the forefront of my mind. I hope that my work will find a home in university classrooms, perhaps as a supplementary text in a course on friendship, sexuality, and/or fieldwork. In addition, my participants, other gay men and lesbians, and their straight associates are an important audience. I'd like my work to be as evocative and useful to them as to my academic colleagues."

"That's a tall order," Art observes, "and a delicate balance."

Marsha speaks next. "My exam question asked you to reflect on rhetorical approaches to studying communication. Much of your answer focused on narrative inquiry. What role has—and will—narrative play in your project?"

"Narrative is the core of fieldwork," I say. "Researchers listen to, record, transcribe, and tell stories. My field notes, essentially, are recountings of, and reflections on, stories shared by and with participants: coming-out stories, family stories, relationship stories, stories of hardship and crisis. Writing ethnography, moreover, involves composing narratives that make sense of fieldwork experience. What my narratives will look or feel like, I don't yet know."

"Marsha's question speaks to the 'how' of your study," Eric observes. "I'd like to hone in on the 'what.' In your response to my exam question, you began to explore the place of identity in your study. Can you say more about that?"

"For two years, I've attended how these men construct themselves and are constructed by others; how they communicatively perform and conceal their gay identities in both public and private spaces; and how gay identities move through the multiple, shifting contexts of their lives. In the process, I've been moved as never before to reflect on the construction, maintenance, and transformation of my own sexual orientation and identity."

"Does that make you an observer of gay men's identity negotiation?" queries Eric. "A participant in that process? A participant observer of your own identity in this gay culture? I don't yet have a clear sense of your position."

"Frankly," I tell him, "neither do I. The more I observe them, listen to them, share my life with them, read about gay identity and cultures, and write field notes, the more invested I become in my research community. Can I speak most persuasively and rightfully as observer? Participant? Friend? Advocate? Some combination? I'm not sure. I know that I have to find my place. It will be difficult to move forward until I do." They all nod.

Shortly after my comps defense, the Cove team resumes practice for a tournament that opens each spring season. Meanwhile, I'm taking a seminar in ethnography, my program's last course. Students are assigned to go into the field and write about "the spirit of a place." Based on my observations the first day of the tournament, I write the following short story.

Men Kissing

Men kissing—it strikes me as wonderfully subversive. In the United States, we tolerate little boys who sloppily smooch their fathers and brothers, but when our little men reach a certain age, such displays induce a cultural squeamishness. Verbally and nonverbally, subtly and not so subtly, we send the message: "You shouldn't do that anymore—especially in public." Our little boys become adolescents whose physical contact we conspire to confine to fields, courts, and rinks. Many grow into men who keep other men at arm's length, communicating to the next generation of little boys, "Kissing me(n) is not appropriate; it's not masculine; it's not *right* "

Three years ago, I'd never seen men kissing—not even in a movie. This weekend, I'm surrounded by male lips pecking, smacking, and lingering on Mayor Dick Greco (Ball Fields, that is, near the University of South Florida in Tampa).

Along with a smattering of women, more than three hundred men come from places as distant as Toronto for the third Gasparilla Softball Classic. The atmosphere is much like a class reunion, only the males don't greet with stiff, distant handshakes. I watch as an Atlanta Heretic puckers for a Virginia Outlaw, and a Birmingham Cub plants one on a Fort Lauderdale Hot Spot.

Four softball fields occupy most of the terrain. Between them sits a sand-cushioned playground with a swing set and a jungle gym. Atop the twist slide, the tongues of two Atlanta Trojans are engaged in an enthusiastic tango.

Players inhabit the eight concrete-block-and-metal-fencing dugouts as the stands fill with spectators, duffle bags, and jugs of Gatorade. Square and triangular banners in a variety of plaids and polka dots line the bleachers. Underneath, an Atlanta Thunder cups the unshaven face of a Cincinnati Comet, laying a smooch dead-on.

The Florida sun tries to warm this early February morning while a cool breeze teases the back of my neck, whipping and turning my ponytailed hair. As I move toward the concession stand, little packs of foil-wrapped Hershey's Kisses entice me, but I settle for a cup of coffee instead. Initially smitten by the robust, roasted scent, my nose crinkles when the bitterness of day-old espresso meets my tongue. Loading down the foam cup with Dixie Crystals sugar and Sam's Club faux creamer, I spot Tim and Rob in line for the men's room. Lip-locked, they gently cradle each other's heads.

Nearby, the rest of the players stretch out. Scanning the group, I ask, "Where's Gordon?"

"State fair," Doug reminds me. I'd forgotten that Gordon's stuck all weekend at a promotion booth. His business partner thought they could scope out clients there; his teammates, however, find that notion ridiculous. What an image—our left fielder peddling hairpieces amid the Zipper and the Scrambler, livestock pageants, and fruit judging.

"Peanuts, popcorn, get your hair here!" quips Al, turning to steal a public kiss from the cheek of his lover, new both to him and to this community. Neil's cheek blushes when Al's lips take their leave.

Laughter, layers of it, can be heard all around—hooting, howling, snickering, snorting, giggling, and guffawing. Spontaneous laughter responds to a struggling player's surprisingly powerful line drive. Solicited laughter follows cheers of "Two, four, six, eight, do it like you masturbate. Whack it! Whack it! Whack it!" Despite the analogy's androcentrism, I smile, wondering how women can play softball "like we masturbate."

In addition to the sometimes campy performances, other markers of gay culture appear. Someone hangs a large rainbow flag on the fence behind center field, and several vehicles parked in the lot display pink-triangle decals and stickers. Community-identifying buttons, jewelry, and T-shirts also help transform this city park into a gay space, where men and women can be collectively out.

When I approach, Jeff and beau un-Velcro their mouths and wave me over. I sit next to them on the hard, patchy ground of clover and browning grass. Prickly burs await anyone not careful about where she places her butt. I discover this immediately.

Thorns removed, I begin examining the contents of a plastic bag received upon registration. The first item provided is a tournament schedule. On the second page, the legend of pirate José Gaspar receives a bit of much-deserved revisionism. "Surreptitiously," it reads, "Gaspar would sail into town. 'Arrrr!' he would growl, while looting the guava trees. Erect went his member as his eyes fixed on the soon-to-be-possessed jewels."

Other surprises await. I find a voucher for one free well drink at Rascals; a packet of Banana Boat Baby Sunblock 29; two LifeStyles lubricated condoms, red; an ad for the Cove's Pirate Fest claiming, "A Pirate's Treasure is his First Mate's Body"; from Barnett Bank a "Mightygrip," useful for safely unscrewing light bulbs and mayonnaise jars; a string of reflective Mardi Gras beads; and a Tootsie Roll Pop, chocolate—my favorite. The mix is eclectic and colorful, much like those gathered here.

People begin filing past, so our group heads to field 1 for opening ceremonies. The Tampa Gay Men's Chorus has been invited to sing the Canadian and U.S. national anthems. Before they begin, Doug unevenly warbles, "Oooo, Canadaaaaa!"

"I know that off-key voice," calls someone from behind. We turn to find Terry, a former teammate who moved to Georgia last year.

I watch Doug and Terry embrace. They don't retain rigid, military postures or slap each other nervously on the back. Jaw-to-jaw, they share a moment of reunion before Terry puckers and plants.

"Jealous?" he teases, peering over my husband's shoulder.

"Grateful," I respond. How beautiful these sights of unashamed men kissing.

Later that week, I present "Men Kissing" to my ethnography class. A male cohort takes issue with the opening line ("Men kissing—it strikes me as wonderfully subversive"). "I assume you've never employed the term 'subversive' before," he tells me, "because your usage strikes me as naïve. What exactly does men kissing subvert?"

My cheeks burning, I reply, "Only all of orthodox masculinity."

The interaction between Doug and Terry is only the first of many significant encounters at the tournament. Later that day, I have this one with Joe.

Swingers

"Let's swing," suggests my congenial companion, pointing toward the playground. "I'd like to talk with you about something."

As Joe and I make our way over, we cross paths with one of the twenty or so women here for the tournament. I look up and into the brown eyes of a gold-jerseyed player with long, shiny curls pulled through the back of her navy cap. "Hi," she greets me in a sultry alto voice. Her mouth opens a bit as she tosses a warm half-smile.

"Hiii," Joe and I chorus. But her lingering eyes are not on him. Her head rotates over her right shoulder as she passes by. She and I exchange a penetrating glance, making the hairs on my neck stand on end. She gives a tiny nod before turning away.

"Hello!" Joe says, feigning insult. "I'm here too!" I just smile and watch her stride to the dugout, her hips swaying breezily.

Having reached the swing set, each of us takes a blue rubber seat, grips the chains tightly, and pushes off from the sand below. Our laughter blends with creaking metal as he secures his khaki FSU cap and sighs, "I met a woman."

His statement seems fitting in light of the previous encounter and in the frame of rolling scenery, where a teal-and-gold parrot perched above the park's lavatories continually approaches and recedes, enlarges and shrinks, while its owner tries to coax the defiant bird down.

"She works at my office," Joe explains, his mocha eyes gazing into the distance. "I find her very attractive, to the point where my heart pitter-patters when she enters the room."

I straighten my body and lay back my head. At this angle, I pass over tiny dunes of sand, then a patch of rye grass, grass then sand, sand then grass. "Have you told her how you feel?"

"No, but I asked a colleague about her. I guess she's involved with someone, but they're having problems. Turns out, she asked about me too."

Returning to an upright position, I comment, "That's a good sign."

"I'm not so sure," Joe replies, digging his feet into the dirt. "My last relationship with a woman ended after I told her I was gay."

With a tennis-shoe brake, I ask, "You said you were 'gay' or 'bisexual'?"

"Gay."

Confused, I say, "But you were drawn to her, and now you're drawn to this woman."

"Yes," he responds matter-of-factly. "I still fall for women, but my primary attraction is to men. My old girlfriend thought she could handle it."

"She couldn't?"

"Could *you*?" he queries, backstepping again, then springing off. Going forward, Joe arches his back, pulls the chains toward his body, and extends both legs high into the air. Coming back, he kicks his feet far behind, almost to his spine.

"I don't know," I say, taking flight again. "If I felt secure in our relationship, I might be able to. But I also might worry that you'd be unfulfilled, especially if you said you were gay as opposed to bisexual or curious. I would wonder if you'd rather be with a man."

Reaching maximum altitude, Joe lets out a howl. "So," he queries, "should I ask her out?"

I pump higher and higher. "If you're that interested, sure." My stomach drops, and I close my eyes to ward off the dizziness. "Wow!" I exclaim, dragging my feet again.

On his next peak, Joe leaps from the swing. Landing safely on the ground, he turns to me. Giddily, he asks, "When should I tell her I'm gay?"

"Not sure I'd do it on the first date. Things might not work out anyway."

"And if things *do* work out?"

"Then you'll tell her."

Approaching his swing, he probes, "Would you want to know?"

"That a potential lover considered himself gay? Yes."

"Another flight?" Joe suggests, giving my swing a push.

"Aaaah," I hedge, still a bit nauseous. "Oh, why not?"

This episode moves me to think about the fluidity of sexual orientation and identity. Given Joe's repeated physical attractions to women, what does it mean to say that he's gay? Why doesn't he claim to be bisexual? Because both straight and gay people police the borders so strictly? Because, for him, being gay is less a claim to a sexual identity than to a political or community one? Undoubtedly, Joe opens himself to more validation and affiliation by claiming to be gay than he would by claiming to be bisexual, but what does he close off? In theory, his gay identity all but precludes cross-sex romance, but what about in practice?

And what about my encounter with the gold-jerseyed woman? My heterosexual identity calls me to deny or explain away the powerful attraction I felt for her in that moment. Pushing at the boundaries feels exciting but also risky. However limiting, our categories bring order to the chaos of human experience and desire. That order undoubtedly is an illusion—but one I'm not yet sure I'm prepared to give up.

"Is He . . . Flaming?"

In its next game, the Cove gets trounced, as it does most of the weekend. This time, an error-ridden defense and a pop-fly offense culminate in a mercy rule. "One, two, three," our players count down before giving their postgame cheer: "Way to lubricate us, Trojans!"

"Very catchy," I praise. "Way to maintain that sense of humor!"

"It's the only thing we *haven't* lost this weekend," Tim observes.

"Two to eighteen," Pat growls, shaking his head. "What a tournament!"

"Forget about it," I encourage, "let's have lunch." When Al suggests Friday's, everyone nods. We collect our gear and head for the parking lot.

Popping the trunk, Doug asks, "Have I told you about Xavier?"

"Who?"

"There's this guy who comes into Walgreens almost every day now. Xavier never has a prescription for me to fill. He comes 'just to talk.' I'm not sure, but I think he *likes* me. He keeps asking me to have a beer with him."

Uncertain why this is the first I've heard of Xavier, and why now, I query, "Does his crush bother you?"

"I'm not sure it's a crush," Doug says. "I'm not even sure that Xavier's gay."

"Does he know that you're married?"

"Oh yeah, I've mentioned you several times, but he's never tried to coordinate a meeting with both of us, if you know what I mean."

Do I know what you mean? "Well, maybe you should coordinate the meeting," I suggest. "I'd be happy to check out the competition."

Opening my door, Doug loudly insists, "He's *not* the competition."

Hmm. Doth the pharmacist protest too much?

At the restaurant, they set up a table for eleven. Just when it's ready, some of our Atlanta opponents walk through the wooden double doors. "Heeeey, Tampa," greets a lanky African American. Counting their turquoise-and-white jerseys, I ask the waitress to expand our party to eighteen. After several table reconfigurations, we at last take our seats. "Introductions!" announces the same man. "I'm William, and to my right is Kurt." He continues listing their names, but I lose track.

We then go around our group. "Hey, I'm Rob."

"Hi, Raaaahb," William fawns. "Please tell me that you're single."

"Actually," Rob says, "I'm with Tim over there."

"I'm Anna," says the former teammate who's joined the Cove for the tournament. "And I'm not with anyone, in case you're interested." William smiles.

"Pat. Ditto what she said."

"And Tiiiim," William says before he can.

Going around our part of the table, Tim says, "Doug, Lisa, Joe, Al, Jeff—"

"Ooooh, Jeff," William flirts, "a sexy Mexican or somethin'."

"Italian," Jeff corrects. "And next to me is Hank. We couldn't talk 'im into another season, but he's helping us out for the tournament." A bit embarrassed, Hank waves.

"So many beee-yoootiful men," William swoons, tugging at his closely cut beard. "Ooh, and ladies. Y'all play softball too?"

"Anna does," Tim explains, "and Lisa's writing her dissertation about the team."

William turns to me, adjusts his round glasses, and purses his lips. "And whuut, Miss Lisa, is so captivating about this team?"

"Their experiences, their feelings, their stories. I'm hoping that my project will foster understanding and community between gay and straight people."

"Straight people?" William repeats.

"Well," I point out, "in our group we have Anna, myself, my husband Doug—"

"Doug!" William exclaims, looking over at him. "I never suspected."

"Thank you very much," Doug says with a grin.

Ever so slightly, I shift in my seat.

"It *is* a compliment," William insists.

"I know," Doug responds.

"He knows," Rob assures him.

"And Hank," I say, completing the list.

"They've been trying to convert me," claims Hank.

Adds Doug in his best James Earl Jones voice, "To another side of the force."

"The *dark* side!" Hank says.

"This ain' no dark side," Jeff counters. "It's *aaawl* sunshine."

Hank begins to protest, but William interrupts with, "That's just two tears in a bucket, so motherfuck it!" No one knows exactly what he means, but we crack up nonetheless.

Their spokesman keeps us in stitches throughout a lunch of slow service and lukewarm food. As we take our last bites, he compliments us, "Y'all have a great sense of humor."

"We laugh at everything you say," Rob observes.

"See what I mean?" William asks, getting up from the table. "'Scuse me a minute. I need to use the little girls' room."

When he leaves, our pigtailed waitress returns. As she distributes checks, clears dishes, and wipes spills, we admire her black, high-cut vinyl shorts. Instead of responding, she says, "That guy who was just here, is he . . . *flaming?*" Her wrist goes limp, and she sways it like a pendulum. The table falls silent.

At last, Rob responds, "Yeah, we *all* are."

Her mouth drops open, and she looks away. "R-really? I'd never guess *you* were gay."

"Thanks," Rob bites. He clenches his teeth, and I wait for him to say something more. He doesn't. No one does.

Before making a quick exit, she weakly tosses out, "Seems like every good-looking guy is gay."

By the time William returns, we're all standing behind our chairs. "Whuut?" he asks. "No one's havin' another cocktail?"

"Nah," Rob answers. "Let's get back to the tournament."

The group talks little on the way to our cars, and Doug and I drive most of the return trip in silence. Only when the ballpark comes into view does our energy pick up.

Rob and Tim arrive at the same time, and the four of us begin raking our server. "'I'd never guess *you* were gay,'" Rob mocks. "Is that supposed to be a compliment?"

"She was clueless!" says Tim. "Had no idea she was being insulting."
"And stupid," Doug adds.

Rob exhales, then, "Forget it. Please, let's just forget it." With that, he strides toward the field.

Watching him, I wonder about his response to our waitress. Was it enough? She was caught in her heterosexist web, and Rob replied sarcastically to her backpedaling remark, but was this teachable moment effective? Did she rethink her assumptions? Should we have been more direct, more expressive of our anger—to her, perhaps even to her manager? Why did so many of my gay companions not respond to her? I could see frustration in their narrowed gazes and tightened foreheads. Are they afraid that if they turn the valve, they'll explode? Is this experience so ubiquitous that they're numb? Why didn't I respond? Was I giving the floor to Rob because it seemed more rightfully his? Was I surprised into silence? Am I numb?

Then I wonder about William. What's it like to be so conspicuously gay? What does he face that men who can pass (like the Cove men) don't? At the same time, how much of this repugnant "third-party" discourse does he not have to hear because few would presume him heterosexual? To pass or not to pass, each seems an equally complex path.

Second Shot

At field 4, I secure the lens onto my new camera and position myself behind home plate. Looking into the viewfinder, I see only black. Confused, I adjust the settings, check the battery, and examine the flash. Still, every time I peer through, I get the same onyx landscape. "Take off the lens cap," suggests a man behind me. I smile, knowing both the voice and the correctness of his diagnosis. How cliché of me, I think, and how dumb!

"Thanks, Colin," I say, turning to greet the former Suncoast player. "How are you?" His appearance speaks for itself: full face, shiny hair, and smooth, rosy complexion. My mind flashes to a different time—just one year ago—and a different Colin, dangerously gaunt, with pale, jaundiced skin.

Colin shows me his camera and explains the features on mine, taking me through aperture and depth of field. Much of it goes over my head, but I play along, happy to see some fire back in his crystal-blue eyes. "By the way," he says, "did you get a team picture from when Michael was alive?"

Studying his newly robust chest and arms, I tell him, "No, do you have any left?"

"I'll send you one," Colin offers. Then, with a quizzical look, he asks, "What?"

"I'm sorry to be staring, Colin, but I can't get over it. You look so . . ."

"Healthy?" he finishes. When I nod, his face flushes a bit.

I watch him return his lenses to their case, and one thought occupies my mind: thank god for protease inhibitors.

Intersubjectivity

Nine A.M. brings a disappointing twelve-run shutout, ending the tournament for the Cove. As we clear the dugout, I remind the grumbling group, "It's supposed to be fun." Grimaces all around. "Besides," I try again, "you lost so early in the day that we can get breakfast!"

Our attentive waitress brings two fresh pots of coffee as ten of us enjoy dishes remarkably unique for a strip-mall café. Dill omelets, banana and granola pancakes, and Spanish frittatas circle the table as we rehash the games. Changing the subject, I ask across the table, "Your mother still in town?" When Al nods, I say, "Maybe your mom and Gordon's mom should get together. Marilyn will be here another week."

"They'd have a lot to talk about," he agrees.

"Gordon said he might disclose to her first," I toss out. "Is it easier to tell moms?"

"Don't ask me," chorus Al, Rob, and Stewart.

"I wanted that over in one shot," Pat tells us.

"How did it go?" I ask.

Pat sets down his fork and takes a sip of cream-and-sugared coffee. "I was home for Easter. I knew I had to do it, but I was really nervous. I remember going into the bathroom and having to take some deep breaths. When I opened the door, my mom asked if anything was wrong. I directed her into the living room, where my father was sitting." He pauses to adjust his oval glasses. "I just said it: 'I'm gay.'

"My mom said, 'We still love you.' But my dad," Pat recalls, mimicking his father's nonverbals, "he dropped his chin, his mouth fell open, and he said, 'Jeeezus Chrrr*rist!*'" Pat laughs at the memory but winces a bit before saying, "I'll never forget that.

"Then he told me three things. 'One, the average life span of a gay man is thirty-nine years.' I said, 'Well, I'm almost there already.' I was thirty-five at the time. 'Two, there's a place in Arizona with an 80 percent success rate.' You know, *conversion.* I said, 'Dad, if conversion were possible, believe me, I would've done it by now.' 'Three, if you're in the closet, you'd better stay there. This will destroy your business.' I thought, 'If anything, coming out would help my business.' A lot of gay people prefer to keep their money within the community.

"The whole time my dad was talking, he wouldn't look at me. He stared at the floor, the chair, anything to avoid eye contact. I had to get out of there. My mom said goodbye, but he said nothing. *He wouldn't even look at me.*"

As I edit this section, a familiar lump settles into my throat, and tears well in my eyes. I feel like I'm right there—in Pat's living room, in his body, in his heart. Each time I read these pages, I hope for a different response from his father. I want him to look at Pat and say, "I love you, son. I'm sorry you've been alone with this for so long." I want him to reach over and hold Pat while he cries (as I'm crying now), releasing years of loneliness and struggle. But some things you just can't revise.

Months after this breakfast, I ask Pat, "In a perfect world, how would your father have responded?"

Looking away, he replies, "My dad would've said, 'I love you no less for it.' That's all I ever wanted from him."

While the server clears his plate, Pat exhales. "From my parents' house, I drove to my brother's place. He was leaving as I was walking up. I said, 'I dropped a bomb on Mom and Dad. I told them I'm gay.' My brother put his arm around me and said it didn't matter. 'However,' he said, 'that does explain why they just called and told me to get over there right away.' We both laughed. So my brother was really cool about it."

This supportive encounter concludes the story of Pat coming out to his family. I finish my meal wondering about the emotions lingering beneath its happy ending.

When Pat spoke his father's words, his voice was strained; when recalling the averted gaze, rivers of tension cut his brow. I heard equal stress in Rob's voice when he told our is-he-flaming waitress, "We *all* are." I saw the same lines on Tim's forehead when that drunk barked, "Your quarterback is a faggot!" But time after time, our group seems to suppress anger, pain, and fear by ignoring a situation, by laughing at it, or by addressing it on the surface and quickly moving on. What are the consequences of these defenses—for emotional health, for relationships, for social change? Don't they keep us estranged from one another?

Since the disclosure in 1995, Pat and his father, now battling cancer, have not spoken about his sexual identity. Why? For Pat, was coming out so painful that he's not prepared to risk any more? For his father, is having a gay son so disconcerting that he erects verbal and nonverbal barriers to knowing more? For them, what else might open, and what might close, by broaching this topic again? Who, if anyone, should take the initiative, and when? For them, as for Al and his father, someday it will be too late.

Practice as Usual

It's been raining much of this Saturday morning, rendering the field a maze of standing water and mud. That may explain why the practice's only attendees are Pat, Stewart, and Scot (an aspiring actor of twenty and the Cove's latest addition).

Squatting behind the home plate fence, I steady my Canon Rebel, zooming in on Pat. He smirks before sending Stewart a grounder. I push the button halfway to focus, and just as I'm about to take the shot, I hear it. *"Fucking faggots!"*

Startled, my right hand releases the camera, but I catch it by the lens with my left. I look toward the crosstown highway, which runs just behind the Hyde Park field. A beat-up, olive Chevy whizzes down the curve, its male passenger leaning out the window and calling, *"Fucking looooosers!"* Wicked howls of laughter follow.

When the car passes, I peer into the viewfinder at Pat, then Stewart, then Scot. I study each closely, searching for any sign of hurt, embarrassment, or anger. No eyes glare, no brows furrow, no jaws clench. Their warm-up continues as usual. Maybe they were distracted, I tell myself, maybe they couldn't hear from the outfield. Maybe.

In the next meeting of my ethnography seminar, I tell the class about this incident. "It's difficult enough for these men to—"

"I don't mean to interrupt," interrupts a male colleague, "but being called a faggot is no big deal. It happened to me just the other day."

"But the term doesn't assault you in the same way it would if you were gay."

"You're making too much of it," he says, "and if you don't mind, I'd prefer to discuss the readings for tonight."

"Making too much of it." The phrase sticks in my mind. Better than being dismissive!

As I impatiently await the end of class, I think about how disengaged I feel from the department. Most weeks, I spend just three hours here. In my first year, it was between twenty and thirty. Each previous semester, I took three courses; now, I have only one. Thanks to a university fellowship, I'm not teaching either, whereas I used to be assigned two classes each term. But my absence isn't merely physical. I'm emotionally estranged as well. I don't feel nearly as connected to my associates or as invested in the departmental community as I once did. What has been lost, and what would it take to regain—from my colleagues and from me?

Bagels with Satan

After practice, we decide to meet at the Village Inn, where a matronly server brings us skillet breakfasts and pancakes. As we sip coffee, I wonder if anyone will mention the "fucking faggots" incident at the field. No one does. Instead, we get into a discussion about Stewart's family.

"Your folks know that you're gay?" I ask.

"Oh no!" Stewart exclaims. "They're not ready for that one."

"How do you know?" I probe.

"Well," he says, stabbing a home-fried potato, "my parents aren't the most tolerant people, my father especially—a real racist. When I was eighteen, I asked this guy over to our house. We were having a party. After a while, one of the guests said to my dad, 'There's some *black* kid here.' My father came up to me and ordered, '*Never* invite him again!' My eyes really opened that day. I saw my father in a whole new light.

"My dad," Stewart continues, then breaks into laughter. "My dad won't eat . . . " he barely can get the words out, "he won't eat bagels!"

"Bagels?" Pat queries. "Why not?"

Hushing his voice, Stewart mocks, *"Jewish thing."* We giggle ourselves silly.

"And my mother, whoa!" he says, throwing his hands in the air. "She told me that Satan, *Satan* has been planting evil seeds in her head." Stewart loses it again. "He's making her think I'm," he looks to his right, then his left, then leans in, as if guarding a secret, "a homosexual!

"But the best part," he tells us, " is that she had a conversation about me—with God!"

I play along. "What did God say?"

"He covered for me," Stewart reports. "So, I've got a dad who won't even eat a bagel and a mom haunted by Satan. Think they're ready to hear their son is gay?"

"Maybe not," I reply, "but at least God's on your side."

Tacit Agreements

When we arrive for Thursday night practice, Little Leaguers have the field. Doug and I cheer as a series of fielding errors and some aggressive running turn a single into four bases. In the half-full bleachers, the young boy's proud parents stand and high-five each other. Stretching out by the fence, Gordon encourages, "That 'a way, kid!"

"Hey," I call as we approach, "how was the state fair?"

"Uh!" he exclaims. "Should 'a been selling *teeth* instead 'a hair!"

I swat his arm and ask, "Your parents still here?"

"Their twenty-first day," Gordon replies, scratching his goatee-in-progress. "But they're drivin' back to Philly tomorrow."

"Did you tell them?" I pry.

"Nah," he responds. "They don't wanna know."

"How can you be sure?"

"In three weeks, the closest either of them came to opening the door was when my mom looked at that picture of us from Lauderdale, the one of you and about twenty guys. She said, 'My, you have a lot of male friends.'"

"To which you said . . . "

"Nothing! Look, I'll tell them when they're ready."

As Gordon picks up his glove, I wonder about his assessment. I think his parents *are* ready. When I met Tex and Marilyn, I sensed that they want to know their son. I saw it in their concerned faces; I heard it in their earnest questioning. So what's Gordon waiting for? The "right" time? From my experience with disclosing bulimia, that time never comes. What does come is a nerve-racking, composure-lacking, hands-shaking, lump-in-your-throat-making experience. It sucks, yes, but what a relief when it's over!

Still, I've no right to judge. I've kept a part of myself hidden for ten years. No one has invented more excuses not to tell than I. Maybe that's why I can't seem to confront my friend more directly.

While Gordon warms up with Doug, I find Al below an old oak, where a slow shower of acorns rains upon the hard ground. He lies down, using his glove as a pillow. "What's up?" I ask, hoping to learn more about Neil, his new lover.

"Been movin' the boy into his house," Al replies. "Neil's brother and friend will be stayin' with him. Neither of them knows." Al raises his eyebrows and shoots me a look that suggests trouble. "I also met The Parents. They were eyein' meeee! I was thinkin' to myself, 'Oh, jus' figure it out!'"

I sense something underneath his light tone. "Is it difficult, Al, keeping this secret?"

"Sometimes," he admits. "I won't lie about it like I used to. These days, my mother and I seem to have an agreement: don't ask, don't tell."

"So what do you do when something important happens in your personal life, like you meet someone, or a relationship falls apart?"

"Whoo!" Al exclaims. "A few years ago, I called home after a breakup. I was *devastated*, cryin' on the phone to my mother. I told her what'd happened, but in my story, I changed the sex of the person I was datin'. I was such a mess that Mom flew me home."

Hesitantly I ask, "Are you, um, are you sad you never told your father?"

"Well," he sighs, "my dad knows now, and there's nothin' he can do about it. I don't think my father could've handled it. My family's pretty fundamentalist. Even dancin' is out. Just imagine how a gay son would go over!"

"I can't."

"Neither can I."

As Al closes his eyes, I ponder "don't ask, don't tell" agreements. How are they formed? When Al and Gordon began coming to terms with their sexual orientation, did they consciously (or unconsciously) decide to stop sharing their romantic lives with their families? When they reached a certain age and no women were coming home or being mentioned, were family members scared into silence? When did these communicative behaviors become rules? How much do their families know? How much do they want to know? Do their families speculate about Gordon and Al's sexual orientation among themselves, or do they "dare not speak its name"—ever? What do such tacit agreements permit? What do they prohibit?

"I Don't Need Change"

Scattered Sunday clouds offer inadequate shelter from a sun that seems ten feet overhead. I feel my lips cracking and my hair fading to brass. "Beverage?" Rob offers.

"I'll go with you. Then you can tell me how things are between you and Tim."

"Hectic," he admits. "I've been traveling a lot for work, and Tim's busy with his last semester of classes. But we're talking about living together in June." I smile.

We approach a large cooler between the home and visitors' stands. Next to the blue chest, this year's league commissioner sits in a folding lawn chair. "Hey there," Rob greets. "One bottled water and a Gatorade, please." The commissioner starts bending down to unhook the metal latch but stops abruptly. Grabbing his lower back, he flinches. Through his T-shirt, the outline of his body becomes visible. He can't weigh 140 pounds. Every rib and vertebra is visible, and yellowish, pallid skin hangs loosely from his triceps and knees.

"I got it," Rob says. "I got it." He reaches into the ice and water to find our drinks, then hands over three dollars.

"Change, " the commissioner wheezes, "you've got change coming." Mucus rattles in his throat as he speaks himself out of breath. "The box on the ground . . . can you hand it to me?"

"Don't worry about it," Rob says, touching his shoulder. "I don't need change."

As we return to the bench, neither of us voices what we both suspect: AIDS will claim this life before the spring season ends.

A Whole Other Dissertation

Later that afternoon, Pat and I make our way through the trendy cafés and galleries of Hyde Park Village. As we round the corner toward Joffrey's Coffee Shop, I ask, "What did you think the first time you met Doug?"

Pat smiles, blushing a little. "When I joined the team, I thought everybody was gay. And I was kind of, ah, interested in Doug. 'Cause he's my type, you know, tall, lanky."

"So you thought he looked gay?"

The question seems to surprise him. "Um, I don't know," Pat says reluctantly. "It just never occurred to me that straight people would play on a gay team."

We find Tim and Rob waiting at an outdoor table. When Pat and I take our seats, I decide to pursue this line with them as well. "Guys, do you think Doug could pass as gay?"

Rob cocks his head and studies me a bit, while Tim crinkles his brow. After thinking about it a second, Rob says, "Doug is handsome, clean-cut, and well dressed enough, but if I saw him walking down the street, he's not someone I necessarily would peg as gay."

Still eyeing me suspiciously, Tim inquires, "Why do you ask?"

"Just wondering," I reply. "It's not a problem."

"Oh good," he says. "I thought maybe you were worried about something."

I smile and tell him no, but I'm not sure he believes me. I mean, I'm just curious about how these men see Doug. Really! Do I seem concerned? I shrug it off . . . for now.

When *Dateline* breaks for its final set of commercials, I check the time on the VCR—10:46 P.M. Where is Doug? He was off work at 10:00. Hung up at the pharmacy? He would've phoned by now. Traffic maybe. But at quarter to 11:00? Car trouble then. I'm sure he would've called. I try not to worry, but at 11:00, I dial his work number. "Walgreens pharmacy," answers a female voice.

"Hello. Is Doug Healy still there?"

"Oh, no," she replies. "He left at 10:15."

Perplexed, I hang up. Did he tell me about an errand? Was he meeting Pat or Gordon?

Eleven-fifteen comes, 11:30, midnight. At 12:30, I swear, I'm getting in my car.

It's now 12:15, and my hand trembles slightly as I put my contacts back in. Moving quickly, I peel off my pajamas and head for the closet, where I throw on a long-sleeved T-shirt. As I'm stepping into stretch pants, I hear a bolt click. I stride toward the living room.

"Hi, honey," Doug says. His sweet smile fades when he sees the all-business expression on my face.

"Where the hell have you been?" I demand.

Doug takes a step back and gives me a puzzled look. "I went for a beer," he answers.

"Where, Orlando?"

"Xavier's house," Doug tells me.

I pause, dumbfounded. *"Xavier?"*

"You know, the guy who keeps stopping by 'just to talk.'"

"I know," I snap. "So you went to his *house?*"

"What's the problem?"

"The problem? I can't believe you! Didn't you say that Xavier is interested in you?"

"I don't know that for sure; I don't even know if he's gay."

"But he comes to see you at the pharmacy every single day."

"Just about."

"Uh!" I exclaim, exasperated. "I can't believe you didn't call to let me know. It's quarter after 12:00! What if he'd tried to attack you? What if he'd slipped Rophynol in your beer?"

"Listen to yourself," Doug says. "If Xavier's gay, then he's likely to victimize straight guys? Aren't you beyond that kind of thinking?"

"Him being gay makes him neither more nor less likely to hurt someone."

Walking away, Doug lets out a prolonged sigh. "You're overreacting."

I follow him into the bedroom. "Here's a scenario for you. For a month, a student of mine has been hanging around after class, making up any excuse to talk with me. I can tell he's interested in more than my theories of communication. One night, I accept his invitation to go back to his place for a beer. I don't call you. You don't know his last name, so you have no way to find me. Would all that be cool with you?"

Doug turns to face me. "No," he says sheepishly, "it wouldn't."

"What you did was not smart! You don't know this man! Weren't you thinking at all about your personal safety?"

"I guess not," Doug admits.

"Besides, what kind of message do you think it sends when you agree to have a beer at the home of someone who's got a crush on you?"

A long pause follows. "Lisa, do you think I'm gay and I'm having an affair?"

Boom.

His question hangs there a moment. I exhale slowly and say, "Douglas, I trust you. But crazy things go through your head when your partner is missing for two hours."

"So the thought occurred to you?"

"Yes," I admit. "It did."

"I love you," he tells me.

"You scared me."

"I'm sorry," Doug says. "I'm really sorry."

Over the next several days, Xavier continues to frequent Doug's store, each time asking, "When can we have another beer?" With every visit, it becomes increasingly evident that he's looking for more than a drinking buddy. As much as I hate to admit it, whenever Xavier's name arises in conversation, an unsettling question turns over in my mind: what does Doug really want?

A week later, I attend my friend Leigh's master's thesis defense. Afterward, she thanks me for coming and says, "I can't wait for *your* defense."

Overhearing, her boss and mentor Harriet approaches. "Leigh tells me you've been studying gay men. How did you become involved with that?"

"My husband plays on a gay softball team."

"Oh, right," Harriet remembers. "Leigh mentioned that." She looks away, seeming to process something. "But, um, your husband, he's not gay, right?"

Her question stirs up emotions from the other night. "Not to my knowledge," I say, trying to feel as light as my words. "That would be a whole other dissertation."

That's It

Al passes me a bite of sausage while I wait for a salmon dijon to replace the overcooked one I sent back. "Here," he says, "the real thang, not the vegetarian stuff you're always eatin'." When I wave in refusal, Al encourages, "Ah c'mon, live a little!" So I do. He catches my slight smile in response to the spicy, greasy meat. "See!"

When I hand over his fork, Al shares, "Talked to my mom the other day. You won' believe this. She said, 'Al, I've been talkin' with your brother, and he and I agreed that we don' need any secrets in this family. We're past that now.'"

"Wow!" I exclaim. "That really opened the door." Al nods but says nothing. "So," I probe, "how did you respond?"

He digs through his mound of pasta and peppers a bit before answering, "I said, 'You're right Mom.'"

I smile, wondering what Al's not telling me. "And . . . what else did you say?"

"That's it," he insists.

"That's *it*?"

"That's it," Al repeats, stabbing another slice of pork. "More sausage?"

"No," I say, looking at him quizzically, "that's it."

In this moment, I want to reach across the table and shake him. I'd like to shout, "Tell them! Confirm what they already know so you all can move on!"

But I don't. I guess Al and I have a tacit agreement of our own.

Men in Pumps

It's Easter Sunday, and I'm about to tackle the reading for ethnography when the phone rings. "Hey, baby," says Doug. "I'm at the house of Rob's friend, Jon. You should come—people to meet, things to see."

"In other words, a fieldwork opportunity?"

"Better bring your camera," he advises.

When I ring the bell, I hear snickering and shuffling inside. Rob appears, about five inches taller than usual. I look down to find black platform sandals on his feet. "I'm the asshole," he explains, referring to a card game where your hand determines your position in a hierarchy that ranges from president to asshole. Any superior can tell you to do anything.

Tim comes over. "Hey! I've been wanting you to meet Kerby," he says, leading me to the table. Wearing a Wonder Woman T, a twentyish man with ultrablond spikes and ear and tongue piercings extends his hand.

The men continue their game. As president, Pat orders everyone into the shoes. He's about to let my husband off the hook when Doug slides his pants legs past his knees and says, "Hand 'em over." He groans while squashing size 10 men's feet into size 9 ladies' pumps. Bunched up and buckled in, Doug climbs onto the piano bench.

"Strike a pose!" Tim instructs.

He turns his back, sticks out his rear end, looks over his shoulder, and tosses a come-hither glance. Letting out a girlish sigh, he says, "They really accentuate my calves, don'cha think?"

"Unbelievable," I remark as his audience whistles and applauds.

Doug's other gender-bending experience is no less eventful. While practicing a Madonna routine with Jeff and Pat for the 1997 Miss Suncoast Softball pageant, he tries to outdo his costars by finishing with the splits. Doug pulls a hamstring and has to sit the bench for a month.

Ironically, Doug's willingness to perform as one of the "girls" seems to solidify his position as one of the boys. Often, like at this Easter party, he chooses their comfort over his own, pushing his boundaries in order to prove himself worthy of insider status.

More and more, I feel like an insider as well. My social life revolves around Thursday practices and postpractice gatherings, Sunday games and brunches, plus phone calls, movies, and meals throughout the week. My academic life, moreover, involves taking notes on the group, recording our interactions, and conducting and transcribing interview sessions. In spite of my efforts, I find that there are limits to the intersubjectivity I can share with these men.

The Lone Ethnographer

Cream candles set in iron chandeliers as big as satellite dishes illuminate the main floor of Odyssey in Orlando. Flashes of red, green, and yellow emanate from dozens of spot- and strobe lights while Tori Amos's "Professional Widow" pumps from refrigerator-size speakers. Recognizing its tune, many standing near the bar down their drinks and pack the already full dance floor.

Our Tampa group has splintered. I spot Al upstairs chatting with a tall guy I don't recognize. Near the stage, Pat—shades on, shirt off—grooves with a young raver. Gordon must be outside or in line for the bathroom, and I haven't seen Rob and Tim since we got here two hours ago. That leaves me dancing with Gregg, a charming new acquaintance who has his eye on a boyish platinum blond. "Where's your husband?" Gregg shouts over the music.

"What?" I ask, placing my hand behind my ear.

"Doug . . . where is he?" he yells.

With a shrug, I mouth back, "No idea."

He takes a step toward me and says in my ear, "You're amazing."

"No," I tell him, pointing at his slinky silver shirt, "that outfit is amazing."

"I mean it. Your husband's wandering a gay club, and you don't seem worried." Is that a bit of foreboding I hear? Before I can ask, he's again making eyes elsewhere.

For a while, I don't mind Gregg's diverted attention; it gives me the freedom to turn inward and enjoy the rhythm. But after several minutes of him looking over my shoulder, I give him a shove toward the male Marilyn and say, "Go!"

I wander through the crowd, looking for Tampa people. Pat comes into view, but when I see him take the Blow Pop from his mouth and place it between the raver's lips, I shy away. I locate Tim and Rob, but they're attached like double-sided tape. Glancing upward, I no longer see Al.

As I step off the dance floor, I feel something I haven't felt in months—left out. Where do I fit, I wonder, when everyone's either paired off or trying to pair off? Perhaps nowhere. Maybe this is how gay men feel in straight clubs. But they could pass as insiders there, an option I don't have here, and besides, we never go to straight clubs.

How dependent I've become on them for a sense of inclusion, and how it stings to be pushed back to the periphery! In this moment, I grasp the limits of my role as participant in this community. A bit melancholy, the "lone ethnographer" ascends the stairs, walks over to the railing, gazes down over the sea of men, and observes.

Standing there, I consider that for some time, I've been thinking of Doug and me as "model heterosexuals." But now I wonder how many could follow our lead. How many straight men could get used to being presumed gay? How many straight women could adjust to the some-times disconcerting mix of conspicuousness and invisibility? How many straight couples would all but leave behind their old worlds; and how many of those wouldn't fit into this one because they don't enjoy the club scene, because they lack disposable income, or because they have family commitments? What *are* the possibilities for border crossing? And what are the consequences?

Not a Massage Parlor

A moment later, Doug startles me from behind. "Been looking all over Odyssey for you. What are you doing?"

"Watching," I tell him.

When he asks, "Want to get some air instead?" I nod.

Taking my hand, he leads me to the L-shaped patio, where we find Gregg. The guys wait under a large potted tree while I purchase two bottled waters from a man working the hotdog cart. Walking back, I pass a raver sitting astride her companion, her legs wrapped tightly around his back. His tongue dueling hers, he grips blond ringlets with one hand as the other ventures up her micro Lycra skirt.

Through the dense 4:00 A.M. crowd, I make my way toward my husband and acquaintance. From a few feet away, I hear Gregg imploring, "Dougie, stretch me. You're the only one tall enough." Obligingly, Doug moves behind Gregg, who sways to the music thundering from inside. Arms high overhead, Gregg puts his palms together; Doug then places his hands around Gregg's. Both go on their tiptoes, elongating their groove-weary backs.

"Excuse me!" a male's stern voice shouts. We turn to find a navy-jacketed security guard. "This is *not* a massage parlor. If you guys need to do that, take it someplace else!"

"*This*," Gregg retorts, "is a gay club, *sir*." The guard stares at Gregg and Doug a few moments before continuing along his patio beat.

Peering over silver-rimmed sunglasses, Gregg marvels, "Of all people, he picks on Doug!" The three of us laugh. "Did he really say, 'This is *not* a massage parlor'?"

Later, the story of this encounter will be repeated so often that the security guard's comment becomes incorporated into our group's vernacular, so whenever people get "a little too close," someone will say, "Excuse me, this is *not* a massage parlor!"

"Enough about him," Doug says disgustedly. "Let's go dance."

As we reenter the club, I watch Officer Anti-Massage pass by the raver couple, still crawling all over each other. He glances at them briefly but says nothing.

"Ya Keep Tryin'"

Knee in the practice-field dirt, I focus for a shot of Pat on the mound. He brings his right arm back and through in a fluid motion that sends the ball in a lazy arc. Click!

"'Scuse me," calls an unfamiliar voice from beside the dugout. "You with this team?"

"I am," I respond, turning around. From his too-long feathered hair and beer gut, I assume he's not gay.

"D'you know if they're lookin' fer guys?" he asks.

I cough through a giggle. "Oh, they're always looking for guys."

"I been wan'n' tah be picked up," says the man.

For real? Smiling, I reply, "Then you came to the right place." I pause, unsure how to handle this. Jeff looks over from first base and grins. "They're almost done with the season," I say.

"I'd shore like tah play," he persists.

"Okay, here's the deal. Are you familiar with Suncoast Softball?"

"No, ma'am."

"It's a gay league," I say, watching his eyes for reaction. Nothing. "Are you gay?"

"No, ma'am."

"There are straight people who play; that's my husband in right center. But you have to be cool with gay people, understand?"

"I jus' wanna play."

"Hold on then," I instruct, cupping my hands around my mouth. "Mr. Manager, could you come here please?" As Jeff strides toward the dugout, I ask the man, "What's your name?"

"E. J.," he replies.

"Jeff, this is E. J. He's interested in signing on."

"Nice to meet ya," Jeff greets him, holding out his hand. He turns to me, "Did ya explain the situation?" I nod. "Ya have gay family or somethin'?" Jeff asks him.

"No sir, I jus' wanna play ball." E. J. runs his hands down his Wranglers.

"All right," Jeff says, "as long as ya accept that the league is centered around our lifestyle. If ya can handle that, great. If ya can't, don't bother."

"I understand," E. J. says, shifting his weight from one foot to the other.

"There is a team with only eight players," Jeff tells him. "Ya could start Sunday."

"That'd be fine, sir, jus' fine."

"Write down your number; I'll get in touch with their coach and have 'im call ya."

"I do appreciate it." I tear a sheet of paper from my notepad and hand it to E. J. along with my pen. He scribbles the information and shakes our hands before returning to his pickup. Jeff and I watch as E. J. pulls away from the field.

"Think he'll show?" I ask.

"I think he will."

On Sunday, Jeff warms up with David while I get settled in the dugout. "Hey, Li," Jeff calls between throws. "You know that guy? The one from last practice."

"E. J.?"

"Rudy called 'im three times."

"And he never called back," I anticipate. When Jeff nods, I say, "I knew it!"

"I didn't," my friend tells me. "I believed 'im when he said he wanted to play."

"What do you do?" I muse.

"Ya keep tryin'," Jeff replies.

I go home thinking about Jeff's last statement. It moves me to consider my feelings of isolation from straight associates. How has my absence affected me? What have I gained and lost? What message has my absence sent my old worlds? That straight and gay lives shall remain separate? No, that can't be the moral of my journey. If Jeff and other gay men can "keep tryin'," then surely I can too.

No Polish

The first Sunday in May, I sit on the bench next to Kerby. He doesn't seem to mind my incessant questions about the chemical conversion of his once-dark locks into flaxen spikes; the violet, green, and lavender tattoo winding around his upper arm; and the silver stud through his tongue. "Did it hurt?" I ask of the piercing.

"Not as much as the Prince Albert," he says.

The closet doors blew open for Kerby ages ago, and he hasn't looked back since—remarkable for a twenty-two-year-old raised Mormon in Salt Lake City. A sharp storyteller who can recall of a long-past event not only who did and said what but also how they were sitting and what they were wearing (accessories included), Kerby keeps me entertained while the Cove struggles to end this inning.

The guttural roar of an old engine intrudes upon our conversation, but we try to ignore it. Then we hear something unmistakable. "*Faaag-goooots!*"

"Not again," I moan, as umpires, players, and spectators turn toward the parking lot.

A gray sedan creeps down the street, along the left field line. Then the carload of males turns the corner onto Swann Avenue, which runs behind the outfield. "Suck me, faggots!" If my stare had the force of Carrie's in the Stephen King novel, their ride would end in a spectacular fireball. Hysterical guffaws fade slowly as the four-door motors away.

I steal a glance at Kerby, whose back has straightened. Looking into his green eyes, I remark with mock surprise, "Wait a minute, there are *faggots* here?"

In a childlike falsetto, Kerby responds, "And me without my good nail polish!" We exchange smiles, but they fade simultaneously. I lay my head on his shoulder, and he pulls me close, stroking my hair.

When I go home to write about this episode, it occurs to me that keeping it locked away in my field notes accomplishes nothing. It doesn't communicate to my gay associates how deeply angry and hurt I was, and it doesn't challenge the structure of homophobia that renders such incidents so commonplace. My gut tells me that I have been a mere witness long enough. Soon it will be time to bear witness.

Other Women

After yet another loss, Pat reminds his frustrated team that we're hosting a fund-raiser at Impulse. We agree to meet there at 4:00.

Doug and I move quickly to the patio, where several Cove players busily set up. Al loads a tray with a can of Redi-Whip and plastic shot glasses of cubed Jell-O in lemon, apricot, and black cherry. Meanwhile, Tim and Rob put out plates, buns, and chips for the barbecue. Gordon stands behind a small bar that David and Pat lean on as they strategize about the sale of raffle tickets. The duo agrees on one dollar each or five dollars for a string extending "from dick to the floor." I don't ask what the "bargain" entails for women.

I feel a tug at my sleeve. "Lisa," says Tim, "there's someone I'd like you to meet." He walks me across the patio and stops by the buffet table. A striking woman I recognize offers a manicured hand when Tim tells me, "This is Mia."

"We met once before," I remind her. "You were wearing a fabulous leather ensemble." She looks equally stunning now: short, sleeveless dress in a summery yellow floral; deep-burgundy locks, perfectly bobbed; flawless makeup. I glance down at my team jersey, denim shorts, and dirty Nikes, then reach back to feel my unwashed, ponytailed hair.

"Anyway . . . " Mia says, turning toward Rob. As they continue whatever conversation we interrupted, I smile at Tim and walk back to the bar.

A few minutes later, Tim comes over again. "Rob and I sensed bad vibes between you and Mia," he says. "What were you thinking when I introduced you?"

Surprised by his analysis, I consider it a moment, then tell him, "The only thing I can remember thinking is that she had a nice, firm hand shake. Why?"

"We thought maybe . . . " Tim hesitates a bit. "Maybe you've gotten used to being the only girl—" Shooting me an oops! glance, he stops to correct himself. "Sorry, the only *woman* around. Maybe you don't like women anymore!"

My mouth falls open. "Is that a joke?"

"*Is* it?" he shoots back.

My first impulse is to tell Tim he's crazy, but then I begin asking myself some tough questions. How long has it been since I wrote Kara—a year? When was the last time I had lunch with Alexandra, Christine, Jennifer, or Leigh, and why don't I ever invite them along when I do things with the softball guys? Am I protective of my position as the only woman in the group? If I am (and women similarly located are), how encouraging can that be for other women who want to cultivate friendships with gay men?

Suddenly, Tim busts out laughing. "I'm kidding!" he assures me. Only a little relieved, I break into a halfhearted chuckle.

Pink Triangles and Personnel Folders

After the barbecue, our group heads inside. Doug makes a run to the bar and returns with Rob, who appears distressed. I walk over and ask, "You okay?"

"Nervous," Rob admits. "I just ran into a coworker."

It takes me a second to grasp his meaning. "Who doesn't know," I add.

"Right. None of them does."

"Could you come out at work?" queries Jon. "This might be an opportunity."

Wringing his hands, Rob says, "I don't think so. The environment is pretty conservative. I like my job; I earn a good living; and I hope to move up in the next year. If they find out, they can refuse to promote me; hell, they can fire me. It's too risky right now."

"I'll go outside with you," I offer, trying to comfort him but feeling ambivalent about engaging in a "passing" conspiracy. "We could hold hands or something."

"Thanks, but my colleagues already think that I'm seeing Tim's friend Linda. Now I've been spotted in a gay bar. Going out there with you might confuse the situation even further."

"Is he your superior?" Jon asks.

"My subordinate, but a troublemaker—not someone I want to have any dirt on me."

"It's not dirt!" Jon and I insist.

"I know," he responds. "I know it's not." Rob smiles but remains distracted.

The word "dirt" sticks in my consciousness. Rob works twelve- and fifteen-hour days, sometimes traveling all week for his company, yet his position feels so precarious that he conceals both his gay identity and his most significant relationship by constructing this lie about Linda. Then tonight, while having a good time with his partner and friends, he runs into somebody from his other world. Instead of the two bonding over the mutual discovery, Rob ends up even more anxious. But the most wrenching part is that he throws the "dirt" not onto an unjust cultural system but onto himself.

A little later, Doug and I stand on the patio catching up with David. He gives us the latest scoop on his peak-and-valley relationship with Chris. Right now, they're in a pack-your-bags crater. When David begs us to change the subject, Doug obliges, "Not to talk shop, but did you hear they may be splitting our district?"

"I did hear that," answers our friend.

"It means a district supervisor position will open up," Doug tells me. Then, turning to David, he says, "You should be ready. What have you got, ten years with Walgreens?"

"Just about," David replies.

"Would you take the job?" I ask him.

"Giirl, I would take it in a heartbeat, in a *heartbeat*. But your husband will be promoted looong before I."

"Why do you say that?"

"Buhcause Doug has you! There's a big ol' pink triangle on my personnel folder."

"You don't think you'll ever be promoted?" I inquire.

"No way, no waaay! I have hit the gay ceilin'!" When I shake my head, David says, "Welcome, girl. Welcome to the real world."

Graduations

When I reach the apartment Tim and Rob just began renting, much of Tim's family is already there. I recognize his mother and brother Joseph from Doug's birthday lunch yesterday, but we really didn't have a chance to talk.

Rob presents me to the group. "Everybody, this is Lisa. Her husband, Doug, who's working today, plays softball with Tim and me. They're close friends of ours."

"Nice to meet you," says a smartly dressed older woman. "I'm Mimi, Tim's grandmother." She smiles sweetly, clasping my right hand with both of hers.

A younger, longer-haired version of Tim approaches. Rob informs, "This is Tim's brother, Matt." He takes my hand a bit reluctantly, his quizzical look suggesting he doesn't know quite what to make of me.

"Your husband plays on their team?" he asks. I nod. "I thought everybody was . . ."

"Gay?" I fill in.

"Most everybody is," Rob explains. "But occasionally, a straight person comes along who doesn't mind hanging with a bunch of gay guys." He winks at me.

"Is Doug, ah, comfortable out there?" asks Joseph with a slightly suspicious scowl.

"He is," I answer. "Like Doug, these guys are educated, professional, athletic. Frankly, they're much more similar to him than different."

Obviously mulling it over, the brothers mutter, "Hmm."

"Lis, would you give me a hand in the kitchen?" Rob asks.

When we're alone, I inquire, "How's the visit going?"

"Well, I think. They're very nice, caring people. I was a little worried about Matt; he's the sibling who seemed to have the most difficulty when Tim came out. Ever since he was a little kid, he always admired Tim, wanting to look just like him, be just like him. When Matt found out Tim was gay, his world caved in. Suddenly, he didn't want anything to do with Tim, and he hated it when anyone compared him to his brother. He changed his hairstyle and took up different activities—anything to be unlike Tim. I can tell that Matt loves his brother, and he's trying to be tolerant, but it's good for him to meet straight people who are at ease with us. Maybe it'll help him move beyond tolerance."

I smile. "And how are the rest of them handling everything?"

"Okay," he says. "They seem a bit taken aback by us living together. They've never had to deal with Tim being gay on his turf before. You remember that we went to his mom's for Christmas, but he was sick and in bed the whole time, so they really didn't see us together. This weekend, Tim's been trying to normalize our relationship for them. He kissed me goodbye before leaving for the University of Tampa. They were all staring, but nobody said anything."

Glancing at the kitchen clock, I gasp, "Ooh! We'd better get going."

Hundreds crowd the campus. Every chair is taken, so Grandma Mimi and I stake out a tree about halfway to the podium while the others try for a closer spot. Cameras ready, we sit through speech after speech, name after name, until finally, we hear it: "Tim Mahn. Accounting. Magna cum laude." Mimi and I let out a collective "Whooo!"

Suddenly, she reaches over to hug me, saying, "I'm glad you're in Tim's life."

Glowing, I reply, "That makes two of us."

New Traditions

The Cove spends Memorial Day weekend at a tournament in Atlanta. Headed to our first dinner out, four of us pile into a rented Bonneville. At a stoplight, I ask Tim and Rob, "What's happening with that same-sex marriage case in Hawaii?"

In 1990, three same-sex couples applied for and were denied marriage licenses from the Hawaii State Department of Health. Attorney Dan Foley filed suit on the couples' behalf. At the trial of *Baehr v. Lewin*, Foley argued that same-sex couples are entitled to equal protection under the law. The case was dismissed. On appeal in May 1993, Hawaii's Supreme Court ruled that the Department of Health's actions had been discriminatory and that unless the state could prove a "compelling interest" in withholding legal status from same-sex unions, it could not do so.

In September 1996, President Clinton signed the federal Defense of Marriage Act. The following May, Hawaii's legislators passed a bill putting a constitutional amendment to the voters: "Shall the legislature have the power to reserve marriage to opposite-sex couples?"[7]

Tim responds, "Believe it or not, the issue is still unresolved. It's been several years since those couples first applied for marriage licenses."

Shaking my head, I observe, "Our culture has tended to stereotype same-sex relationships as less meaningful and committed than heterosexual ones, yet we close off the very avenues that lend support to such bonds."

"To tell you the truth," Tim says, "I'm not sure that most gay people care that much about marriage. It's an institution rooted in a life we left behind."

Along these lines, Michael Warner suggests that marriage works by legitimating some forms of relationships and delegitimating others. This "program of privilege," he argues, is no answer to sexual or gay liberation.[8]

Looking at his partner, Rob replies, "That doesn't mean we shouldn't have the option; we may want that someday."

A picture comes into my mind. "I can see it now: tropical flowers, tiki torches and moonlight, Birkenstocks instead of wing tips, Don Ho strumming Handel's '*Hallelujah*' on the ukulele, and a suckling-pig luau reception!"

Tim laughs. "Still want to be a—what did you call it?"

"A groomsmaid. Absolutely!"

"We'll need help changing the man/woman parts of the ceremony," adds Rob.

"No problem! I'm an expert at wedding revisionism."

"That's the truth," Doug agrees. "Will you get wedding bands?"

"Maybe Claddagh rings," Rob says, "the ones with the hands, heart, and crown."

"For friendship, love, and loyalty," I recall. "Very Irish, Rob Ryan. What about your names? Will you keep your own? Hyphenate? Ryan-Mahn or Mahn-Ryan? You could combine them. Let's see, Ryahn works, or Mayan."

"I'm not sure," Rob says. "I'd have to think a long time before changing my name."

"Tell me about it," I concur.

"Black-tie affair?" Doug suggests.

"Yes!" they respond together.

"And the women?" I inquire. "Will we wear gowns, cocktail dresses, grass skirts?"

"Cocktail dresses," Tim replies, "definitely."

"I don't know," Rob says, "I'd like our wedding to be traditional."

"A traditional gay wedding," I ponder. "I like the sound of that."

On November 3, 1998, Hawaiian voters approved a measure giving their legislature the power to reserve marriage to opposite-sex couples.

In December 1999, the Hawaii Supreme Court dismissed the *Baehr* case, saying that the constitutional amendment rendered it moot.[9]

Many eyes have since turned to Vermont. In 2000, the state supreme court ruled in *Baker v. Vermont* that the state has an obligation to extend the same legal rights and economic benefits to same-sex couples as to married couples.

Blasphemy

After dinner, we find our way to a bar called Blasphemy, "a must-see" according to Pat. There, a rotund female officer checks our IDs and ushers us inside. The line to pay the cover moves quickly, but when the giant, scraggly-haired bouncer spots me, he holds out his hand and shouts, "Whoa! No women! No women before two o'clock!"

Tim steps in front of me. "We called ahead and told the guy we were bringing her. He said it wasn't a problem."

"She's our softball sponsor," Rob fibs. "We're in town for the Armory Classic."

"Well . . . all right," he concedes. "But our policy is no shirts on the dance floor."

"I'm brave," I tell Tim and Rob, "but not that brave."

"That's why we called ahead," Tim says, getting impatient. "We asked if she had to take off her shirt, and the guy we spoke to said she didn't."

The bouncer handling the other line comes over. "What's the problem?"

"This lady doesn't want to remove her shirt," the first tells him.

"She can't!" the second insists. "Don't you remember that time? All those lesbians! They started baring their chests; the whole place was in an uproar! No way, honey. Your shirt stays on!"

Shrugging his shoulders, the first says, "You heard 'im."

I smile. "If it makes you more comfortable, gentlemen, I'll keep it on."

We move inside the bar, which is illuminated only by black lights. All the shirtless men blend into the darkness, but my white tank top acts like a giant reflector panel. It must be visible from a hundred yards. My breasts never so conspicuous, I cross my arms protectively in front of my chest. Meanwhile, Doug peels off his shirt; less than enthusiastically, Rob and Tim follow suit.

"I have to pee," I tell the guys, so Rob and Tim wind us through the thick forest of men toward the bathroom. When we reach it, Tim bypasses the twenty-man line to check out the facilities.

He returns with a crinkled nose. "You definitely don't want to go in there."

"Why not?" I ask.

"Trust me," he says.

When Rob queries, "Can you hold it?" I give a nod.

We then try finding space on the dance floor, but it's wall-to-wall sweaty chests and backs. When Pat sees us, he waves us over. "Have you visited that room?" he asks me, pointing to the abyss in the back.

"No," I respond.

"You don't want to."

"Why not?"

"Trust me," he says.

So many places not to go, so much not to see. I turn to Rob and Tim. "Listen, I don't mean to wimp out. I know what you went through to get me in here, and I appreciate the fact that you thought enough of me and of our relationship to show me this place rather than assuming that I couldn't handle it or wouldn't want to go. I make no judgments about this bar, about the men here, or about whatever's happening in all the areas I'm supposed to avoid. But as a woman—as the *only* woman at Blasphemy—I don't sense that I have a place here. I think I'd like to leave."

"I'm glad you said something," Rob tells me, slipping his shirt back on. "To tell you the truth, Blasphemy isn't my first choice either. This meat market might be fun if I were single—"

"But there isn't much appeal if you're in a monogamous relationship," adds Tim.

I turn to Pat. "You said Blasphemy was a must-see. I hope I've seen enough of it to earn my gay card."

Pat laughs. "You earned your card a long time ago," he assures me, kissing me goodbye. With that, we blaze a trail out of Blasphemy.

Crossing the Line

The weekend after our return from Atlanta is Gay Disney, a gathering each June that brings to Orlando a hundred thousand gay men and lesbians and a few hundred Southern Baptists. Doug has to work, but with the guys' encouragement, I decide to attend the festivities anyway. Pat and I drive to Orlando together, meeting Tim, Rob, and Kerby at their hotel. We pass the afternoon sunbathing and "club wear" shopping. Around 9:00 P.M., the group begins to shower and dress for the night.

At Odyssey, we head straight for the dance floor. The music progresses from "gay anthems" (dance mixes of popular songs) to house (techno) music to a more industrial hard house. Hours pass without notice.

From across our circle, Rob smiles at me. When I smile back, he grooves my way. The music kicks in, and Rob takes my hand, pulling me close. About the same height, our bodies fit well together.

He tucks his head between my neck and shoulder, blowing lightly onto my back. In my ear, he says, "There's no substitute for a woman's body." My heart begins to pound. Rob pulls back, staring intently into my eyes. He eases closer, until our noses almost touch. When his lips part, I tell myself, "You'd better decide now where you want this to go." I peck the side of his mouth, as if to say, "I like being with you; perhaps I'm even attracted to you, but we're approaching dangerous territory."

Suddenly, Rob spins me around, then reaches behind my back, unhooks my strapless bra, and pulls it out the side of my dress. My jaw drops, and I recall a line I just read in Rauch and Fessler's *Why Gay Guys Are a Girl's Best Friend*: "A gay guy hugs you to show he cares. A straight guy hugs you to determine if your bra is front- or back-opening."[10] Perhaps I should lend my copy to Rob. With a devilish eyebrow flash, he leans in and says, "I was a straight man for a long time." Hand on my thigh, Rob tugs at my stockings and informs me, "These are coming off next."

Okay, I think, as exciting as this "research" experience is, we have to stop now. "My friend, I assure you that those are staying on." Perhaps feeling he took one liberty too many, Rob sheepishly hands over the white satin.

"What can I do with that now?" I ask with a smile. "It doesn't go on the same way you took it off." A bit guiltily, Rob folds one cup atop the other and stuffs my brassiere into the back pocket of his jeans, where it remains until morning.

When I get home at 9:30 A.M., Doug's already up and out running. I head for the bathroom to wash up and brush my teeth.

Doug passes by just as I'm peeling off my contacts. "Have fun?" he asks, kissing my cheek.

"Yeah," I tell him. "You really should have been there." I kick my shoes away, remove my stockings, and pull my dress over my head. It's then I realize I'm still braless. "Honey," I say, "Rob, um, well, he has my bra."

"Rob has your bra?" he repeats.

"It was amazing," I report with all the nonchalance I can muster. "He undid it with one hand, and before I knew it, he'd yanked it out of my dress." Doug laughs. Looking up at him, I inquire, "Are you mad?"

"I'm not mad," he says.

"Not at all?"

"I guess not."

"Is that because Rob's gay?"

Doug thinks about this a moment. "Yeah, that's at least part of it. Also Rob's my friend; I trust him. And I trust you."

Kissing him tenderly, I silently query: But do I trust myself?

In the literature on friendship between gay men and straight women, there are two competing narratives about sexuality.[11] One holds that friendships between gay men and straight women are relatively free of the sexual tensions that complicate many interactions between heterosexual men and women. Women in particular, so the story goes, "appreciate the companionship of men who are not attracted to them for sexual reasons."[12]

The other narrative, however, recognizes that even these friendships can be erotic. It suggests that women often develop powerful physical attractions to gay men and that gay men and straight women do have sexual relationships.[13] In his survey of 161 gay men, Nardi indicates that about 20 percent of his respondents had had sex with a straight woman who was a best, close, or casual friend.[14]

As I reflect on my encounter with Rob, my inner voice tells me that we crossed the (albeit blurry) line between friendship and a more explicitly sexual relationship. It's something I've never said of my interactions with these men. At first, my dance with Rob felt much like the dance with Tim two years ago—playful and flirtatious but still within the realm of friendship. But as we stood there, poised to kiss, I realized that even with a gay man, I can't ignore boundaries. Perhaps I felt free to explore such attractions because I assumed that they couldn't be reciprocated. Now I recognize the possibility of mutuality (and the risks, especially for two people already involved in monogamous relationships).

Then again, isn't the line between friendship and sex, at least to some extent, arbitrary and fictional? What purposes—and whose interests—does monogamy serve?[15] Is this arrangement negotiable, for Rob and Tim, for Doug and me? With what possible consequences? Could either couple agree on the terms? And, perhaps most difficult to answer, am I so willing to explore these thoughts because, at least for now, it is I—and not my husband—who has an attraction to another?

Two weeks later, boundaries again are tested. This time, however, the desires in question are Doug's.

Gay Tendencies

I take a stool at the breakfast bar. Across from me, Kerby leans on the counter, anxiously tugging at his bib overalls. His gaze narrows when he says, "I need to tell you something."

"Uh oh."

Kerby places his fingers on my left hand, caressing and squeezing lightly. The gesture feels like one of sympathy, and I cock my head. He straightens my wedding band, then looks into my eyes, saying, "I think you deserve to know that there's been some discussion in the group about Doug's . . . " My mouth opens slightly as I await the last word. Lowering his voice, Kerby adds, "sexuality."

Eyes widening, I ask, "What do you mean?"

He smiles nervously and clears his throat. "Some people are worried about him going to Odyssey." Confusion crinkles my brow. Seeing I'm not getting it, Kerby explains, "They think if Doug has gay tendencies, they might come out while he's partying."

My pulse picks up. "What do you think?"

"I told them, 'You're fucking crazy! Don't you think if Doug were gay he would've revealed this by now?' I said it was their own wishful thinking."

"Whose wishful thinking?"

"Now I'm really in deep," Kerby says with a sigh. "Gregg's made comments on more than one occasion, but Gregg thinks every man is gay. Jon also has his concerns. And Pat—"

"Pat?" I respond. "He's known us well over a year!"

Just then, a friend of Kerby's approaches from the patio. I recognize Gary from the clubs; his dark skin, black hair, and muscular build always have reminded me of ice skater Rudy Galindo. "I said something once," he confesses. "The last time we were at Odyssey, Doug came up and told me I was beautiful. I was so shocked hearing that from a straight man, I didn't know what to think."

"Please!" Kerby exclaims. "Doug once told me that if he were gay, I'd be his boyfriend. I said, 'Thanks, but that really doesn't help me out!'" Then Kerby turns to me and says, "If I thought for a minute that Doug were gay, sister, you'd have been off the nearest cliff!"

"Gee, thanks, Kerby," I respond.

"You know I'm kidding," he says, planting a kiss on my cheek. "God, I shouldn't have said anything."

"No," I reply, "I think this is important. Maybe for some people in the group it's easier to believe that Doug's in the closet than it is to believe that he's straight yet comfortable in a gay community. Maybe they're even afraid that he's primarily attracted to men, because that would throw out our evidence that a straight man can be truly close to gay men."

"In my experience," Kerby says, "that *is* rare."

"Very rare!" affirms Gary.

In Dwight Fee's study of friendship between gay and straight men, gay male respondents reported feeling highly aware of how threatening many straight men find their homosexuality. "Every once in a while an exceptional straight man would come along," writes Fee. "But this is exactly what he was—an exception." He continues, "Gay men saw definite contrasts in gay and straight friends, and obviously did not seek out straight men. They only had rare instances where they felt they could meaningfully connect with straight men, finding little appeal in their usual instrumental approach to friendship, if they even got that far." Later, Fee reports, "Sometimes they even wondered why the straights were open to them, questioning their sincerity as well as, occasionally, their sexual preference."[16]

Similar conclusions are drawn by Jammie Price in *Navigating Differences*. Price interviewed twenty-five pairs of gay and straight male friends. Only nine of the twenty-five straight men reported that they socialized with their gay friend's gay associates. Of these, six indicated that the gay man's friends and acquaintances had expressed doubts about the straight friend's heterosexuality. [17]

"You mind if I talk with Doug about this?" I ask Kerby.

"Ooh boy," he hedges. "I guess it wouldn't be fair to tell you and then expect you not to inform your husband."

"I'm glad you shared this," I say.

"I probably won't be glad tomorrow," he predicts.

I arrive home past 3:00 A.M. Having to work at 8:00, Doug's been asleep for hours. When I crawl in bed, he turns from his left side onto his back and asks if I had a nice time.

"It was fine," I report, wondering if I should leave it at that. But of course I don't. "Want to hear something interesting, or should I tell you in the morning?"

"Tell me now."

The room is completely black; my eyes haven't yet adjusted, so I can't see him at all. Facing him, I lie on my left side and put my right hand on his chest. Into the darkness, I say, "The group has been discussing your, ah, sexuality."

Abruptly, he rolls onto his right side, leaving my hand to rest on his pillow. "My *what?*"

Swallow, breathe. "Well, some are worried that if you have . . . gay tendencies, they might come out while you're partying at Odyssey."

Silence. At last, he queries, "They think I'm in the closet?" We both snicker, a little nervously perhaps. "Who are we talking about here?"

"Gary admitted saying something after you told him he was beautiful."

"I said that? I don't remember, though maybe I did."

"And Jon, and Gregg, and uh, Pat—"

"*Pat?*" he responds, taken aback. "What about Kerby?"

"Kerby told them they were 'fucking crazy.'"

Doug laughs. "Good for him."

A question forms in my head, one I've never asked him directly. I pause, not sure I want to go there. At last, I just spit it out: "*Are* you curious?"

"Sure."

Surprised by the immediacy of his answer, I inquire, "H-how so?"

"I've wondered what it's like to be with a man. I mean, what do they do to each other? How does it feel?" When I say nothing, Doug adds, "I'm sure you've thought about being with a woman."

"Yes," I reply, "but it's mostly conceptual for me."

"What do you mean?"

"Well, when I watch a film with two women making love, for example, or I imagine myself being intimate with a woman, I find it more intellectually interesting than physically exciting. Is that . . . is that how it is for you?"

"No," he answers, almost apologetically. "I think for me it's a little more physical."

I pause again, then decide to push on. "Do you feel you need to . . . act on any of your curiosities?" I try to swallow my brewing anxiety.

"No," Doug says emphatically.

"Have you ever, um, experimented sexually with another male?"

"Never."

Deep breath, then, "*Would* you experiment if you weren't in a relationship with me?"

"I . . . I seriously doubt it," Doug responds. "Besides, I *am* in a relationship with you. I'm fully committed to that. If I weren't . . . hmm. Can you imagine? The guys really would think I was in the closet. Still, I'm certain that, if we weren't together, I'd be dating women or in another relationship with a woman."

"How do you feel about what they said?"

With a note of sadness, he tells me, "I don't know how to take it. Does it mean they think little of me?"

"Thinking you might be attracted to men is thinking 'little' of you?"

"That's not at all what I meant. Do they think I'm not genuine, that I'm using their friendships only as a means to 'test the waters' or to fantasize about desires I'm too ashamed to bring to the surface?"

"I suspect that they don't know what to do with you. The level of your ease is so singular that the only way they can make sense of it is to think that you might be suppressing your 'true' sexuality. Maybe they're afraid of the consequences of that—for you, for me, for our marriage, and for our relationships with them."

"So what should I do?" he asks. "Should I not compliment them? Not hug them?"

"Don't second-guess yourself. You've been open and kind and affectionate. There's nothing wrong with that."

"If that's true, then how could they think that I've been in the closet all this time?"

"Cut them some slack. They endure so much, especially from straight men."

Closing his eyes, he says, "They need exposure, I guess."

As we settle in for sleep, I tell him, "To men like you? Definitely."

For some time, I watch Doug approach our friends with more reserve than I've seen in years. He greets less openly and embraces less tightly (if at all). When I point out my observations, Doug admits intending the distance. Several of our friends notice the change and seem equally uncertain about how to interact with him. The scenario reminds me of Fee's study. He indicates that, in these kinds of situations, both the straight and the gay male friends are asking themselves, "How do I communicate affection without threatening him?"[18]

Perhaps their physical restraint isn't something to be concerned about. All relationships involve both reaching out and pulling back. Still, I worry that they'll start pulling back emotionally as well. What then?

Slowly, Doug and our friends work their way back. Over the next few weeks, their interactions become less and less hesitant. As a group, we emerge from the experience a bit rattled at first, but stronger.

Members of the 1996 Cove team

A Call from Home

My mother calls from Minnesota. Though she catches me in the middle of constructing a paragraph, her tales of painting the shed, weeding the flower beds, and getting the dog shaved for summer offer a welcome break from the buzz and glow of my computer. As usual, we eventually get around to dishing about the relatives—how some have changed, how some should change, and how some will never change. "Your father said something interesting to me the other night," Mom recalls. "He said, 'If one of our sons came home and told me that he was gay, I'd be okay with it.'"

With a good dose of disbelief, I respond, "*Dad* said that?"

"Surprised me too," she says. "I don't think he would've said that two years ago."

I process a moment, then ask, "Mom, do you think that has anything to do with me?"

My mother laughs. "Lisa," she answers, "I think it has *everything* to do with you."

When I hang up, I reflect on my old and new worlds. I've known for some time that the Cove men have changed me, rendering me more open to new ideas and less tolerant of old prejudices. My marriage also has evolved, becoming one of the most daringly honest unions I've ever encountered. Now I see that my old worlds have been changing too, altering their assumptions to accommodate mine. Maybe I *can* go home again.

In 1999, my parents (without prompting from me) began attending seminars on the Christian church's evolving perspectives on homosexuality. That same year, my mother, a school nurse, began campaigning for the inclusion of representatives from PFLAG (Parents and Friends of Lesbians and Gays) in the next community health fair.

While I continue to receive such reinforcement for my life project, my academic project has yet to be written. One morning in May 1997, I meet my adviser for breakfast.

Finding My Place

Rolling the ball of butter off my apple-oatmeal pancake, I say, "I have so many feelings about the project and so many materials to go through, I don't know where to begin."

"Just talk for a while," Art suggests. "Share what your fieldwork has meant to you."

"These men have become my best friends, my family; they've expanded and deepened my relationship with Doug. They've moved me to examine our cultural constructions of sexual orientation and identity; they've strengthened my political commitments to people who are marginalized; and they've changed who I am as a scholar and teacher."

"Are you writing about all that?" he asks.

A question leaves my lips: "Should I be?"

Art sets down his coffee cup. "I don't understand. Why would you ask that?"

"If I take a traditional ethnographic stance, I'm supposed to be objective and distanced. But I'm emotionally attached to these men and politically invested in their welfare. If I take an autoethnographic stance, I can recognize and write from my interests and sympathies, but I'll be focusing on my own experience. I value and want to feature their experience as well."

"But you're making a false distinction," he says. "Even the most traditional ethnography is, in some ways, autoethnography. The culture an ethnographer studies, the sites she visits, the issues she investigates, the methods she employs, the perceptions she has, the lessons she gleans, and the way she writes all relate to her personal and emotional biography. At the same time, all good autoethnography draws from, and teaches about, cultural life.

"Besides," Art continues, "what you always have seemed most passionate about is what happens *between* you and them. Perhaps you can approach your project as what Tedlock calls 'narrative ethnography,' where the ethnographic dialogue becomes the focus of investigation and you represent fieldwork experience and relationships in the form of stories."[19]

I exhale. "I've been searching for my place—as a person and as a researcher—in this community, and you're right. What I really have to offer others is an account of what's happened between us."

"So go back to your field notes and write." And that's exactly what I do.

A Journey into Narrative Ethnography

Art gives me Tedlock's monograph. Reading it, I learn that narrative ethnography combines the researcher's lived experience in the field with ethnographic data, reflections on fieldwork, and cultural analysis. For the first time, I can envision how to write thoughtfully, passionately, and ethically about my fieldwork.

To review my research experience, I first print out a copy of my field notes. For several days, I pore over these, reexamining my descriptions of, and my emotional and analytic responses to, social actors, scenes, and conversations. I highlight all turning-point experiences, from asking Tim for permission to study the team to my discussion with Doug about "gay tendencies." On a sheet of paper, I begin listing key episodes.

While inspecting my notes, I realize that many significant moments had occurred when I wasn't studying this community in an academic sense. Looking over my experiences in the field triggers thoughts of my childhood; my secondary, undergraduate, and early graduate education; meeting David; and the first encounters Doug and I had with David's community. Who we were before stumbling onto this path thus becomes an important part of the story.

In order to tell that part, I spend hours in quiet contemplation and in conversations with Doug and David. Using systematic introspection, I try to recall every instance I thought, heard, or talked about homosexuality prior to September 1995 (when I began taking field notes).[20] Certain experiences, like going to Tracks, return in vivid flashes; others creep back slowly, enveloped by fog.

My list of key episodes with me at all times, I make additions while I read, eat, and drive. I keep a notepad next to my bed to record ideas that surface as I drift off to sleep. After a week of intense introspection, my inventory of encounters spans several pages. It's now time to write.

The First Draft

I begin crafting ethnographic short stories.[21] In these, I attempt to show my encounters with my research community through dramatic tension, strong characterization, (re)constructed dialogue, thick description, and a discernible moral or message.

For episodes not covered in my field notes, I rely on what Stanislavski terms "emotional recall," a process similar to Lee Strasberg's method acting.[22] According to Bruner, this works by reliving the past and recalling an experience in all its sensual and affective detail.[23] For actor and author alike, emotional recall evokes a response in oneself in order to create a powerful and convincing scene for others to engage.

To create "Lesbian Thanksgiving," for example, I close my eyes and experientially return to my childhood home. I ask myself, "What can be seen, heard, and felt here? Who's present, and what are they doing and saying?" Eyes still closed, I begin typing. I list the foods and how they taste, the rooms and how they appear, the people and how they move and talk. A half hour later, I've exhausted my memory. I open my eyes and begin examining the two pages I've entered. These become my field notes for that event.

For episodes that occurred between September 1995 and May 1997, I rely heavily on field notes written from tapes and jottings. Before composing an ethnographic short story from field notes, I read over the relevant passages several times, highlighting sections and making notes in the margins. I then engage in emotional recall to see if further detail or reflection can be gleaned. Only after I feel sufficiently "inside" an episode do I begin to set the scene.

I also listen closely to the eight hours of interactions and reflections I recorded. Hearing my participants' voices helps me return to the past, to sense and feel previous experiences. The tapes prove invaluable in writing dialects as well. Throughout the episodes, I try to mimic David's combination of camp and Kentucky drawl and the hints of a Staten Island Italian upbringing still evident in Jeff Grasso's speech.

In certain cases, interview tapes and transcripts are crucial resources. Preparing to write about my first life-history session with Gordon, for example, I listen to the tape and read the transcripts several times. Our words and voices take me back to that night, enveloping me in the issues and emotions. When I begin reconstructing our dialogue, I strive for readability, cutting conversational threads that seem extraneous and weaving together related threads. Nonetheless, the tapes and transcripts allow me to stay close to the actual words spoken.

The tape from a session with Pat Martinez also provides materials for a short story. When preparing to write what I later title "Intersubjectivity" (where he offers his coming-out narrative to a group of us gathered for breakfast), I remember that Pat shared further details during a focused interview. For this episode, therefore, I study my field notes from the restaurant and the related section in both the interview tape and the transcript. As a result, "Intersubjectivity" contains some of the most detailed storytelling by one of my participants.

The first draft takes more than two months to complete. Each day, as I scan the list of turning points, an entry strikes me, and I immerse myself in that experience, using all the available materials.

As I work, I make constant "member-checking" phone calls, where I question my participants about events, take down their responses, and incorporate their recollections into the text. While out with these men, moreover, I open many discussions with, "Today I wrote about . . ." or, "Remember the time . . ." Again I note their reactions, and when I return home, I make additions and corrections to the manuscript. Both strategies bring a co-constructedness to the project.

By July 1997, I have 196 typed pages of individual scenes—dated, organized chronologically, and separated by asterisks. As I print out a copy for Art, a smile of accomplishment crosses my lips for the first time.

But it quickly fades. I realize, as never before, that moving toward the end of this project probably means *moving*, away from a community that has become mine. With more than a little ambivalence, I meet Art for breakfast and turn over the manuscript.

"For having completed so much," he observes, "you seem pretty down."

"I am down," I admit. "It's ironic. At long last, I feel like this project is happening. I should be ecstatic."

"But?"

"But the sooner I finish, the sooner I leave the field."

Art reassures, "Many graduate students become attached to where they attend school."

"It's more than that. I've always liked USF and living in Florida. But until recently, being here felt transitory. Tampa was just a stop on the way to somewhere else."

"And now?"

"Now it's my *home*." I reluctantly add, "And I'm not sure I can leave."

Art strokes his beard a bit, asking, "What are you saying?"

I swallow my rising emotion. "I'm saying I've begun to question what kind of life I want and who I need in it. Do I hope to be an academic? Yes. Do I think I can be that here? I don't know. My options certainly are limited. But every time I think about leaving—not leaving USF, not leaving Tampa, but leaving *them*—I get a sick feeling in my stomach."

Art sits back and sighs.

"I want to finish my Ph.D.," I tell him. "I'm committed to that. I suspect you don't like what I'm saying. You have high hopes for me—a great job at a fine university. I want that too. But I also want a *life,* and I have that here."

Our session ends with a promise not to close off my options. Art takes my manuscript home, and I spend the next month trying to imagine how he'll respond. Will my narratives intrigue him, shock him, disappoint him?

One afternoon, Art asks that we meet in the conference room at school—the moment of truth.

He leans forward in his chair. "I had no idea you were so . . . immersed in this culture."

I take a deep breath. For weeks, I've been squirming. I'd written from the center of my personal and academic selves, offering my whole being to this project, but what if it wasn't enough? What if my encounters with my research community are only interesting and important to me?

"We should discuss form," he says. "Journal entries are okay, but the storytelling lacks variety."

"*Form,*" I repeat. "Is that your major concern?"

"At this time, yes. Later, you'll also need to work through the theoretical issues at stake."

A few moments pass before the significance sinks in. "But this is it; this is the project?"

"It's the beginning," Art tells me. "I'd say 80 percent of what's here will end up in the final version. But there's a lot of work left. What I'd like you to do now is make the text read more like an ethnographic novel than a series of episodes. Continue developing the plot and subplots and increase the dramatic tension."

As soon as I arrive home, I rush to my computer and begin work on the second draft.

The Second Draft

Making the text more novelistic requires another round of performing emotional recall, studying field notes and transcripts, listening to tapes, and holding conversations with participants. The sequence remains chronological as I fill in what happened between the episodes and work toward more literary transitions.

In addition, I dispense with the dated-entry format and begin thinking about significant blocks of time (which later become chapters), such as the period before Doug and I met David, our early explorations of this community, and my initial fieldwork semester. Since the first section covers twenty-three years (in which I had few significant encounters with homosexuality), I decide to intersperse the present-tense episodes with past-tense commentary. To give the remaining text a sense of continual unfolding, however, I maintain present tense in the chapters that follow.

The Third Draft

After I receive Art's comments on the second draft, the following weeks require fewer returns to my original fieldwork materials and more attention to modes of storytelling. Art reports difficulty keeping track of the characters (over 120 in the second draft). At his urging, I begin deciding who would receive greater, and who lesser, attention.

After much reflection, I determine that my main characters are Lisa, Doug, David, Tim, and Gordon and that my supporting characters (those at the center of three or more scenes) are Brandon, Rob, Al, Pat, and Art. I also keep several minor characters (those central to one or two scenes), including Bob, Kerby, and the other members of my doctoral committee. Painfully, I eliminate about forty "extras" (those with no or virtually no lines); the ones remaining are those that help develop other characters more thoroughly.

By this time, the central questions of my project seem to be: what does friendship across sexual orientation require, mean, and do; and how can friendship be a method of inquiry? To ensure that all episodes speak to one or both questions, I study the manuscript from beginning to end, making notes about each story's function.

When finished, I make another pass, this one to eliminate text that either doesn't fit or that addresses an issue portrayed elsewhere similarly and/or more evocatively. To help flesh out the issues, moreover, I add layers of emotional and intellectual reflections within and following several episodes.

For a more readable and engaging text, I also bring together scenes separated in time through the use of flashbacks, flash-forwards, and thematic groupings. Finally, I add titles to many of the episodes to offer a sense of things to come.

Toward an Analysis

It's 1:00 A.M. and I've just finished yet another pass at this narrative ethnography. I've studied every episode, dissected every line, and quibbled over every adjective. I feel an unparalleled sense of accomplishment as I save the file.

But when I turn off my computer, I'm left with the question, What does it all mean? What do my travels suggest about gay communities, straight communities, the people who inhabit them, and their/our relationships? I decide to sleep on it and begin again tomorrow.

7

Talking through Meaning

I've been on a mission of avoidance. The past several hours I spent screening videos for a media class I'm teaching this summer, catching up on my journal reading, and cleaning everything in sight. I scrubbed floors by hand, dusted light fixtures, even washed beneath the refrigerator. But here I am at last, in front of my computer, pushing on (and fighting the urge to go rotate my tires).

I'm afraid of endings. I'm afraid of what the close of this project will mean for me, for my husband, for the men I've befriended and studied, for *us*. I'm afraid of leaving the field and leaving them. Perhaps I'm even afraid of some difficult issues left to process. I stare into my blue screen, wondering how I can best convey what I've learned along this journey.

Doug appears at my office door. His mouth drops open when he sees my academic bunker—knee-high piles of books, articles, field notes, transcripts, literature summaries, and printouts of the narrative chapters. "Dare I ask what you're doing?"

"Trying to write a conclusion," I say with a sigh. "For months, my purpose has been to show readers a series of lived moments, to draw them inside scenes, conversations, and relationships. I'll continue to tweak the narratives, of course. But I think that much of the hardest work on that dimension of my project is behind me."

"So what's the matter?"

"I've been immersed in the stories for so long that I'm having trouble stepping back. How does everything fit together? What makes our experiences significant, and how can others put them to use in their own lives and communities?"

He glances down at the Post-It labels atop each stack of materials: Friendship, Narrative Ethnography, Queer Theory, Gender. "You look pretty organized."

"I *feel* scattered. I've studied the narratives so closely that I can recite many chapter and verse. I've read and reread articles and books on gay–straight relationships, qualitative methods, and sexuality. I've summarized findings in computer files and memos. In spite of my efforts, I'm still grappling with two major questions: what does friendship across sexual orientation require, mean, and do; and how can friendship be a method of inquiry?"

"At least you can articulate the questions," Doug reassures me. When I only manage a halfhearted smile, he clears a path and takes a seat next to me. Caressing my shoulder, he says soothingly, "A step at a time. What's one way that you could begin to answer these?"

I let this sink in. Hesitantly, I reply, "Well . . . I could try to articulate implications of my fieldwork."

"That's a start. Implications for whom?"

"The friendship-as-method question is directed mainly toward other qualitative researchers."

"And the question about friendship across sexual orientation?"

"I think that could have implications for everyone—gay, bisexual, straight."

"Okay. If a straight person came to you and asked, 'Why should I read your book?' how would you answer?"

I exhale slowly. "Hmm . . . I would say that each of us has a vested interest in recognizing and working through our heterosexist attitudes, behaviors, and practices. Anxieties about homosexuality poison us at every level. They inhibit personal growth; they close off relationship possibilities; and they weaken our social fabric."

Doug nods. "What if this person retorted, 'And how can your story help?'"

The words come easily: "By showing the transformative power of friendship."

"Ah, but won't some resist transformation? Many straight people aren't open to the *presence* of nonheterosexuals, let alone to friendship with them."

His statement resonates with much of what I've been reading. From my computer's folder of literature reviews, I pull up a file on homophobia. Scrolling down, I say, "A lot of research supports your observation. Look at this. Woog cites a survey of high school students in which only

18 percent of boys and 35 percent of girls said they would remain comfortable with a friend who came out as gay.[1] And here, Singer and Deschamps report that, in a survey of first-year college students, 22 percent admitted they had verbally harassed gay men, 51 percent said that lesbians and gay men should try to be heterosexual, and only 8 percent described themselves as 'approving' or 'very approving' of homosexuality."[2] I scan further. "There was one more, Herek and someone . . . yes, Herek and Capitanio. Of their 538 heterosexual respondents, 54 percent agreed that 'male homosexuals are disgusting,' and 70 percent agreed that 'sex between two men is just plain wrong.'"[3]

More recently, a 1999 Gallup poll on homosexuality found that people in the United States are becoming more supportive of gay and lesbian economic and political rights, but many remain ambivalent about same-sex relations and marriage. Eighty-three percent believed that gay men and lesbians should have equal job opportunities (up from 71 percent in 1989 and 58 percent in 1977), and 79 percent said that gay men and lesbians should be allowed to serve in the military, either openly or under the current "don't ask, don't tell" policy (41 percent and 38 percent, respectively). In contrast, only 50 percent thought that same-sex relations should be legal, and just 34 percent supported equal status and rights for same-sex couples.[4]

"While disturbing," Doug says, "those responses don't surprise me. The first two studies involved high school and college students, who feel enormous pressure to think and act in conventional ways—as you did when you broke up with Trent, the guy your peers called a 'femme' and a 'fag.' I also suspect that most of those surveyed had had limited exposure to openly gay people."

Pointing at my computer screen, I reply, "Herek and Capitanio confirm that. Their results suggest that homophobic attitudes tend to precede rather than follow interpersonal contact with lesbians and gay men."[5]

This exchange sparks an idea. With an eye toward my Sony recorder, I query, "Do you mind?" When he shakes his head, I insert a new tape and press "record."

Doug taps my computer's down arrow key. Reading on, he asks, "How did we come to think in these ways about homosexuality?"

"Our apprehensions have roots in everything from traditional family ideology to orthodox religion to popular culture—each a primary source of cultural scripts. It's a vicious circle: if heterosexuals don't question the scripts, they're unlikely to have meaningful encounters with gay people;

and if they have no meaningful encounters with gay people, they're unlikely to question the scripts."

"Do you think we were open to befriending gay people *before* meeting David," he asks, "or do you think meeting David was what opened us?"

I ponder this a moment. "I think both are true. Meeting David undoubtedly was serendipitous. He gave us our first real exposures to openly gay people and to a gay community. At the same time, we must have been looking for something—new ideas, new experiences, new friends. In his interview study on friendship between gay and straight men, Dwight Fee describes his heterosexual respondents as 'searchers.'[6] That term stuck with me because it seemed to fit each of us. What do you think?"

"I would agree, though David certainly broadened the parameters of our search. How else would you explain our visits to places like the Vice?"

"If you think about it, Doug, what we saw of the Vice was pretty tame."

"Ha!" he responds playfully. "It wasn't *your* pectoral that was groped."

"Ha!" I respond in kind. "But my backside has been handled at the Cove, Odyssey—"

"And there was the famous bra incident with Rob," Doug adds. "Hmm . . . a gay man approaching me sexually seems less surprising than a gay man approaching you. What do you make of those encounters?"

"They subvert the equation of sexual orientation and sexual identity." When he wrinkles his brow in confusion, I begin riffling through the stack by his feet. "Where is that Katz book? I had it out yesterday . . . got it! Jonathan Katz points out that the terms 'heterosexual' and 'homosexual' were *invented* by psychoanalysts in the nineteenth century.[7] Ironically, the term 'heterosexual' originally referred to a *pathological* fixation on someone of the other sex."[8]

"I always knew there was something funny about you," he quips.

"About *us*," I retort. "Anyway, prior to the invention of these terms, sexual behaviors were practices we *engaged in*. They did not confer a status, an identity that defined who we were. Since then, the terms have become reified, making this humanly constructed distinction appear 'natural' when it's arbitrary. Instead of hetero- and homosexual, we could classify people as male-oriented or female-oriented. Under that system, lesbians and straight men would share a sexual orientation, because both have primary attractions to women.[9] We also could expand our conception of sexual orientation beyond the sex/gender of one's object choice. We could categorize sexual practices as the early Christians did—in terms of procreative and non-procreative.[10] We could distinguish between orgasmic and nonorgasmic sex, between public and private sex, between spontaneous and scripted sex.[11] The possibilities are endless, but we seldom see outside the boxes that we ourselves have created."

I continue, "In our culture, we tend to think that people *have* sexual identities. But an identity is not a *thing*. It's a construct, a *claim*. In theory, when we claim a gay or straight identity, we open a set of relational options and close off another set. In practice, that claim may not—probably cannot—encapsulate the expansive nature of any human's desires."

"What do you mean?"

"Well, I call myself a heterosexual woman, but my associations with gay men have moved me to recognize and value my amorous attachments to women, like my old friend Kara. You claim to be a straight man, but you now redefine a connection with a friend from home as an 'attraction' of sorts. Likewise, Joe and Rob identify themselves as gay yet continue to respond erotically to women. Not all gay-identified men seem to; David is a good example of that."

"How do you explain such differences *within* a category?" Doug queries.

"We can question the utility of the category system itself. There are alternatives to the dominant, dichotomous construction of sexual orientation. Instead of two categories, Kinsey's scale has seven, with zero indicating that one's fantasies, desires, and behaviors are exclusively heterosexual and six indicating that these are exclusively homosexual.[12] So, at the risk of putting too much weight on numbers, we might say that David is a six while Joe and Rob are fives or fours."

The two-dimensional model proposed by Storms and discussed by Stein is even more nuanced. One problem with Kinsey's scale is that it implies that one's level of attraction to women varies inversely to one's level of attraction to men (in other words, the more attracted one is to women, the less attracted one is to men, and vice versa). According to Storms and Stein, these measures should be separated, because the degree to which someone is attracted to one sex/gender is not related to the degree to which that person is attracted to the other. Any combination is possible, from a high level of attraction to both (or neither) to a high level of attraction to one sex/gender and a low level of attraction to the other.[13]

"So why don't Joe and Rob call themselves 'bisexual'?" asks Doug.

"Perhaps because there are more identity and community resources available to gay men than to bisexuals. You notice that, in spite of the openness we've cultivated to same-sex attractions, we don't call ourselves bisexual either. Ours is a dichotomized society."

"Do you think that can change?"

"I do, but such a change requires us to imagine a world beyond the categories that keep us estranged. That doesn't mean denying the unique insights and experiences that stem from particular standpoints; it doesn't mean total assimilation of one group into another. It means *completely altering our notions of self and other.* In *The Book*, Alan Watts says that the Western conception of self as separate and autonomous is an illusion, and one that doesn't serve us well.[14] For him, the only 'true' self is the whole of creation. He calls us to see our fundamental interconnection with everyone, with all of life. This won't come easily or quickly. It will demand openness and commitment; shared experiences and meaningful conversations; mutual questioning, disclosure, and critique; and sustained interpersonal contact."

"So how do you convince people to participate in that?"

"By showing others where we've been and what we've seen, felt, and learned. In the company of these men, we've experienced friendship across, through, and beyond sexual orientation and identity. We recognize that 'their' well-being and liberation are woven into the same tapestry as 'our' well-being and liberation, because 'they' are now *us*."

"I understand what you're saying," he responds, "but are there reasons *not* to step outside our categories?"

"Good question. For gay communities, stepping outside could mean losing a place on the margins—where some might prefer to stay, especially if they believe the price is total assimilation. Critics like Harris suggest that while increased mainstream acceptance brings social and political clout, it also files away the edge associated with gay cultures' unique spaces, characters, and discourse.[15] That edge defies and contests heterosexist norms and practices, and the more we lose it, the harder it may be for *any* of us to make peace with the shame our culture induces on virtually all sexual matters."[16]

I go on, "For straight people, stepping outside requires giving up the power resources that come with being the norm. It's hard enough to recognize one's own privilege, harder to concede it, and harder still to convince others to do the same."

"What privileges do you think we've conceded?" Doug asks.

"Oh, we're still privileged—legally, politically, culturally. But we've given up the comforts associated with our prior ignorance of gay men's experiences and stories. Our connections have fostered a radically new consciousness about many issues."

"Like HIV and AIDS," he says.

"Exactly."

"All through pharmacy school, AIDS was about drug protocols and patient compliance. Then I met Michael. I played ball with him, laughed with him. I got to know *the person*. I heard him gasping for breath, saw him wasting away, and then he was gone. Twenty-nine years old. God, I can't believe that was three years ago."

"Since then," I respond, "we've seen our associates grieve for lovers and friends, and we've watched some battle HIV themselves. I often wonder how different our lives would have been without the drug cocktails that are holding the virus at bay."

"For now," Doug says. "Their long-term efficacy and side-effects are still unknown." His statement hangs there a moment.

I take in a breath. "Listening and responding to these men's stories has helped me develop profound respect and compassion for gay people. But it's hard sometimes to watch them struggle, with HIV—"

"With coming out," he adds.

"Yes!"

"Revealing the secret, not revealing the secret, all the implications of disclosure." He shakes his head. "The whole process just amazes me."

"Is there an example that stands out in your mind?"

"Look at Al," Doug says. "Since his father's death, his mother and brother have all but told him that they know he's gay. But no one will say the words."

"Gordon's recent disclosure to his mother revealed a similar dynamic. He sat her down and said, 'Mom, I have something to tell you: I'm gay,' and she replied, 'Well yeah, I kind of figured.'"

"Rather anticlimactic after five years of tormenting himself," he remarks.

"I feel conflicted about Al, Gordon, and Rob refusing to confirm what others indicate they already know. On one hand, these tacit agreements allow straight associates to hold on to old hopes and plans, and in some ways, they protect gay people from the consequences of revelation. On the other, what levels of intimacy might be closed off by these silent contracts? How do you truly know Rob without knowing that his deepest commitments have been with men?"

"But who are we to judge?" Doug asks. "It took you ten years to begin sharing your struggles with bulimia. You knew that others might react negatively, so you kept quiet."

"And in keeping quiet, we do nothing to contest our marginalization. Besides, it's not a perfect parallel. I consider bulimia peripheral to my identity. I think you can know me without knowing that I've lived with an eating disorder."

"Then what does it mean to *know* you?" he questions. "Maybe some of them consider being gay peripheral. Besides, how can you expect more gay people to come out given the social conditions? In Florida, lesbians and gay men cannot legally have sex; they cannot marry or adopt children; they have no state civil rights protections against housing or employment discrimination."

"True, but how do those conditions change if gay people don't stand up—even to their own families, even to those who already seem to know—and say, 'This is part of my experience'? I'm not suggesting that it's easy. According to Weston, coming out is almost universally perceived as a family crisis.[17] But lesbians and gay men bravely confront that every day. Look at Pat. Telling his parents was perhaps the hardest thing he'd ever done. I'll never forget the scene he described: him catching his breath in the bathroom, then sitting his parents down and spitting out the words, and his father growling, 'Jeeezus Chrr*rist!*' Still, he got through it."

"Not without cost," Doug points out. "Imagine your father reacting that way: being unable to look you in the eye, telling you not to reveal your secret to others, and suggesting radical 'conversion' therapy." He pauses, then adds, "Of course, the process can't be a simple one for parents either."

"No. Many have internalized our culture's associations of homosexuality with illness and sin, and they have to grieve the loss of a future most parents project for their offspring: heterosexual marriage, perhaps children of their own (and grandchildren for their parents)."

"Plus, as Pat says, any parent who's made antigay comments has to eat crow when his or her own child comes out."

"I've done that myself," I reply. "In my growing intolerance of intolerance, I came face to face with others' heterosexist assumptions. But even more uncomfortably, I came face to face *with my own*. I had to confront my prejudices, my privilege, and my complicity in a cultural system that suppresses and marginalizes gay and lesbian experience. My fearful reaction to having Pat's blood on my hands, for example, was one of the most painfully revealing moments of my fieldwork."

Doug responds, "It wasn't long after I met David that I deeply regretted every gay joke I ever told and every time I called someone 'fag' or 'queer.' In high school and college, the jabs seemed funny only because I didn't see 'those people' as part of my life, part of myself."

"How do you feel now when you hear an antigay comment?"

"It stings. My approach has changed somewhat. I've become more confrontational. Two summers ago, you and I didn't verbally object when my college buddy used the word 'faggot' at Stan and Cindy's barbecue. I wouldn't let that go today."

"That episode, for me, is just one example of how my new consciousness colored return trips to straight circles. While some family and old friends seemed quietly puzzled by our connections with gay men, others approached us as usual, meaning that our interactions with them continued to include their occasional antigay commentary. Sometimes we sat in silence—like at the barbecue—but often I dove into confrontation head or gut first. In retrospect, I was too slow to empathy, forgetting who *I* had been not long before, and I was too quick to defensiveness. The anger I felt toward heterosexism and homophobia was justified, but the anger I *expressed* toward particular individuals often was unproductive. I can't serve as a bridge or ambassador if I alienate straight associates."

Mulling it over, Doug observes, "It's certainly true that we don't have many straight friends here."

"Is that a source of regret for you?"

"No, we have enough friends. That almost all of them are gay is just the way things evolved."

"But we also *allowed* things to evolve that way. After we got to know David and Tim, it felt as though we were bringing our straight and gay communities together, but eventually I saw that, in many ways, we'd simply exchanged the former for the latter. David told me once that no one thinks of you as straight, and Pat has said to me, 'Spoken like a true fag.' While such comments show the level of our integration, I wonder how progressive it is to trade one separate, limited domain for another."

Doug says, "For related reasons, I've started to worry about leaving Tampa. You'll be applying for jobs soon, and in this market, your only offer could take us across the country. I try to imagine what our next circle of friends will be like."

Nodding, I reply, "We've been living a gay life—gay softball, gay clubs, gay parties, gay dinner groups—for some time now, and like you, I wonder what kind of life we might live elsewhere. Would we seek out another gay community? Would it accept us? Would we establish more connections with heterosexuals than we currently have?"

I continue, "Many straight couples our age are largely unavailable because they're caring for young children. In this culture, a child-free straight couple is constructed as 'queer.'[18] Perhaps this lifestyle is part of what attracts us to the gay men we know (almost none of whom have children), and part of what separates many heterosexuals from gay— especially gay male—communities."

"Lifestyle issues are relevant," Doug agrees. "Both we and our friends have the time, energy, and disposable income to invest in multiple close friendships. Still, I think other factors might be more significant in keeping those communities apart, especially for straight men."

At this, I pull up another file from my folder of literature reviews. "Check out this summary I've written on male friendship. Research by Fee and Kirch suggests that friendships between straight and gay men are quite rare when compared to same-sex, same-sexual-identity friendships.[19] I also recall something from Hassett and Owen-Towle's *Friendship Chronicles: Letters between a Gay and a Straight Man*.[20] The book is in the 'Friendship' stack on the far right, if you're interested. The authors call themselves 'revolutionary friends,' a term that draws attention to the unconventionality of their relationship."

"According to the available research, why is it so unconventional?" asks Doug.

"One factor is our culture's taboo against male intimacy.[21] Generations of men grew up with strong, silent (or absent) fathers and in households where touch needs were met almost exclusively by women.

"Popular culture is another factor." I hit the page-down key, looking for a remembered list. "Here we go. Male protagonists continue to be portrayed as, in Wood's terms, 'hard, tough, independent, sexually aggressive, unafraid, violent, totally in control of all emotions, and—above all— in no way feminine.'[22] Think about it. In media, male friends often are unexpressive cops and cowboys who touch only through combat and weapons.[23] And consider that most of those men are constructed as straight. How many TV dramas or sit-coms, popular films, or novels feature a deep and abiding relationship between a straight and a gay man?"

"There was *Kiss of the Spider Woman*," Doug recalls.

"But the two men become sexually involved, and the gay character dies at the end."

"*Philadel*—no, the gay friend dies there too. We just rented . . . what? *Kiss Me Guido*."

"A potentially groundbreaking film, but how many people saw it? I don't even remember it being in theaters."

"I see your point," he says, "but the climate seems to be warming. Movies like *Basquiat* and *The Full Monty*, while not centering on friendships across sexual orientation, have them in the background. And what about *As Good As It Gets*? That was a blockbuster Hollywood film in which a gay man befriends both a straight woman and a straight man."

"I hope you're right about the climate," I tell him. "Still, in both popular culture and everyday life, we find few straight men who journey into gay communities—and even fewer who achieve honorary membership."[24] Again referring to the literature summary on my screen, I say, "Michael Kirch writes about staying at the apartment of David, a heterosexual friend, and socializing with him in a college pub, and Michael

Rowe describes being immersed in the family of his straight friend Chris.[25] In other words, Kirch and Rowe have found acceptance with straight men, but in mostly straight contexts. Therefore, in these 'cross-over friendships,' to borrow a term from Dwight Fee, it is the gay men doing much of the crossing over."[26]

"To what do you attribute that?" asks Doug.

"It may be the path of least resistance. 'Crossing over'—into straight contexts of work and family—is an everyday experience for many gay men. For most straight men, crossing over is unfamiliar and even threatening, because gay contexts challenge the performance—and the link-age—of heterosexual-masculine identity."

"Is this what happened to Bruce the night of my bachelor party?"

"I believe so." Pointing at the pile labeled 'Gender,' I say, "In that paperback on top, Fitzgerald argues that orthodox masculinity is defined less by what it *is* than by what it is *not*, specifically not feminine and not homosexual.[27] Bruce's encounter can be seen as violating both aspects of his 'oppositional identity'—Fitzgerald's words, not mine. Another man first assumed that he was gay and then made a pass at him, which put Bruce in a position usually occupied by women."

Thomas and MacGillivray discuss orthodox masculinity in terms of impenetrability. Part of masculine identity, they posit, is being impene-trable—emotionally and physically. This explains some of the anxiety many heterosexual men feel in the presence of gay men, who remind them that men, like women, *are* penetrable.[28]

I continue, "Bruce probably never had (knowingly) experienced being an object of the male gaze. In our culture, we expect men to be gaz-ers, not those gazed upon—especially by other men. He felt as women often do: on display, maybe even vulnerable."

"Yes," Doug says, "but over time, that gaze can become flattering and validating."

"I even think you *court* it. Before we go out to gay clubs, you spend extra time on your hair and are careful about your wardrobe, which now includes body-hugging shirts and flashy pants."

"Some nights, I do feel like dressing in a way that will attract atten-tion, even if most—all—of that attention comes from men."

"Gay men offer a kind you won't get from most women."

"Unless they've learned, what did you call it? A gay gaze."

I shuffle through the papers cluttering my desk until I spot a field-work memo on gazing. "Malone and Pearlberg and Wilder write about the 'playful cruising' women can learn from gay men.[29] As a woman, I

wasn't socialized to objectify others, but in the presence of our gay associates, I became an active spectator. Unlike a dominant male spectator
(straight, white, middle-class), we were gazing from the margins—looking across, perhaps even up rather than down, not to possess and control but to admire."

"But what about the objects of your gaze?" queries Doug. "What if
they feel, as you often have—on display and vulnerable? Or what if they
also are marginalized, say by race or social class?"

"That gives me pause. On one hand, it feels progressive to reclaim
and revalue gazing as a normal part of sexuality; on the other, perhaps
it's unethical to reproduce for others a shadow side of women's public
life, however valuable exposure to that might be for some. Can there be
ethical gazing? I suppose it would depend on the relative social positions of the gazer and the gazed-upon, on their relationship, and on the
context."

"What about you?" I then question. "If there is something we might
call a gay gaze, do you think you've learned it? Of all the straight men I
know, you seem the most comfortable and open about looking at other
males."

"Looking at men now feels natural to me," Doug says. "I can see them
as attractive, even beautiful. All straight guys study men. Some of that is
competition—is he bigger or taller than I? Some of that is admiration—
wow, he's well built or has a cool haircut. But these are things most
straight men wouldn't say in the presence of other men."

Returning to my notes on male friendship, I respond, "And, as writers like Miller, Hassett and Owen-Towle, and Kirch indicate, for all
straight men's unease about looking at men, nothing compares to their
reticence about *touching* men."[30]

Doug nods. "Before I met David, I wasn't nearly as open physically
with other men. Ever since graduation, my Drake buddies and I always
hug 'hello' and 'goodbye.' What the hell? It's only once a year! But our
embraces always seem a little stiff and withdrawn, and my straight male
friends are a bit quick to pull away. In contrast, when I hug David or
Rob, it's warm, strong, and close. There's a different level of comfort—
for them and for me."

"I think that friendship with gay men has a lot to offer straight men.
Dwight Fee says that such relationships help straight men face and even
transcend their fears about being close to other men."[31]

"That certainly has been true for me." Doug pauses a second, then
asks, "And what about straight women? They—you—don't appear to
have such anxieties about connecting with gay men."

"Straight women do seem to have an easier time forming friendships with gay men,[32] perhaps because women's attitudes toward homosexuality tend to be more favorable than men's.[33] But heterosexism isn't absent from straight women's consciousness. The ubiquitous saying, 'What a waste!' implies that, at some level, many women think that all men—or at least the 'best' men—rightfully belong with women."

He responds, "I've even heard women who already are involved or married make this statement, and I always think, 'Why do you care anyway?'"

"Ironically, it seems to be intended as a compliment: these fine men would've added something to the—or *my*—gene pool. But it's hard not to read it as naïve and self-serving."

I continue, "Besides heterosexism, other issues may complicate relationships between straight women and gay men. My experience contests the popular wisdom, espoused by authors such as Rauch and Fessler, that the sexual tensions of straight cross-sex friendship are absent in friendships between gay men and straight women.[34] Early on, I believed that wisdom and felt free to explore my sexualized feelings toward gay men. I assumed that these couldn't be reciprocated and therefore wouldn't be acted upon. But my talk with Joe on the swings and my crossing the line with Rob taught me that a straight woman and a gay man *can* become erotically attracted, and whether the attraction is one-way or mutual, it has implications, both for the friendship and for any romantic partnerships involved."

"What else do you think your experience can teach straight women?" he asks.

I collect my thoughts a moment, then say, "Because we lack the anxieties associated with masculine identity, straight women are more likely than straight men to serve as bridges between gay and straight communities. We can and should help straight men—and other straight women—cross over. That's a responsibility I haven't always fulfilled."

Doug replies, "We've only known one other woman so deeply immersed in this community, and that's Mia. At the time you were introduced, you both were accustomed to being a diva, so neither of you knew how to react to the other."

"I agree, though I think my crime is more of omission than commission. I don't believe I actively pushed away Mia, your teammate Anna, or Tim's friend Linda; I just don't think I made extraordinary efforts to get to know them."

I go on, "The past year changed my thinking about my 'special' status. In August, my colleague and close friend Christine moved to Texas, and Jennifer, our old housemate, died in February. I *pine* for feminine closeness like never before. I miss the gut-level empathy. I miss my mom! I think I expected my friendships with gay men to fill the void of feminine companionship. I thought our speech communities and our ways of experiencing relationships and expressing emotions would be more like female friendships than straight cross-sex friendships."

"Now what do you think?"

"I think the gay men we've befriended are strikingly similar to my straight male friends. My relationships with them are playful, active, and intellectually stimulating, but I find myself, as Wood says many female friends do, giving more emotional support than I receive.[35] You remember how crushed I was when Al responded to my disclosure of bulimia with, 'I'd have no problem telling my parents something like *that.*' When I was grieving over Christine's departure, none of these men noticed; when Jennifer died, no one sent a card or called to check up on me. In contrast, I've spent hours at a time counseling Rob and Tim about their relationship, hours shoring up Pat after his love interest moved to Memphis, hours listening to Al and Gordon talk about their struggles to come out. Don't get me wrong. I love these men; they're brothers to me. But sometimes *I* don't feel loved in that deep, feminine way, and given the masculine socialization and identities of these particular gay men, that's something I probably cannot expect."

"Would you expect it from other gay men?" Doug asks.

"Possibly. We met most of our friends through your softball team. On one hand, the Suncoast league was founded as an alternative to the hypermasculinity and homophobia often associated with athletics. On the other, a competitive sports league tends to attract traditionally masculine people. Had we become part of a gay community through a political group or an AIDS support network, we might have encountered men with more varied mixes of masculine and feminine qualities. In any case, I'm not pulling back from these relationships, but I am committed to developing more female friendships.

"What about you?" I then query. "Do you like being the only straight guy around? It does confer an exalted status. Everybody's always fawning, 'Doug is so great; he's so rare!' You must find that flattering."

"More than anything, I find that sad. At the same time, I like to think that I've given our friends some hope when it comes to straight men. Maybe my example will move them to keep reaching out, to keep giving straight men a chance at friendship. I like to think that I've given Suncoast Softball that same hope.

"However," Doug adds, "there's no denying the unique position each of us currently occupies in this community, and the one we occupy together, as a straight couple."

"As I read over my account of this journey," I reflect, "I'm struck by how deeply ours the project is. This community is a shared community. Neither of us could have become part of it without the other."

He predicts, "If I'd been single when I met David, we still would've connected. Maybe I even would've gone to Tracks that first time. Beyond that, it's hard to say. I do think that some of my willingness to venture out came from you and our relationship."

"When I married you," I tell him, "the differences in our educations and careers concerned me. I wondered what we would have to talk about. What would be ours? Part of my motivation for studying this group was that it enabled me to get to know and spend time with you, time I otherwise would have spent in places removed from your life and experience."

"I had those concerns too. We often talk about ourselves as bridges from our friends to straight circles, but in a sense, *they* have been a bridge between you and me. They've become our common interest."

"These connections also have engendered a radical honesty," I say. "They've moved us to confront each other's repertoire of desires and talk through fear and uncertainty. Asking if you were curious about sex with men and disclosing my crossing the line with Rob felt unsettling and risky, but on the other side were mutual learning and growth."

Doug reaches over and rubs my hand. Then, glancing at the rolling tape, he asks, "Where are we?"

"Well, we've talked about how these friendships have affected our identities and relationship and what implications our experiences might have for other heterosexuals."

"What about gay men?" he asks. "What lessons does your project draw for them?"

"Hmm. For a time, I thought that heterosexuals bore all responsibility for improving the cultural climate. Such one-way blaming denies that the chasm between gay and straight communities is what Bateson and other systems theorists might consider a *relationship* problem.[36] That doesn't mean that straight and gay people contribute equally to this problem, but it recognizes that gay people's attitudes and behaviors play some role in the construction and maintenance of the cultural systems that keep us divided."

"So what are you asking gay men to do?"

"This is such an old argument, but first, I'm asking them to come out."

"I know you understand their reluctance."

"Of course. Some fear for their relationships with straight people." I take a book from the floor and turn to a marked page. "This is Chris Shyer in *Not Like Other Boys*: 'I had convinced myself not only that my homosexuality would decimate my family, but that coming out of the closet would mean losing all the straight friends I had. It meant being kicked out of my safe and solid universe for keeps.'"[37]

Doug replies, "And even if straight associates don't reject a gay person, they still may be unable to provide the kind of support needed for close friendships."

"That's true. I remember this from Kirk and Madsen's *After the Ball*: 'Few straight women, and fewer straight men, will be bold enough to defend homosexuality.'"[38] I return to *Not Like Other Boys*. "Along these lines, Chris Shyer says that 'being accepting falls a bit short of being my advocate. Telling me to roll with the punches is not like throwing one, or wanting to, when I am reviled or stigmatized. Supporting me is different from expecting me to conform to community standards when they're repressive, unenlightened and unjust.'[39]

"So, yes," I continue, "coming out entails vulnerability. But what's the alternative? Take this case: Rob's brother and sister-in-law are staying with Rob and Tim this weekend. Rob just came out to his brother, but the two agreed not to tell the sister-in-law because they don't believe she'll be accepting. Tim's furious because Rob offered to sleep on the couch for the duration of their stay so that this woman will think that the two are only roommates. Apparently, Rob and his sibling have little faith in her perceptive abilities. The Ryan brothers may be right about her attitudes. She may react negatively, but if she does, perhaps she has no business staying at their house. Then again, she may surprise them. My point is this: how can true friendship develop between gay and straight people if gay people don't give heterosexuals the chance to know them *as gay?*"

"Their coming out could affect more than just their own relationships," Doug says. "There are too few examples of openly gay men in general and even fewer of openly gay men—and I stress *openly* here— who defy the stereotypes, who are, for example, masculine and athletic."

"Key components of many straight men's identities," I respond.

"Right! I know you hate the terms, but it may be the 'straight-looking' and 'straight-acting' gay men who have the most potential for bridging gay and straight male communities."

"Not long ago," I recall, "our brother-in-law was talking about your bachelor party. He referred to Tim and Brandon as 'good exposure' and the entertaining-yet-purse-carrying Barry as 'bad exposure.' I don't like those categories, but the conversation made me think about timing."

Doug nods. "Perhaps meeting Barry would have been less shocking if he and my college buddies already had experienced several interactions with gay men who looked, talked, and acted more like them."

I put my hand to my forehead, trying to call up a thought. "Oh, what's the quote from Kirk and Madsen? Could you hand me that book by your right knee?"

"This one?" he asks, holding up *After the Ball.*

Nodding, I take it from him. "It was in the middle someplace . . . here: *'You hammer in the wedge narrow end first.'"*[40]

But then I reconsider this line of reasoning. "On the other hand, how do you know what's good or bad exposure until you've had it? What does 'bad exposure' mean? Bad for whom? Is exposure 'good' only when it keeps you safe and comfortable? How does that constitute exposure? And how much homophobic commentary, like Bruce's about his experience at the Cove, stems from genuine negative feelings, and how much from internalized expectations to perform orthodox masculinity?"

Doug responds, "So Bruce may not be reporting what he felt so much as reporting what he thinks others *expect* him to feel as a straight man in a gay context."

"Sounds plausible to me."

On a different note, I predict, "In terms of potential relationships with both straight women and lesbians, I think that gay men could benefit from a more feminist consciousness. As Hassett and Owen-Towle observe, sexism can be as rife in gay male communities as in straight ones.[41] Misogynist labels like 'fish,' one of David's favorite terms for me; drag shows that many believe caricature femininity, like the Miss Suncoast Softball pageant; and spaces that all but exclude women, like Blasphemy, do little to foster cross-sex connections."

"Not many men are well versed in feminism," Doug says, "and there aren't enough women in gay male communities to point out assumptions and correct offenders. As a result, the locker-room mentality can run amok."

"Hadn't thought of it that way," I reply. "I guess what's needed are feminist women and sensitive gay men committed to bridging our experiential worlds and working together to combat sexism and homophobia."

I then posit, "Another limiting factor is gay men's adoption of our culture's obsessions with appearance and youth. Perpetual anxiety and dissatisfaction sap us of the kind of energy it requires to build and maintain strong relationships and communities."

"I know what you mean," he says. "The frequent talk of weight lifting, the Zone, and steroids made me more conscious about my physique than ever before. I sometimes wonder, 'How do they see *me*? Can *anyone* measure up to their standards?'"

"This is a potential dark side of a gay gaze. When projected outward, it can feel empowering, but when turned inward, it can feel debilitating."

Doug suggests, "Maybe gay men turn inward because, in so many ways, their outward reality is difficult to face. They see and experience rejection, harassment, even violence. Perhaps the body is something they believe they can control; perhaps some women turn to bulimia for similar reasons."

"The 'body projects' of straight women and gay men do seem to share roots," I say.[42] "They have similar consequences as well. Media circulate impossible physical ideals. Straight women and gay men acquire cultural capital by striving toward those ideals, but the process promotes little more than an internalized sense of 'never enough.' We exhaust our emotional and financial resources on superficial pursuits, leaving none for the bigger fights: cultural harmony, civil rights, social justice. In the end, our self-absorption serves no one but our political enemies."

"And whatever sense of control you gain is illusive and temporary anyway. After all, bodies age, become ill, and die."

"Maybe that's part of it too. Wrinkles, HIV, an 'undisciplined' body— these are signs of mortality. Perhaps our body projects are also what Becker considers immortality projects—means to repress our sense of finitude."[43]

"That doesn't sound healthy."

"Becker might disagree. He believes repression is central to our survival because we're not equipped to face the human condition. But I suspect he'd recommend less destructive campaigns."

When I say nothing more, he asks, "Have we covered what friendship across sexual orientation requires, means, and does?"

"For us, at least."

Doug settles further into his chair. "What about your idea of friendship as method?"

"I've written a series of memos about that. Could I run them by you?"

He smiles. "Go ahead, but qualitative methods isn't exactly my area."

I dig out the pages, remove the paper clip, and put my notes in order. "Okay, here goes."

In many ways, friendship and fieldwork are similar endeavors. Friendship, after all, is fieldwork. It's being in the world with others. To both friendship communities and fieldwork communities, we first must gain access. We might stumble in accidentally, or we might find an 'informant' who introduces us to her or his collective. But somehow we've got to get in. Once there, we negotiate roles. How much do we participate; how much observe? Will we be relative insiders or outsiders? We learn new ways of speaking and new codes for behavior. Then, as we deepen our ties, we meet trials and challenges, and we cope with relationship dialectics, negotiating how private and how candid we will be, how separate and how together, how stable and how in flux. One day, depending where life takes us, we even may face "leaving the field."

I look up from my notes to gauge his reaction.

"I think I understand," Doug says slowly, "but what does it mean to say that friendship is a *method* of inquiry?"

"In terms of my study, friendship is not only a subject but also the way I conducted it. Friendship as method is not a completely new idea. It builds on several established approaches to qualitative research."

"Like what?"

Shuffling through papers, I respond, "Let me find that page. All right. First, it's based on the principles of interpretivism, which according to Schwandt, stem from the German intellectual traditions of hermeneutics (interpretation) and *verstehen* (understanding), from phenomenology (a research tradition focused on the everyday meanings that construct, maintain, and transform a social world), and from the critiques of positivism."[44]

"Can you explain those critiques?"

"Sure. Positivism is a philosophy of science based on several assumptions: that there exists a single, universal, and fixed reality; that inquiry should be neutral, dispassionate, and apolitical; and that our purposes as researchers are to discover unmediated facts and causal relationships, to predict and control the physical and social world, and to formulate general laws and grand narratives. Interpretivism rejects all of these.

"If you'll permit me to read again," I say.

Interpretivists take reality to be both pluralistic and constructed in language and interaction. Instead of facts, we search for intersubjective meanings, what Geertz calls the 'webs of significance,' and instead of control, we seek understanding.[45] According to Denzin, we research and write not to capture the totality of social life but to interpret reflectively and reflexively slices and glimpses of localized interaction in order to understand more fully both others and ourselves.[46]

"Does feminism factor in somewhere?" Doug asks.

"Ah, you're right with me. Much of feminist thought draws from this tradition, combining interpretivist assumptions with political commitments to empowerment, consciousness-raising, and social justice. I'll read you what I've written on this next page."

Feminists like Cook and Fonow, Reinharz, and Roberts have been instrumental in debunking the myth of value-free inquiry; in calling researchers to acknowledge their interests and sympathies; in questioning the traditional, hierarchical separation between researcher and respondents; in promoting caring and just relationships in the field; and in encouraging as much emotional sharing and vulnerability from the researcher as from those researched.[47]

Feminist standpoint theory has been especially instrumental in showing how one's location in cultural categories (such as sexual identity) influences social position.[48] This position, in turn, shapes and constrains what one can know and do. Because each person views the social world from her or his unique standpoint, intersubjectivity between researcher and participants only can occur when each understands the other's social position and its emotional, relational, and political consequences.

"Keep going," he encourages.

I say, "The next section pulls together my sources on queer theory, which has been equally instructive."

"Read it."

"All right," I say.

A project or text is "queer" if it challenges heterosexism and heteronormativity—the idea that heterosexual is normative and all other sexualities deviant—[49] and it problematizes the binary construction of hetero- and homosexualities.[50] "The key to liberation," writes Gamson, is "muddying the categories rather than shoring them up, pointing out their instability and fluidity along with their social roots."[51]

"How has queer theory influenced your work?" Doug asks.

"Like feminist theory, it has encouraged me to be reflexive about the challenges and opportunities of studying a marginalized community to which I don't belong. It has moved me to recognize my heterosexual privilege and to work against cultural practices of 'othering,' where we silence, suppress, and shame experiences and people that somehow challenge the dominant ideology."

Scanning ahead, I say, "Along similar lines, I've been influenced by Fine's notion of 'working the hyphens.[52] Like other interpretivist approaches, hers rejects scientific neutrality, universal truths, and dispassionate inquiry and moves toward social justice, relational truths, and passionate inquiry. Through authentic engagement, the lines between researcher and respondent blur, permitting each to explore the complex humanity of both self and other. Instead of 'giving voice,' researchers get to know others in meaningful and sustained ways.

"I'll read you the next passage," I say.

Fine's philosophy shares much common ground with participatory action research. According to Reason, this type of inquiry emerged from the tradition of liberationist movements.[53] Through genuine collaboration, it promotes the understanding of knowledge as an instrument of power and domination, honors lived experience, and aims to produce knowledge and action *directly useful* to those being studied. Research, under this model, can be judged by what Lather calls 'catalytic validity,' the degree to which it empowers those researched.[54] Key to this approach is dialogue, where the subject–object relationship of positivism becomes a subject–subject one, in which academic knowledge combines with everyday experience to produce new and profound understandings.

Nodding, Doug inquires, "Is that what you were trying to accomplish in your interactive interviewing project with Carolyn and Christine?"[55]

"That project differed from traditional participatory action research because all subjects involved are academics. Also, interactive interviewing demands more sharing of personal and social experiences on the part of the researcher than does PAR. But, like participatory action research, interactive interviewing is an interpretive practice, calls for intense collaboration, and privileges lived, emotional experience."

"After interactive interviewing, is friendship the next step?"

"Methodologically, yes."

"What does it involve?"

Consulting my notes, I say, "First, we research with the *practices* of friendship. This means that although researchers might use traditional forms of data gathering, like systematic note taking and informal and formal interviewing, our primary procedures are those we all use to build and sustain friendship: conversation, everyday involvement, compassion, giving, and vulnerability.

"Second, it demands that we research at the natural *pace* of friendship. As with interactive interviewing, often this is slow, gradual, and unsteady. Both cultural immersion and true friendship are long-term commitments. It's difficult to know others in meaningful and sustained ways when feeling rushed or pressured by deadlines. I suppose I could have tried to begin writing sooner, but the result wouldn't have been this narrative ethnography. With friendship as method, a project's issues emerge organically, in the context of going for walks and sharing meals. The unfolding path of the relationships becomes the path of the project. This approach may frustrate a researcher who needs everything spelled out in advance. I know, I used to be one of those. But if we have or can cultivate an openness to—and a patience for—surprise and serendipity, new and unexpected dimensions are added to fieldwork experience and relationships.

"To other qualitative researchers, I would say that the most important aspect of this methodology is that we research with an *ethic* of friendship—a stance of mutuality, caring, justice, and even love. I realize that 'friendship as method' sounds somewhat tactical. But what I'm suggesting, and what I've been trying to practice, is not a program strategically aimed at gaining deeper access. It's a level of investment in participants' lives that requires putting the relationships on par with the project. We give up a day of writing to help someone move—and are grateful for the opportunity. We set aside our reading pile when someone drops by or calls 'just to talk.' We keep secrets, even when they'd add compelling twists to the narrative. We consider our participants an audience and struggle to write both honestly and compassionately *for them.* We put ourselves on the line—going virtually anywhere, doing almost anything, pushing to the furthest reaches of our being. We never ask more of others than we are willing to give. Friendship as method demands *radical reciprocity,* a move from studying them to studying *us.*"

"What do you see as the benefits of this approach?" Doug asks.

"Personally, the most significant benefit has been the relationships themselves. My 'subjects'—and it feels strange to call them that— became our best friends, our family. Academically, the friendships permitted a level of understanding and depth of experience I don't know how else I could have gotten."

I then say, "Throughout the cycles of talking, reading, and writing, my researcher and friendship roles wove together, each adding depth and breadth to the other. Because I was studying them, these men always could assume that I wanted to understand their experience. But because I cared about them so deeply, they always could assume that I would value their stories and try to use them in ways that promoted liberation and justice. When I talked to my classmates and students about our experiences and wrote about them in conference papers, I felt I was doing just that.

"In addition, my writing seemed to foster conversation and connection among *them,* as illustrated by the encounter at Gordon's apartment, where my papers were being passed around the room. My hope is that someday my work will spark such dialogue outside our friendship circle."

"Are there any risks or drawbacks to approaching research this way?" Doug queries.

"Such fieldwork carries all the risks that friendship carries. Both researcher and participants will be vulnerable to one another, and that means they can be profoundly disappointed, angered, or hurt. Distanced, 'objective' ethnographers might experience embarrassment at their initial ignorance of 'native' customs; they might feel disoriented or lonely in the field. But they never bare their souls and therefore never risk the pain of being disconfirmed by someone embedded there.

"When I told Al of my bulimia, it wasn't a strategy aimed at inducing disclosure from him. I opened myself because I sensed that my friend was hurting, and I wanted him to know that I could be his companion in pain. I wanted to comfort him; perhaps I even wanted *him* to comfort *me*. It just didn't work out that way.

"But often it did work out," I reflect. "Not long ago, a chapter to which I'd contributed was published.[56] Pat was over when I brought the book home. When he asked to see it, I hesitated because the piece contained an excerpt from my autoethnographic account of bulimia.[57] I couldn't get Gordon's and Al's reactions out of my mind. Pat took the book home and called me as soon as he read it. 'It brought tears to my eyes,' he said. 'I've never known anyone bulimic before. I had no idea what it was like. Even though our situations were completely different, I saw my struggles with sexuality in your struggles with food. I understand what it's like to feel so completely alone—when you're dying for someone to come to you, when you don't know how to tell others what's wrong.' It was a risky but deeply affirming conversation. Sometimes vulnerability brings closeness—but not always."

I continue, "Another uncertainty of this kind of research is that you never know what you'll learn about yourself. When your life and experiences are some of the 'primary data,' to borrow Jackson's words, you must examine yourself in ways not required by traditional qualitative inquiry.[58] I learned, for example, that in spite of my ardently feminist sensibility, I haven't yet shed my ties to traditional feminine beauty and my need for male validation. To recognize my continued complicity in our culture's obsession with appearance was a difficult and discrediting process. It brought to light a chasm between who I've been and who I'm trying to become. Sometimes I would have preferred not to look so deeply into myself.

"I've also considered how this project might have affected our marriage," I share. "In probing our own and each other's identities and desires, we may have opened Pandora's boxes for which we weren't prepared. What if you'd discovered that you needed to experiment sexually with men? What if I'd discovered that I needed to explore other attractions?"

"But we didn't discover those things," Doug replies.

"No, but we *could* have. Perhaps we don't *have* desires so much as we *find* or *create* them through certain kinds of experiences.[59] It's something that might give others pause.

"In terms of the writing," I say, "friendship as method has additional considerations. Relationships are ongoing, but at some point, the writing has to stop. That point always is arbitrary and involves leaving out what comes after."

"What's been left out that you'd like in?"

"I ended the narrative section in the summer of 1997. In the fall, two lesbians joined the Cove. Holly and Kelly played only one season, then moved away, but I shared some interesting moments with these strong, talented women. Because I had to stop somewhere, those moments were not included, so as it stands, this project is disappointingly devoid of lesbian experience, voice, and cultures."

"Unfortunately," Doug suggests, "I think it's fairly understandable given that lesbian and gay communities can be as separate as gay and straight communities."

"A topic worthy of another project," I say. "In addition, I've been asked to keep secrets about attractions, relationships, and crises that would have added significant layers to this account. There are a number of experiences and conversations I'd love to invite readers inside, but I can't because I value the friendships as much as the project. A traditional researcher probably wouldn't feel such a forceful pull."

"Remember, though, a traditional researcher might not know those secrets in the first place. You have that information because you're also a trusted friend."

"That's true, but the dual role of friend–researcher often made it difficult to decide what to divulge. I've had the most trouble writing about incidents that potentially discredit or stereotype my participants. I felt much more uncomfortable *writing* about the Vice, for example, than I did experiencing it.

"Unlike a conventional researcher," I say, "I assumed that my participants would read—and care about—what I wrote. In part, my project was a testament to our friendships. So how could I admit that I felt disconfirmed or disturbed?

"But writing an honest account required me to deal with my negative feelings. On early drafts, Art kept commenting, 'You're romanticizing them. Is that *all* you felt? Didn't that hurt you, make you mad?' Adding the darker aspects of my experience was really difficult for me. It felt as though I were betraying the friendships."

"I have to admit," Doug shares, "that's something I've been concerned about. While Art sometimes thought you didn't push them far enough, I sometimes thought you pushed them *too* far. I worried that your questions would make them uncomfortable, that your encouragement for them to come out would backfire, and that they might not like what you wrote. If any of those proved true, it could impact not only your relationships with them but *our* and *my* relationships with them as well."

"I was troubled by those prospects too, and I see how your position differed from mine. I had to juggle the demands of a study with the demands of the friendships. You didn't.

"For me," I say, "weighing those demands required a sometimes difficult balancing act. After all, this became more than just my life or just a project. It became a *life project,* and one that projected us toward an uncertain future. These men gave us a sense of home, and sometimes I thought it would be easier to leave higher education than to leave the field of their friendships."

"What do you think now?"

"I'm torn by what Art describes as a dialectic between two worlds of experience: the academic and the personal. In 'It's about Time: Narrative and the Divided Self,' he reflects on how these collided for him when he received word at an academic conference that his father had died.[60] Art recognized a gulf between his successful yet 'tame' professional life and the profound emotional intensity of his personal loss. His interests in lived experience and narrative grew out of a desire to bridge that gulf.

"As a student of his, I've always been encouraged to bring together my personal and academic selves. This project certainly reflects that. However, the grand narrative of academia still dictates a rather inflexible path: graduate students are socialized by one institution and hired into another, often one geographically distant. Art's mentoring has allowed me to merge the personal and the academic for my dissertation, but once the project is finished, those worlds, in all likelihood, will be ripped apart. In a sense, I've done what he asked so well that no academic job seems worth the sacrifices."

I go on, "On the other hand, these men have changed my professional interests and investments. What I've learned from them is too important not to share, and perhaps the best place for me to accomplish that is the university, where I can be an agent of and for social change. But to do that, we will have to leave this community, and that will tear my heart from my chest."

Glancing at the clock, Doug assures me, "We'll cross that bridge when we come to it. Right now, it's late. Shut off your computer and come to bed."

"I will," I say. "But first, I have to write up our conversation."

With an exasperated sigh, Doug asks, "*Then* will you be finished?"

"I'm not sure I'll *ever* be finished," I reply as he disappears into the darkened hallway. "That's the thing about life projects."

Epilogue: Defending Life

October 16, 1998: a day of endings and new beginnings. Ten minutes before 2:00 P.M., my mother and I take the elevator to the third floor of the communication building. Putting her arm around my waist, she says, "This doesn't seem real."

I rub my palms together and reply, "I was thinking the same thing."

"Are you, um, nervous?" she asks, sounding a bit jittery herself.

"I'm getting there." When we reach my office, I open the door for her. "I need to check on the room—number of chairs, arrangement. You can wait here, if you like." She takes a seat at my desk.

Down the hall, I find Art in the performance lab. "Hey!" he calls out. "How are you feeling?"

"Aside from the knotted stomach and dry mouth?"

With a chuckle, he remarks, "I know what you mean."

"I guess for an adviser, a dissertation defense is the academic version of your kid getting married."

"Something like that," he smilingly replies. I join him in moving chairs, but Art shoos me away, saying, "I'll handle this. Go collect your thoughts. *Try to relax.*" I take a dramatically prolonged nasal inhalation before heading back to my office.

Turning the corner, I see my mother looking at an open copy of my dissertation, which she has read. When she faces me, her gray-blue eyes fill with tears. "I'm proud of you," she says softly. She pauses, then, "I . . . I know we don't have time now, but sometime soon, I'd like to talk with you . . . about the bulimia." My heart drops. "No one in our family really knew."

My mouth opens but no words come. This isn't a conversation for which I was prepared. "I know, Mom," I reply at last. "I guess in some ways, this was my coming out story, too." Drawing her close, I take in the familiar scent of her White Linen perfume. We pull away far enough to look at one another; in her face, I see the curve of my brow and the shape of my eyes and jaw. She smiles and tucks strands of hair behind my left ear.

"This way?" she asks, pointing toward the performance lab.

"Yes. I'll be there in just a minute." I watch her walk down the hall and turn into the room.

Taking several deep breaths, I begin looking over my notes. A mass settles into my throat the instant I see his name: Matthew Shepard. In most of my presentation run-throughs, I broke down by the third paragraph.

His story has been front-page news for the past six days: the brutal beating, his parents' desperate return from Saudi Arabia, the round-the-clock vigil as he lay in a coma, the arrests of Russell Henderson and Aaron McKinney, Matthew Shepard's passing on Monday, and the planning of his memorial service.

Almost every report has included the same photograph. In the profile shot, an introspective Matthew Shepard gazes downward and grins slightly. I try to imagine how Aaron McKinney could look at his soft, boyish face and deliver eighteen blows with the butt of a gun.

The tears that have come so easily this week well and spill onto my cheeks. I grab a tissue, dab my eyes, and blow my nose. My fingers tremble as I straighten my long white dress.

Closing the door behind me, I begin the walk from my office to the performance lab. "It's okay if you cry during the presentation," I tell myself. "Surely lots of 'defendants' have cried at these things."

I crack the lab door and peek inside. Art already is seated with the rest of my committee: Carolyn Ellis, Eric Eisenberg, Marsha Vanderford, and Barney Downs. Jim King, a professor of education and appointed chair of the meeting, looks over and waves me into the room. When he smiles, I remember meeting him a year ago. Responding to a colleague's self-description as a "dust-bowl empiricist," Jim proclaimed himself a "fruit-bowl interpretivist." I liked him immediately.

"Please be seated," Jim tells the audience. I hear my heart thumping in my chest. "In a few moments, Lisa will give a brief presentation about her project, then her committee will ask their questions, and finally the discussion will be open to everyone."

I move to the podium and look out at those gathered: my mother and husband, current and former students, several peers from USF, and about a dozen of the men I've befriended and studied. David and Chris sit together, both smiling warmly. To their right are Tim, Rob, Al, and Pat, who look excited and perhaps a bit anxious for me. When I make eye contact, Gordon raises his hand slightly and grins. My body floods with emotions: excitement at the impending transition from graduate student to Ph.D., pride that nearly fifty friends and colleagues are here, and a lingering sadness for a man whose promising life was extinguished just four days ago.

"Last Saturday," I begin, "as I was thinking about what I wanted to say to you today, I picked up the *St. Pete Times*. It was there that I first learned about Matthew Shepard." I pause and try to clear the quake from my voice.

"On October 6, Matthew Shepard was doing something remarkably ordinary for a twenty-one-year-old college student—having a beer at a popular hangout. Around midnight, Russell Henderson and Aaron McKinney approached.

"The three men left the Fireside together and got into a truck belonging to McKinney's father. It was there that the beating began. They drove to a secluded area and ordered Matthew Shepard out of the truck." I pause, knowing what comes next. "As he . . . as he cried, 'Please don't,' Henderson and McKinney tied Matthew Shepard to a fence, kicked and pistol-whipped him into unconsciousness, and set his body on fire." I exhale and swallow hard. "They stole his wallet and shoes and left him tied to that fence, where he remained for eighteen hours."

I push on. "As Matthew Shepard lay dying, a homecoming parade float at Colorado State University featured a scarecrow, a reference to early reports of what the first passerby had mistaken Matthew Shepard for. 'I'm gay' was sprayed across its face." The room is still and silent.

"Matthew Shepard never regained consciousness. He spent six days in a coma before dying this Monday, October 12. His memorial service will be held this afternoon." I look out at Tim, whose eyes brim with tears. He nods reassuringly.

"These past few years, I have been on a journey. Perhaps it's not one every person would take. But when I think of Matthew Shepard—a young man who spoke three languages and dreamed of becoming a diplomat—I wonder what he could have been thinking, feeling, or doing right now. Practicing his German? Writing a homesick letter to his dad? Having a happy-hour beer at the Fireside? How might Matthew Shepard's fate have been different if Russell Henderson and Aaron McKinney had been where I've been, seen what I've seen, felt what I've felt—even just a little?"

No one moves or even seems to breathe. I pause before shifting into the more formal portion of my speech.

About half of those here have not read my dissertation, so I provide an overview of its history, consequences, and implications. "This work centers on two major questions," I explain, "what does friendship across sexual orientation require, mean, and do, and how can friendship be considered a method of inquiry?

"My project is a narrative ethnography, which is both a way of conducting and a way of representing fieldwork. Narrative ethnographers explore the creation, maintenance, and transformation of fieldwork relationships. We also write about those relationships and their turning points in the form of stories that invite readers inside the ongoing dialogue between ourselves and our participants.

"Through narrative ethnography, I show how my husband, Doug, and I—a straight couple from the rural Midwest with not a single gay friend between us—came to be immersed in a community of gay men; how the bonds changed over time; how they affected our sexual, personal, and professional identities, our marriage, and our positions in straight circles of family, friends, and colleagues; how networks *outside* the friendships were affected; and what unique conversations were provoked along the way.

"To explain how we all came to be here today, I must take you back to a beginning. It is June 1994. My then-boyfriend Doug comes home from work and tells me how 'cool' his pharmacy supervisor is. 'David's been so helpful,' Doug says, 'a real mentor. He tells great stories; we laugh all the time. Oh yeah, and I think he might be gay.'" David grins.

"I suspect that David has a parallel conversation with his partner, Chris. Perhaps it goes something like, 'My new intern seems all right. Doug's very eager, a real go-getter. He's pretty green, though. I think he's prob'ly straight.'" Chris and David lean toward one another, chuckling softly.

"David and Chris get to see firsthand just how naïve the intern and the intern's girlfriend are. What must our faces look like as we enter our first gay dance club? See our first drag show? Visit our first leather bar?" David laughs.

"And what must *David's* face look like when Doug later asks about his softball team? What is David thinking and feeling as he explains to Doug that both the Cove team, and indeed, the whole Suncoast Softball league are gay identified? Is David surprised that his 'green' intern is not deterred?"

I smile at David. "The first time Doug comes up to bat at his very first Suncoast Softball practice, David says to him, 'I'm glad you're my friend.' It is the understatement of understatements to stand up here today and say the same to you, David." With tears in his eyes, David smiles back.

"Fast forward to September 1995. The setting: a graduate seminar in qualitative methods. Needing an 'alternative' fieldwork site, I go to Tim Mahn, the Cove's coach, and ask if I can study the team. Only for a moment does he look at me as if I might be crazy." Tim laughs. "At the time, neither of us has any idea how much this last-minute, last-ditch pitch will change our lives.

"Beginning that semester, my life with these men becomes a research project—and then a *life project*. Tim and his partner Brandon Nolan invite me inside their relationship and its difficulties. Al Steel talks with me about concealing his gay identity from coworkers and his family. David tells me of Christmas cards returned—unopened—because yet another friend has been lost to HIV-related illnesses. Later, Gordon Bernstein and Pat Martinez share their struggles to come out to themselves, to be intimate with men, and to reveal their homosexuality to their parents; and Rob Ryan helps me envision and experience a place *beyond* categories like sexual identity."

Looking at the group, I say, "Your stories and friendship have been among the greatest gifts of my life. They forever changed how I move through the social world, how I teach my classes, how I practice research, and how I write. In return for those gifts, I offer this project as a counternarrative to the cultural fears and anxieties that moved Russell Henderson and Aaron McKinney to treat Matthew Shepard with such inhumanity, to tear apart his family, and to destroy their own lives and families in the process."

As I scan the audience from left to right, tears return to my eyes. "Individually and collectively, we have a long way to go and much work to do; perhaps some of that can begin here today. Thank you for coming." I take a seat and await the first question from my committee.

Professor Marsha Vanderford speaks first. "I want to ask about the notion of a counternarrative. You say you want to offer a story that contests much of what's disseminated about homosexuality. But you also refer to the project as a dialogue—between you and your research community, and between you and readers. This implies that you want to keep the text open, so readers are free to bring their own experiences to bear on the episodes you describe. As I read, I often felt guided by you. I would have felt almost disloyal—even immoral—to interpret the scenes in any other way than you did. So I wonder if you can create both a counternarrative—which has a specific agenda—and an open text."

"Like all writers," I say, "narrative ethnographers have reasons for creating and sharing texts. One of my purposes is to question the scripts that construct heterosexuality and homosexuality as mutually exclusive polar opposites and that regard homosexuality as something to fear, hate, and/or suppress. I try to show how I have grappled with these scripts in my own life and how my evolving friendships with gay men have helped me write new ones. In short, I'm trying to convey what happened to me, to us, not what will—or should—happen to you. Readers will come with their own experiences, make their own meanings of our experiences, and decide for themselves what to do with what they read."

Marsha responds, "I can see how the stories leave some things open, but what about the analysis chapter? In a sense you do lay out specific points and lessons. How does this differ from a standard argumentative conclusion?"

"I am making arguments," I reply, "though I try to present them in a dialogic form. Because of this, the issues raised can be taken as conversational starting points instead of definitive conclusions, which tend to close off discussion."

Art considers this and asks, "Would the text have been more open to alternative interpretations had you simply ended with the last narrative chapter?"

"Perhaps," I say, "but then Eric would be asking me, 'Where is the analysis?'" I wink at Eric, who returns the gesture. "I think different readers will be attracted to different sections. Some may be drawn to the stories, others to the more explicitly theoretical discussions, still others to the metanarratives and methodological discourse."

On that note, Carolyn jumps in. "I have a methods question. In your work, you ask if there can be 'ethical gazing' in the context of objectifying others in public life. I'm interested in ethical gazing and the practice of ethnography. I wonder if we always have to sell out somebody, and if we choose not to sell out our participants—as you try not to do through the methods of narrative ethnography and friendship—might we then be selling out our *readers*? Readers have to believe that we're telling the truth, or at least *a* truth."

Nodding, I reply, "Like any text, mine is selective, partial, and incomplete. Its truths are multiple and experiential. That is, the work is true to my experience; it represents who my participants and I have become together. For readers, its truths—or nontruths—will depend on their experiences and interpretations. Readers can ask themselves, 'Does it ring true to *me*? Does it provoke *me* to think, feel, and/or act differently than before?'

"That said," I continue, "let me return to the notion of ethical gazing. The term 'gaze' carries a lot of ethnographic baggage. Traditionally, 'we' ethnographers were supposed to be distanced, neutral, apolitical, and value free, reducing 'them'—those we researched—to mere objects of study. Such a stance makes it difficult to be engaged by others' humanity. Perhaps the move I'm making as a narrative ethnographer is from gaze to *engagement*. I'm striving to practice ethical engagement."

Carolyn responds, "A well-known sociologist once wrote to me, saying, 'You can be *friendly* with research participants, but you can never be their friend.'"

"Friendship as method is meant to supplement, not replace, the research traditions from which that assumption emerges," I say. "We learn important and useful things about physical and cultural worlds *both* from a critical distance *and* through direct personal and emotional engagement."

I lean forward. "This approach demands that we get inside others' lives and stories. But it also involves stepping back from experiences and relationships, identifying points of connection *and disconnection*, examining those points analytically, and determining what can be learned from them."

Art asks, "For what kinds of research might friendship as method be inappropriate?"

"Hmm . . . I think *any* study involving human subjects could incorporate some aspect of it. Even in the most empirical, double-blind drug trial, for example, researchers can treat participants with an ethic of friendship. They can solicit fears and concerns, listen closely and respond compassionately, and use such exchanges to refine the study and direct its implications."

"So researchers need not study the *topic* of friendship to utilize this as a method," Jim says.

"Right. The study of close relationships—including friendship—is well suited for friendship as method. In contrast to one-time, retrospective surveys—the primary means of studying relationships—friendship as method involves sustained immersion in participants' lives, offering a processual and longitudinal perspective. But most any topic could be investigated with the practices, at the pace, and/or with an ethic of friendship. Emotional topics, like divorce, serious illness, or the birth of a child, probably lend themselves best to friendship as method, because the more emotional the topic, the more critical it becomes to have an open and trusting relationship between the researcher and participants."

"In this kind of work," queries Carolyn, "must the researcher and participants actually *be* friends?"

"I don't think so. To expect a mutual, deep, and/or lasting friendship to develop between every researcher and all participants is unrealistic. Regardless, we always can approach respondents from a *stance* of friendship, meaning we treat them with respect, we honor their stories, and we try to use their stories for humane and just purposes."

"But what if *they* are not humane and just?" asks Jim intently. "Would you study Matthew Shepard's killers this way?"

I exhale slowly. "That would be extremely difficult. When something like this murder happens, 'we'—the nonperpetrators—often are so shocked and disheartened that we distance ourselves from 'them'—the perpetrators. We tell ourselves that they must be crazy or evil. Such explanations come quickly and easily. The hardest question to ask is this: what kinds of personal, familial, and cultural conditions have to exist for this act to make sense somehow, to seem almost *rational*? We don't ask this because it implicates us in the problem; it forces us to identify with the killers, to bring them close and see them as part of us. Russell Henderson and Aaron McKinney were unable to experience their interconnection with Matthew Shepard; that's exactly what made him so disposable. But if we dispose of them in the same way, we come no closer to creating the kind of world where such actions become less possible. It would be profoundly uncomfortable and disturbing to study Henderson and McKinney with the practices and/or with an ethic of friendship, but that may be what's most needed."

Eric speaks next. "I want to start with a public apology. Frankly, when you proposed this study, I didn't think it would work. I didn't know how you would find a place from which to speak. I thought about traditional, realist ethnography, but I knew that you wanted to do more than merely collect 'data' from and theorize about a gay culture—about 'them.'[1] Then I thought of autoethnography, where one's own experience becomes the basis for cultural analysis, but I had trouble imagining what a straight woman's experience could teach us about gay men."

He continues, "The move you made, however, was to narrative ethnography, where you weren't studying so much 'the gay experience' or 'Lisa's experience' as the *relationships*, which is something you *could* experience. Sitting here, I realized that my doubts about this project are part of the problem you're identifying. For one human being to speak *through* and *for* relationships with other human beings is the heart of your study. Now I feel blown away by its success. You've moved us toward the ideal of communication, which is to free us from the illusions of our separateness."

Eric then says, "I do have a question, and this is something I probably should be asking my therapist rather than you."

"Is she here?" quips Art.

"She could be," Eric replies. "This is starting to feel like therapy. Here's my point: every time I hear the expression 'friendship as method,' I cringe. I cannot get over this. Years ago, my grandfather told me, 'Don't poop where you eat.'" This unexpected phrase stirs the audience into laughter. "What I mean is that we associate pleasure with *unselfconsciousness* and anxiety with self-consciousness. This study brings so much self-consciousness to your marriage, to your participants' and your sexualities, and to the friendships that I want to scream, 'No!' Why would you contaminate all that love with all this reflexivity? Give me an answer that makes me feel better!" Again we laugh.

"I don't think reflexivity 'contaminates' love," I say. "I think it makes it real and *useful*. What moved me to continue doing this as a project was the belief that our experiences could communicate something important and meaningful. Yes, to do that required me to examine and analyze their stories and our relationships. But in the process, I came to believe—and I think *they* came to believe—that what we could say about—and through—friendship needed to be said."

I go on, "The presumption of heterosexuality is so strong that many parents never open a discussion on these issues. Sexual orientation and identity are not sufficiently part of the curriculum in primary and secondary school, and they're not addressed adequately at the university level either. Matthew Shepard was a university student at a university hangout. So whatever unselfconscious pleasures I may have given up or asked these men to give up, I did because it *matters*. If I didn't feel strongly that assumptions could be challenged, that conversations could take place, and that people could think, feel, and act differently, I never would have asked this of them."

Eric responds, "Are you saying that you were willing to subject the friendships to this kind of scrutiny because of the greater good, or did this kind of analysis actually *enhance* the friendships?"

"I think in many ways, the relationships deepened not *in spite of* the research, but *along with* the research. As an ethnographer, I was moved to ask certain kinds of questions, to be open to a wide range of experiences, and to process and write about those experiences. Sharing papers with them provoked new conversations, which moved me to refine my analysis. The research and the relationships were mutually enhancing, not always, perhaps, but overall, definitely."

The next comment is Barney's. "I have a question that also has to do with reflexivity. I'm very intrigued by Eric's notion of 'don't poop where you eat.'" He lowers his voice to an intense stage whisper. "I think we have great fears about being self-aware, yet it is in our self-awareness that we are most crucially connected." Moving his hand in front of his eye, Barney implores, "What about this iris out of which I peer? How is it shaped? How is it distorted? These are questions we seldom pose. So I ask you, Lisa, how has this project shaped your iris, your reality, your awareness, your humanity?"

I reply, "The metaphor I will invoke is that of awakening. Before I met these men, I was peacefully and comfortably asleep. Waking up was—and is—a sometimes startling experience. If I hadn't been where I have in the last four years, I doubt I would have responded so personally and viscerally to the murder of Matthew Shepard. There is grief in that, but there's also a calling unlike any I've ever felt. That calling comes through in every facet of my life. For example, in the past three years, I've had several students come out either in my classes or to me privately. That never happened before. Something must be present now in my classrooms, something that helps them feel safe. So, while waking up moved me out of a restful place, I would never go back. I now see what's at stake."

We've come around to Jim, who appears deep in thought. "I want to return to the narrative," he says slowly. "I told you before that I read all of it in one sitting." Jim inhales deeply. "A couple of times, I lost my composure." He pauses, looking at his feet. "I'm not sure I can talk about it." Silence, then, "At one point when I was reading, you brought Michael back to life." His voice cracks when he says, "And I broke down." Jim looks up at me. When the tears come, he lets them slide down his face. "It was so . . . it was so good to see Michael again. My friends Peter and Jim, who've been dead for a few years now, came up and were reading with me behind my back." A lump forms in my throat. "I just wanted to thank you for that."

Jim smiles through the tears, then looks around at my committee members. When each indicates that there are no further questions, he says, "We now invite the audience to participate."

Murmuring ensues for nearly a minute, but no hands go in the air.

"I have something that might provoke responses," Art offers. "One of the things that Lisa and I have wondered about is how she is perceived and constructed by members of her research community. Originally, she planned to conduct follow-up interviews and incorporate the conversations into the text. I encouraged her to hold off because the project already had become quite an undertaking."

I look at my participants and say, "It's important for me to understand, from your perspectives, what this project did to us and for us."

John Giancola, a professor of communication at the University of Tampa and a fellow Ph.D. student, speaks first. "I'm not a member of Lisa's research community, but I am somebody whose life was changed by reading this. I started taking straight friends to gay places for the first time in fifty-five years. After a movie, a straight male friend and I were standing outside of the Hyde Park theaters. I asked if he wanted to get a drink. He said, 'Sure.' Normally we would go to Four Green Fields or some other straight bar. But I'd just read Lisa's dissertation, so I asked, 'A straight bar . . . or a gay bar?' 'Either,' he said. When I asked if he'd mind going to the Cove, he said no, and we went. Since then, I've had several other adventures because I took risks that I didn't take before and wouldn't have taken without reading your work and letting it inform my life."

John then says, "I do have a question. As you moved through this particular group, how did you feel about their stability as a *community*? Coming from the late sixties and the gay liberation movement, I've been somewhat disappointed by the recent emphasis on gay men's *economic* viability. Obviously for many gay men and lesbians, 'gay wealth' is a myth, but perhaps in some ways, others of us *have* become too aligned with middle-class values. Should the political climate turn very bad, did you get a sense that this group would know how to pick up the phone, discuss, and rally? Is this a responsible set of persons, socially and politically? Or is it all material culture and softball?"

"A couple of these men are card-carrying members of the Republican Party," I begin.

"Oh boy," says Al with a good-humored grin, "here we go."

"Four years ago," I continue, "I had no idea that it was possible to be both gay *and* Republican. I suppose I wasn't yet cognizant of the diversity *within* this community. Regardless of political affiliation, though, fiscal concerns—tax rates, income, job security—often do seem to take precedence over civil rights and cultural climate. So I'm not sure that *these* are the gay men who would organize politically and rally for liberation."

I then say, "As masculine-identified gay men, they can and do pass easily in multiple contexts of their lives. To render themselves visible as gay men, they must consciously and actively come out. Each time they opt for visibility, they make homosexuality harder to dismiss or marginalize.[2] But they also concede the privileges that come with being seen as heterosexual.'[3]

"The Cove has its own unique and local culture," I say. "The team is predominantly gay, male, athletic, masculine identified, white, educated, and middle to upper-middle class. Though perhaps not consciously, the group is exclusive, in some ways for its own protection. Limiting participation by outsiders, particularly straight men, may make it easier for them to manage a gay identity that also is masculine and athletic—qualities more traditionally associated with heterosexual men. But the group's exclusionary practices also may close doors to friendships across many kinds of difference, including sexual identity, gender, social class, and race."

"As I was reading," John replies, "I saw that you were prying open those doors, and it made me want to do the same. Keeping our worlds separate becomes habit. Your work made me realize that, in part, the segregation was my choice. I have so much acceptance around me, yet habit has kept me from reaching out for it."

"But I understand the constraints on that choice," I tell him. "Social, political, and legal conditions render it an act of courage to say to a friend, even one you've had for a long time, 'Would you mind going to the Cove?'"

A fellow graduate student, Jay Baglia, raises his hand. "I'd like to return to the issue of reflexivity and to how these men have been affected by the project. I'm a lifelong softball player. I played with the same team for a long time but left them in order to pursue my education here. I rejoined the team this fall, and perhaps because of my coursework on gender, I began to notice an incredible amount of subtle and explicit misogyny. My question is, as your research community has gotten to know you and has read your portrayals, is there any reflexivity on *their* part? For example, how have they responded to the sexism you point out?"

"Maybe we should ask them," I suggest.

They whisper among themselves, perhaps nominating someone to speak up. At last, Rob says, "Lisa pushes all of us on these issues. Whenever someone makes a sexist remark, we correct each other, even if she's not around. We ask, 'What would Lisa say?'"

Al raises his hand and adds, "I now try to correct *myself*, and do so *before* making a remark that could be heard as sexist. I don't know that Lisa's project changed my *thinking* on these issues so much; I've always considered women my full equals. But I am more conscious of the *words* I use. I try to imagine how a woman might interpret what I'm about to say."

Rob then looks at me and says, "Early in our relationship, I remember talking to you about what it meant to be gay and some of my hang-ups about it. You were the first person—whether you knew it or not—who clarified for me that being gay related to my sexual orientation and not necessarily to being masculine or feminine. I didn't see myself as feminine, but my upbringing was that if you were gay, you were feminine, and that was a bad thing.

"A year later, I asked if you saw me as 'the woman' in my relationship with Tim. Your answer was: 'If you're asking whether I see you as the one who tends to be more sensitive and nurturing, then yes, I see you as the woman.' You turned being 'the woman' from a weakness—as I unknowingly had made it out to be—to a strength. Suddenly, it dawned on me: I should value *all* my good qualities, masculine and feminine."

"I also have a comment," Gordon says. "It relates both to access and to Lisa's role. I grew up playing baseball, played it in college for a couple years. Was very much socialized with middle-class, beer-drinking, heterosexual ideals. Socialized that way all my life. Our group has thought and talked about things since meeting Lisa that we didn't before. Our conversations were very unemotional. I don't know how often we expressed ourselves—what we thought, how we felt, how we came to terms with things. Lisa facilitated those kinds of conversations, and I don't think anyone else here could have facilitated them. I know that I couldn't have been as open, pushed the envelope that often, and really shared my views, because I was socialized not to feel pain. 'Deal with it, suck it up, and move on.' But Lisa made it comfortable for us, and that made it possible for her to establish the kind of friendships we have with her." His words leave me almost breathless.

Tentatively, Pat raises his hand. "I think that I have benefited more from Lisa writing her dissertation than *she* has, or will, even by getting a Ph.D." My eyes well with tears, as do his when he sees my response. "Becoming involved with Lisa and the work she was doing, . . ." he pauses and lowers his head for a moment, "it enabled me to deal with my coming out. It helped me combine my old athletic, fraternity-brother self and my emerging gay self. I saw that I could be a *gay* athlete, a *gay* man with gay *and straight* friends."

I make eye contact with David, who raises his eyebrows, as if asking for permission to speak. When I nod, he says, "I never imagined that the dissertation would have such an impact on all of us as friends. My friendships with these guys were pretty solid before, but the project has brought us even closer. Reading the dissertation, we all learned about each other. Since then, we've talked about the events Lisa wrote about, and those discussions have reforged the bonds between us. This was a very, very unique experience that we all shared."

"Some of you have talked about potential benefits of this project," I reflect. "For you, what were the risks, drawbacks, or considerations?"

"Truth be told," David says, "until I read the dissertation, I didn't know if you were writing a comic book or a textbook. I guess I didn't know what to expect."

Tim adds, "I definitely wondered what episodes you would include and how I would be portrayed."

"Did you see yourself in your character?" I ask.

"Oh yeah," he responds, "but it wasn't always my 'best' self." Then, in true Tim fashion, he says, "I'm really much nicer in person."

"And better looking," I add playfully.

"At first," Al says, "I was concerned about my privacy. Since I'm not out at work or officially to my family, I asked you to call me Adam in the dissertation. But over the past couple years, I've become more comfortable with who I am. Maybe the project had something to do with that; maybe I've simply matured. But if you publish this as a book, you can use my real first name." Surprised by his request, I nod and smile.

Pat clears his throat. "The only 'drawback' for me is that I wish the project would have started earlier. We met just as I was coming out at thirty-five. I wonder how different my twenties would have been had I crossed paths with someone like you, had I been asked to look within myself and discuss my inner struggles—as I have in my late thirties."

Dennis Loutsakas, a Ph.D. student, responds, "From listening to all of you, I get a sense that this work resonated with members of Lisa's committee and with her participants. But I'm still not clear on how it would resonate with the general population. You started out by talking about Matthew Shepard, and I'm wondering how your work could have affected those who committed the murder."

"In our culture," I say, "gay men are perceived as threats to the gender order: men on top, women on bottom, literally and figuratively. As Rob indicated, we tend to associate homosexuality and femininity, perhaps because we have been socialized to think and talk about sexuality and gender only in dichotomous and hierarchical terms. When two men are intimate, we assume that one takes the position of the man—the top— while the other takes the position of the woman—the bottom. This is a limited—and limiting—view of sexuality, I know, but these terms—and their hierarchy—are reproduced in gay male cultures as well.

"Because I feature a masculine-identified gay community, my work challenges our culture's linkage of sexual orientation and gender identity. Moreover, by critiquing hegemonic masculinity in both straight and gay male cultures, I'm attempting to draw attention to the emotional, relational, and political consequences of privileging masculinity and disparaging femininity.

"That in mind," I continue, "let's talk about Matthew Shepard's murder. Aaron McKinney's peers considered him small and weak. In spite of this, or perhaps *because of this*, he was known to pick fights, usually with men smaller than he.[4] McKinney also is reported to have had sexual experiences with men, experiences that profoundly disturbed him.[5] Had he read about these friendships, it might have made no difference. But what if McKinney had looked deeply into these men's lives and stories? Could he have seen positive versions of himself? What if encountering Gordon, Pat, Al, or even Doug had moved him to feel less ashamed of his homosexual experiences?"

I then say, "But more than individuals must change. Families must change. Perhaps had Henderson's and McKinney's parents participated in conversations like the one we're having today, they might have been encouraged to examine and alter the discourses they circulated about sexuality, gender, and prejudice. Discriminatory laws and the media also must change. The cultural terrain is shifting—but not everywhere. In the same culture, we have texts that valorize gay–straight friendships—like the film *My Best Friend's Wedding* and the NBC sit-com *Will and Grace*— and episodes of utter brutality, like the murder of Matthew Shepard.[6]

"Art recently asked me what will make Doug's and my journey attractive to other heterosexuals. In my response, I talked about personal growth, potentially fulfilling relationships, and the possibility of greater social accord. But, in the wake of Matthew Shepard's murder, we now must turn the question on its head and ask, 'What are the consequences of *not* confronting our fears of difference, of remaining closed off from one another?' Ask a gay man who can't bring himself to say the words. Ask the parents of a gay or lesbian teen who commits suicide. Ask Matthew Shepard's relatives and friends. Ask Henderson's and McKinney's parents. Ask Henderson and McKinney. The conversations we need to have may feel uncomfortable. But the price we will pay for our continued estrangement is much higher."

"Many of us here teach college students," says Linda Laine-Timmerman, a friend and colleague. "What can we do to start these conversations and keep them going?"

"We can be self-conscious about every aspect of our teaching," I respond. "We can ensure that the readings we assign are not heterosexist in their portrayals of sexuality and relationships. We can have students encounter texts by authors with a range of backgrounds, identities, and experiences. We can speak in nonheterosexist terms and confront homophobic discourse. We can develop course activities and assignments that move students out of their comfort zones and that require them to study and interact with groups to which they don't belong. Research in the area of anti-oppressive education suggests that students don't so much *lack* knowledge about other groups as much as they *resist* knowledge that disrupts their taken-for-granted assumptions.[7] Perhaps our major challenge will be to convince students that education is not the repetition and affirmation of the status quo but its *disruption* and change. Ideally, we can move them not only to accept such disruption but to *desire* and actively *seek* it."[8]

"When we see an episode of brutality," remarks Linda Andrews, another colleague, "that's disruption. All of us are searching. 'Why? How? What could we do differently?' As teachers, we can learn to create spaces of safety in which we may not *solve* crises, but we can begin *working through them* in collaboration with students."

"I think Lisa's dissertation provides a space of safety," says John Giancola. "In such a context—and when the moment is well shared—the reader *knows* what to do for him- or herself."

"Yes," Eric concurs, "because the reader doesn't take everything literally—that's the power of story. While reading this, I didn't think to myself, 'My wife and I have to do exactly what Lisa and Doug did.' But some piece of this, some lesson like this, I can make my own."

Tim raises his hand. "As a reader, I kept thinking, 'I want to do something; I *have* to do something.' It gave me energy. I feel like I'm now a bit of an activist. So my question is, how, specifically, do you think we in the gay community can help?"

I respond, "I really appreciated what John had to say about reaching out for the acceptance and friendship that already may surround you. Heterosexuals can be ignorant and naïve. We say the wrong things; we do the wrong things. But don't be deterred. Your fears are not unfounded, though sometimes they take over, and they close us off from one another. *Keep trying.* Give us opportunities to say no—or to say *yes*—to friendship with you as a gay person. None of us would be here today had David not had the courage to take a chance on a couple of bumpkins from the Midwest."

David laughs. "Girl, it wasn't like that at all. *I* was a bumpkin from Kentucky. If you want to know the truth, I didn't feel so separated socially from Doug. We both went to pharmacy school; we both had been in fraternities; we both were in our twenties."

"Sometimes we get too focused on our differences," Doug remarks.

Rob speaks next. "This project says to me, as it did to John, 'It's okay to open the door to my straight friends.' *We* have to build the bridge too."

"And we shouldn't put down those willing to cross it," Pat adds. "A lot of gay men I've met have a difficult time with heterosexuals. At gay clubs, I've heard comments like, 'Too many *straight* people here tonight.' I never understood that. We should *welcome,* not criticize, those who can enjoy being part of 'our' scene."

"If we cross the bridge," Kerby says, "there are going to be painful experiences. We will encounter uncomfortable straight people; we may even lose a job. But there will be more people, more experiences, and other jobs. We *have* to come out." The room buzzes with electricity.

Standing, Barney says, "We can help each other do that." His voice rises in pitch and intensity. 'Coming out' is a metaphor for everyone. *Everyone* has to come out, yet we fear this and resist it. It's such a difficult process because it requires us to abandon our previous maps of reality and construct new ones. This is our challenge."

He then turns to the members of my research community and says, "As gay men, you and I go through the anguish of coming out. But remember, *they* are coming out, too. So we must treat them with sensitivity and compassion. It's much easier for all of us to live the way we always have and never to crawl out of our closets. We have too many closets—one for every category that divides us."

We silently absorb Barney's comment for several seconds.

When it is clear that no one has another question or remark, Art says, "At this time, we will ask Lisa and the audience to leave the room."

"I know it's unconventional," Jim suggests, "but there are fewer of us, so why don't *we* leave the room?"

Smiling, Art shrugs. "Why not? It's been an unconventional defense." With that, Marsha, Eric, Carolyn, Art, Barney, and Jim step outside to discuss my academic fate.

When I stand, I am so overcome that I nearly lose my balance. My mom approaches, her eyes red and watery. We embrace, and she says in my ear, "I'll never forget this—as long as I live."

Doug is right behind her. "Well," he announces, "I guess I'll soon be the 'Mister' of 'Doctor and Mister.'"

"Ooh!" I reply, pecking his mouth. "Let's hope."

Rob and Tim walk toward me, looking dazed. "Unbelievable," Tim says, shaking his head.

"I feel like I know you better," Rob tells me. "It was like seeing you teach—a whole other dimension."

Al gives me his usual bear hug, picking me up a bit. I run my fingers through his short, coarse hair.

Gordon catches my gaze. We stare at each other a moment, and I reflect on the things he said earlier. "What can I say, Gordon? Thanks."

"Thank *you*," he replies.

Pat comes over to me. He seems filled with thoughts, but no words come.

Smiling, I look at him and say, "I know. Me too."

"When we walked in here two hours ago," David reports, "I said to Chris, 'This looks like it has the potential to be really *boring*.'" I laugh.

"I guess you surprised us," Chris remarks, "*again*."

Kissing my cheek, David asks, "How do you feel?"

"Blown away. The discussion, the support—it was better than a dream. The only other time I can remember feeling so completely overwhelmed was the night of my wedding."

"That's ironic," says Linda Laine-Timmerman. "Some of us were just saying that this felt like a wedding. And look at you: white dress and all!"

Just then, the door creaks open. One by one, my committee files into the room.

Art clears his throat; everyone falls silent. "*Doctor* Tillmann-Healy, congratulations." The cheer is as loud as any I've heard on the softball field.

Suddenly, I am engulfed by each of my families—my husband and mother, my family of friends, and, for what feels like the first time in years, my academic family. It's good to be home.

Postscript

On April 7, 1999, Reverend Fred Phelps and his followers from the Westboro Baptist Church returned to Wyoming to picket the courthouse where Russell Henderson would plead guilty to murder. The protesters were surprised by a gathering of supporters for the Shepard family. Dressed in white costumes, seven feet high with eight-foot wingspans, the "Angels of Peace" surrounded the Phelps group so that they would not be seen by Judy and Dennis Shepard as they entered the building. In a remarkable gesture, Matthew Shepard's parents approved of a plea bargain that many believe spared Henderson the death penalty.

Six months later, Aaron McKinney stood trial. His "gay panic" defense failed, and he was found guilty of first-degree felony murder. During sentencing, Dennis Shepard read a statement. "I would like nothing better than to see you die, Mr. McKinney," he said. "However, this is the time to begin the healing process. To show mercy to someone who refused to show any mercy."[1] Both Henderson and McKinney are serving two consecutive life sentences.

Shortly after my dissertation defense, and with much trepidation about leaving home, I went on the academic job market. I applied to colleges and universities as far away as Seattle, and I interviewed in upstate New York and San Francisco.

In March 1999, I got a call from the Department of Communication at Rollins College, a picturesque liberal arts institution in Winter Park, Florida, about an hour and a half from Tampa. The tenure-track job offer came a month later. In July, Doug and I bought a house and moved to Orlando.

Tim Mahn and Rob Ryan also have relocated to the Orlando area, where both have successful careers. Though neither is out at work, Rob has told all his siblings and his parents. I saw Brandon Nolan on New Year's Day, 2000; he has a new love and a new job in Atlanta. Pat Martinez still lives in Tampa with his partner of two years, Chris Smith (though they too are considering a move to Orlando). Each is getting to know the other's family members, including Pat's father. Gordon Bernstein has stayed in the hairpiece business and has come out to his entire immediate family. Al Steel continues to advance in his company. Both he and Gordon have entered long-term relationships. Al assumes that his brother and mother know that he's gay, but the words remain unspoken. David Holland and Chris no longer are together. We don't see much of Chris, but we think of him often. David continues to mentor us, of course, and perhaps we now mentor him as well.

In August 2000, David, Doug, and I traveled to New York City to see *The Laramie Project* at the Union Square Theatre. Following Matthew Shepard's murder, members of the Tectonic Theater Project made six trips to Laramie, Wyoming, to interview townspeople. The play is based on interview transcripts and public documents. Each of the actors plays him- or herself as well as several characters from Laramie. As we sat in the audience, mesmerized by this complex, breathtaking performance, I was struck by how multilayered and *human* everyone seemed—even Aaron McKinney (who, upon learning of Matthew Shepard's death, collapses in what appears to be shock and grief). Twice, McKinney laments the impending loss of his relationship with his young son. I somehow had forgotten that he was a father. How easy it would have been to caricature or demonize the perpetrators and Laramie itself. But *The Laramie Project* was friendship as method at its best, seeking not to glorify, gloss over, or excuse but to *understand* so that we can heal and move forward—together.

David, Pat, Gordon, Al, and Jeff still play softball together every Sunday. There is a gay league in Orlando, too, so who knows? Maybe Doug, Tim, and Rob will join forces again someday (and I'll start a new phase of this project). Doug and I see Tim and Rob almost every week, the Tampa crew about once a month. For this, and for everything they've given us, we are grateful.

These men and many others have taken me on the most important and educational journey of my life. Is it a journey I think every person could—or should—take? I don't know.

But you don't have to go everywhere I've been to understand that the violence Russell Henderson and Aaron McKinney inflicted upon Matthew Shepard was rooted in our *collective* fears about difference. You don't have to see all I've seen to know that our fears, and our fear-based actions and *in*actions, stand between us and a more loving and just world. And you don't have to feel all I've felt to believe that in that loving and just world, maybe Russell Henderson, Aaron McKinney, and Matthew Shepard could have been friends.

Notes

Introduction

1. Phelps and his followers also have developed an astoundingly cruel website, which I will not cite here. Clicking on a headshot of Matthew Shepard surrounded by flames produces the sound of a young man screaming, "For God's sake, listen to Phelps!"

2. For a detailed account of his murder, see "Billy Jack Gaither: Assault on Gay America," www.pbs.org/wgbh/pages/frontline/shows/assault/billyjack/ (accessed June 15, 2000).

3. See G. Delsohn and S. Stanton, "I'm Guilty of Obeying the Laws of the Creator," *Salon.com News*, November 8, 1999, www.salon.com/news/feature/1999/11/08/hate/index.html (accessed June 15, 2000).

4. See J. Gamson, *Freaks Talk Back* (Chicago: University of Chicago Press, 1998).

5. In 1998, there were four hundred cases of antigay harassment in the U.S. military, a 120 percent *increase* since the implementation of the infamous "don't ask, don't tell" policy. See C. Poynter, "Soldier to Be Tried in Slaying," *Courrier Journal*, September 25, 1999, www.temenos.net/winchell/news0925.htm (accessed June 15, 2000).

6. See Poynter, "Soldier to Be Tried."

7. For an account of Steen Fenrich's murder, see D. Elliot, "Murder of Gay, African-American Reflects Twin Diseases of Racism, Homophobia, NGLTF Says," *National Gay and Lesbian Task Force News and Views*, March 24, 2000, www.ngltf.org/news/release.cfm?releaseID=277 (accessed June 15, 2000).

8. See D. Cullen, "The Reluctant Activist," *Salon.com News*, October 15, 1999, www.salon.com/news/feature/1999/10/15/laramie/index.html (accessed June 20, 2000). For information on the educational climate for gay, lesbian, bisexual and transgendered youth, see GLSEN (Gay Lesbian, and Straight Education Network), www.glsen.org (accessed June 20, 2000).

9. Similar legislation is pending in several other states.

10. For updated information on legislation pertaining to gay men and lesbians, see NGLTF (National Gay and Lesbian Task Force), www.ngltf.org/index.cfm (accessed June 20, 2000).

11. See "Tinky Winky Comes Out of the Closet," *NLJ online,* February 1999, www.liberty.edu/chancellor/nlj/feb99/politics2.htm (accessed June 20, 2000).

12. See "Words of Dr. Laura," 2000, www.stopdrlaura.com/laura/index.htm (accessed June 20, 2000).

13. See "National Coming Out of Homosexuality Day," www.kerusso.org/ (accessed June 20, 2000).

14. See L. Stux, ed., *Imagine That: Letters from Russell* (Chicago: Lambda Publications, 1999), 239.

15. See D. Elliot, "One Year. Twenty Dead. No Action," *National Gay and Lesbian Task Force News and Views,* October 11, 1999, www.ngltf.org/news/release.cfm?releaseID=277 (accessed June 15, 2000).

16. See S. B. Wallace, "Kids' Town Hall Airs Opinions on Tolerance," *DenverPost.com,* October 27, 1999, www.denverpost.com/news/news1027g.htm (accessed June 20, 2000).

17. Both GSA and GLSEN are dedicated to raising awareness about, and offering services to, gay, lesbian, bisexual, and transgendered youth.

18. On the growth of coalitions, see D. Cullen, "The Reluctant Activist," *Salon.com News,* October 15, 1999, www.salon.com/news/feature/1999/10/15/laramie/index.html (accessed June 20, 2000). Thanks to a Critchfield grant from Rollins College, I was able to attend the stunning production of *The Laramie Project* at the Union Square Theatre in New York City. See also "Journey to a Hate-Free Millennium," 1999, www.newlightmedia.com (accessed June 20, 2000).

19. See K. S. Breald, "Falwell, Gays Pray for End to Violence," *Detroit News,* October 25, 1999, detnews.com/1999/nation/9910/25/10250136.htm (accessed June 20, 2000).

20. In her analysis of Matthew Shepard's murder, JoAnn Wypijewski writes: "Before it came to signify the highest state to which straight society could aspire, tolerance was something one had for a bad job or a bad smell or a nightmare relative who visited once a year. In its new guise, tolerance means straight people know of gay men and women, but there is no recognizable gay life." J. Wypijewski, "A Boy's Life: For Matthew Shepard's Killers, What Does It Take to Pass as a Man?" *Harper's Magazine,* September 1999, 67.

21. At their request, most of the primary characters' names are real.

22. Tracks is the real name of an establishment now closed. Names of bars and clubs still in business have been changed (and, in some cases, merged).

23. Throughout this book, I use the term "sexual orientation" to refer to one's sexual fantasies about, and desires for, men, women, or both. I use "sexual identity" to refer to the (verbal and nonverbal) claims a person makes (or elects not to make) about her or his sexual orientation.

24. Since 1995 the team has had four different sponsors. For readability, I will refer to them as the Cove throughout the book.

25. In 1999 this rule was relaxed. There no longer is an official limit on the number of straight players a team can have on its roster or can field at one time.

26. See C. Geertz, *The Interpretation of Cultures* (New York: Basic Books, 1973).

27. For a foundational text on queer theory, see J. Butler, *Gender Trouble*, 10th anniv. ed. (New York: Routledge, 1999). For a review of queer approaches to qualitative research, see J. Gamson, "Sexualities, Queer Theory, and Qualitative Research," in *Handbook of Qualitative Research*, ed. N. K. Denzin and Y. S. Lincoln, 2d ed. (Thousand Oaks, Calif.: Sage, 2000), 347–65.

28. See E. K. Sedgwick, *Epistemology of the Closet* (Berkeley and Los Angeles: University of California Press, 1990).

29. See B. Tedlock, "From Participant Observation to the Observation of Participation: The Emergence of Narrative Ethnography," *Journal of Anthropological Research* 47 (1991): 69–94.

30. On realist ethnography, see J. Van Maanen, *Tales of the Field* (Chicago: University of Chicago Press, 1988). On autoethnography, see A. P. Bochner and C. Ellis, "Introduction: Talking over Ethnography," in *Composing Ethnography*, ed. C. Ellis and A. P. Bochner (Walnut Creek, Calif.: AltaMira Press, 1996), 13–45; and C. Ellis and A. P. Bochner, "Autoethnography, Personal Narrative, Reflexivity: Researcher as Subject," in *Handbook of Qualitative Research*, ed. Denzin and Lincoln, 2d ed), 733–68.

31. See Tedlock, "Observation of Participation."

32. See E. M. Bruner, "Experience and Its Expressions," in *The Anthropology of Experience*, ed. V. W. Turner and E. M. Bruner (Urbana: University of Illinois Press, 1986), 3–30; and N. K. Denzin and Y. S. Lincoln, "Introduction: Entering the Field of Qualitative Research," in *Handbook of Qualitative Research*, ed. N. K. Denzin and Y. S. Lincoln (Thousand Oaks, Calif.: Sage, 1994), 1–17.

33. See M. Fine, "Working the Hyphens: Reinventing Self and Other in Qualitative Research," in *Handbook of Qualitative Research*, ed. Denzin and Lincoln, 70–82.

34. See P. Reason, "Three Approaches to Participative Inquiry," in *Handbook of Qualitative Research*, ed. Denzin and Lincoln, 324–39.

35. See D. Conquergood, "Rethinking Ethnography: Towards a Critical Cultural Politics," *Communication Monographs* 58 (1991): 179–94.

36. See M. Jackson, *Paths toward a Clearing* (Bloomington: Indiana University Press, 1989).

37. See Y. S. Lincoln and N. K. Denzin, "The Seventh Moment: Out of the Past," in *Handbook of Qualitative Research*, ed. Denzin and Lincoln, 2d ed., 1047–65.

38. See N. K. Denzin, *Interpretive Ethnography* (Thousand Oaks, Calif.: Sage, 1997).

39. See Denzin and Lincoln, "Introduction"; and Lincoln and Denzin, "The Seventh Moment."

40. See Conquergood, "Rethinking Ethnography."

41. See Jackson, *Paths toward a Clearing.*

42. See P. Stoller, *The Taste of Ethnographic Things* (Philadelphia: University of Pennsylvania Press, 1989), 156.

43. See Denzin, *Interpretive Ethnography.*

44. For an ethnographic short story, see, e.g., C. Ellis, "Speaking of Dying: An Ethnographic Short Story," *Symbolic Interaction* 18 (1995): 73–81. For fiction, see e.g., M. V. Angrosino, *Opportunity House* (Walnut Creek, Calif.: AltaMira Press, 1998). For poetry, see, e.g., D. A. Austin, "Kaleidoscope: The Same and Different," in *Composing Ethnography*, ed. Ellis and Bochner, 206–30; and L. Richardson, "The Consequences of Poetic Representation: Writing the Other, Rewriting the Self," in *Investigating Subjectivity*, ed. Ellis and Flaherty, 125–37. For a layered account, see, e.g., C. R. Ronai, "Multiple Reflections of Child Sex Abuse: An Argument for a Layered Account," *Journal of Contemporary Ethnography* 23 (1995): 395–426.

45. The June 2000 issue of *Qualitative Inquiry* includes a forum on evaluating alternative approaches to qualitative research.

46. On narrative truth, see D. P. Spence, *Narrative Truth and Historical Truth* (New York: W. W. Norton, 1982); and A. P. Bochner, "Perspectives on Inquiry 2: Theories and Stories," in *Handbook of Interpersonal Communication*, 2d ed. (Thousand Oaks, Calif.: Sage, 1994), 21–41. On consequences of research, see Jackson, *Paths toward a Clearing*.

47. See R. Coles, *The Call of Stories* (Boston: Houghton Mifflin, 1989).

48. See Bochner, "Perspectives on Inquiry 2."

49. See Denzin, *Interpretive Ethnography*, 247.

50. See A. P. Bochner, "Criteria against Ourselves," *Qualitative Inquiry* 6 (2000): 266–72.

51. See Coles, *Call of Stories;* on social change, see Denzin, *Interpretive Ethnography*.

52. See chap. 7 and the epilogue for expanded discussions of friendship as method.

53 See Fine, "Working the Hyphens."

54. See R. Behar, *The Vulnerable Observer* (Boston: Beacon Press, 1996).

55. See, e.g., J. Malone, *Straight Women/Gay Men* (New York: Dial Press, 1980); and C. Whitney, *Uncommon Lives* (New York: New American Library, 1990).

Chapter 1

1. But, as Mohr indicates, "In 1986, the Catholic church, in a major ideological shift, branded as 'an objective moral disorder' the mere status of being a homosexual, even when congenitally fixed and unaccompanied by any homosexual behavior." R. D. Mohr, *A More Perfect Union* (Boston: Beacon Press, 1994), 67–68.

Chapter 2

1. For an excellent and exhaustive analysis of homosexuality in the movies from the turn of the century through the 1980s, see Vito Russo, *The Celluloid Closet* (New York: Harper & Row, 1987) or the HBO film by the same title.

Chapter 3

I borrow the title of this chapter from the paper I wrote about my first semester of fieldwork. Some episodes recounted here were adapted from that piece; others were written later, from field notes.

1. R. Rodi, *Fag Hag* (New York: Dutton, 1992), 201.
2. See C. A. B. Warren, "Women among Men: Females in the Male Homosexual Community," *Archives of Sexual Behavior* 5 (1976): 157–69.
3. Rodi, *Fag Hag*, 96.
4. P. M. Nardi, *Gay Men's Friendships* (Chicago: University of Chicago Press, 1999), 118.
5. W. J. Mann, "One of Us," in *Sister and Brother*, ed. J. Nestle and J. Preston (San Francisco: HarperSanFrancisco, 1995), 171.
6. M. F. Shyer and C. Shyer, *Not Like Other Boys* (Boston: Houghton Mifflin, 1996), 176.
7. See M. Foucault, *The History of Sexuality*, vol. 1 (New York: Vintage Books, 1990).
8. See A. C. Kinsey, W. B. Pomeroy, and C. E. Martin, *Sexual Behavior in the Human Male* (Philadelphia: W. B. Saunders, 1948).
9. See E. Stein, *The Mismeasure of Desire* (New York: Oxford University Press, 1999); and M. Storms, "Theories of Sexual Orientation," *Journal of Personality and Social Psychology* 38 (1980): 783–92.
10. See A. Rich, "Compulsory Heterosexuality and Lesbian Existence," in *The Lesbian and Gay Studies Reader*, ed. H. Abelove, M. A. Barale, and D. M. Halperin (New York: Routledge, 1993), 227–54.
11. Rob, a respondent in R. H. Hopcke and L. Rafaty's book, *A Couple of Friends* (Berkeley, Calif.: Wildcat Canyon Press, 1999), says this about gay men's identification with women: "When we gay men hear sappy love songs on the radio, it is the female part we sing along to, because it is women who express our own feelings about loving, losing and desiring men" (66).
12. Writes lesbian author Merril Mushroom: "I resented [gay men's] caricaturing of women. I resented their flaunting of their privilege. . . . Don't they realize they are demonstrating the same loathing toward women that straight men exhibit, the same loathing that straight people in general show toward queers?" Merril Mushroom, "Gay Girls and Gay Guys: An Old Past, a New Future," in *Sister and Brother*, ed. Nestle and Preston, 69–70.
13. See J. Butler, *Gender Trouble*, 10th anniv. ed. (New York: Routledge, 1999).
14. Pearlberg and Wilder assert that from gay men, women can learn "a whole new—and very enjoyable—way of gazing" that offers them a means to express themselves as sexual persons "without apologizing for or rationalizing it." G. G. Pearlberg and S. Wilder, "The Cultural Exchange," in *Sister and Brother*, ed. Nestle and Preston, 323–31.
15. In professional sports, it has been over twenty-five years since former running back Dave Kopay publicly acknowledged his homosexuality. Few have followed suit. Notable exceptions include retired major leaguer Glenn Burke, Olympic champion diver Greg Louganis, retired tennis superstar Martina

Navratilova, former New York Giants tackle Roy Simmons, and U.S. National champion ice skater Rudy Galindo. Of these, only Navratilova and Galindo came out while at the top of their sports. This is not surprising, suggests Bull, given the "stranglehold homophobia retains" on athletics and their sponsors. C. Bull, "Disclosure," *Advocate*, March 21, 1995, 29.

16. Stein, *Mismeasure of Desire,* 329.

17. Stein, *Mismeasure of Desire.*

Chapter 4

1. See R. D. Mohr, *A More Perfect Union* (Boston: Beacon Press, 1994), 54.

2. See C. A. B. Warren, "Women among Men: Females in the Male Homosexual Community," *Archives of Sexual Behavior* 5 (1976): 157–69.

3. Fee argues that entering gay worlds "means to transgress *the* normative standard of manhood: not appearing queer to other men." D. Fee "Coming Over: Friendships between Straight and Gay Men" (Ph.D. diss., University of California, Santa Barbara, 1996), 25.

4. For a review, see J. T. Wood, *Gendered Lives,* 2d ed. (Belmont, Calif.: Wadsworth Publishing, 1997).

5. M. Fine, "Working the Hyphens: Reinventing Self and Other in Qualitative Research," in *Handbook of Qualitative Research,* ed. N. K. Denzin and Y. S. Lincoln (Thousand Oaks, Calif.: Sage, 1994), 70–82.

6. J. Malone, *Straight Women/Gay Men* (New York: Dial Press, 1980), 4–5.

Chapter 5

1. See D. Pallone, *Behind the Mask* (New York: Viking, 1990).

2. In R. H. Hopcke and L. Rafaty, *A Couple of Friends* (Berkeley, Calif.: Wildcat Canyon Press, 1999), a gay male respondent talks about how his friendship with a straight woman affected his father's perceptions of him. He says, "I think his seeing my friendship with her reassured him I could have a normal life— something he was worried about" (199).

3. See C. Ellis, C. E. Kiesinger, and L. M. Tillmann-Healy, "Interactive Interviewing: Talking about Emotional Experience," in *Reflexivity and Voice,* ed. R. Hertz (Thousand Oaks, Calif.: Sage, 1997), 119–49.

4. See L. M. Tillmann-Healy, "A Secret Life in a Culture of Thinness: Reflections on Body, Food, and Bulimia," in *Composing Ethnography,* ed. C. Ellis and A. P. Bochner (Walnut Creek, Calif.: AltaMira Press, 1996), 76–108.

Chapter 6

1. See M. Fine, "Working the Hyphens: Reinventing Self and Other in Qualitative Research," in *Handbook of Qualitative Research,* ed. N. K. Denzin and Y. S. Lincoln (Thousand Oaks, Calif.: Sage, 1994), 70–82.

2. See L. M. Tillmann-Healy, "A Secret Life in a Culture of Thinness: Reflections on Body, Food, and Bulimia," in *Composing Ethnography*, ed. C. Ellis and A. P. Bochner (Walnut Creek, Calif.: AltaMira Press, 1996), 76–108.

3. Barney Downs, an associate professor of communication, joined my committee shortly after the oral defense of my comprehensive exam.

4. B. Myerhoff, *Number Our Days* (New York: Simon & Schuster, 1980).

5. D. A. Austin, "Kaleidoscope: The Same and Different," in *Composing Ethnography*, ed. Ellis and Bochner, 206–30.

6. K. Cherry, "Ain't No Grave Deep Enough," *Journal of Contemporary Ethnography* 25 (1996). 22–57.

7. See "Marriage Project–Hawaii," members.tripod.com/~MPHAWAII/ (accessed June 15, 2000).

8. M. Warner, *The Trouble with Normal* (New York: Free Press, 1999), 117.

9. See "Marriage Project–Hawaii."

10. K. Rauch and J. Fessler, *Why Gay Guys Are a Girl's Best Friend* (New York: Fireside, 1995).

11. See R. Nahas and M. Turley, *The New Couple* (New York: Seaview Books, 1979); J. Malone, *Straight Women/Gay Men* (New York: Dial Press, 1980); and R. H. Hopcke and L. Rafaty, *A Couple of Friends* (Berkeley, Calif.: Wildcat Canyon Press, 1999).

12. See Nahas and Turley, *New Couple*, 123.

13. See Malone, *Straight Women/Gay Men*.

14. P. M. Nardi, *Gay Men's Friendships* (Chicago: University of Chicago Press, 1999).

15. In his book *On Flirtation* (Cambridge: Harvard University Press, 1994), Adam Phillips suggests that in order to commit to a relationship, we must first commit to commitment itself. While not seeking to dispense with commitment, Phillips asks us to embrace life's contingency and uncertainty and to imagine the many lives within each of us competing to be lived.

16. D. Fee, "Coming Over: Friendship between Straight and Gay Men" (Ph.D. diss., University of California, Santa Barbara, 1996), 198–99, 221.

17. J. Price, *Navigating Differences* (New York: Harrington Park Press, 1999).

18. Fee, "Coming Over," 229.

19. B. Tedlock, "From Participant Observation to the Observation of Participation: The Emergence of Narrative Ethnography," *Journal of Anthropological Research* 47 (1991): 69–94.

20. See C. Ellis, "Sociological Introspection and Emotional Experience," *Symbolic Interaction* 14 (1991): 23–50.

21. See C. Ellis, "Speaking of Dying: An Ethnographic Short Story," *Symbolic Interaction* 18 (1995): 73–81.

22. See also C. Ellis, "Emotional Sociology," in *Studies in Symbolic Interaction*, vol. 12, ed. N. K. Denzin (Greenwich, Conn.: JAI Press, 1991), 123–45.

23. E. M. Bruner, "Experience and Its Expressions," in *The Anthropology of Experience*, ed. V. W. Turner and E. M. Bruner (Urbana: University of Illinois Press, 1986), 3–30.

Chapter 7

1. D. Woog, *School's Out* (Los Angeles: Alyson Publications, 1995).

2. B. L. Singer and D. Deschamps, eds., *Gay and Lesbian Stats* (New York: New Press, 1994).

3. G. M. Herek and J. P. Capitanio, "'Some of My Best Friends': Intergroup Contact, Concealable Stigma, and Heterosexuals' Attitudes toward Gay Men and Lesbians," *Personality and Social Psychology Bulletin* 22 (1996): 412–24.

4. See F. Newport, "Some Change over Time in American Attitudes towards Homosexuality, but Negativity Remains," www.gallup.com/poll/releases/pr990301b.asp, 1999 (accessed June 1, 2000).

5. Herek and Capitanio, "'Some of My Best Friends.'"

6. D. Fee, "Coming Over: Friendship between Straight and Gay Men" (Ph.D. diss., University of California, Santa Barbara, 1996).

7. J. N. Katz, *The Invention of Heterosexuality* (New York: Plume, 1996).

8. Of course, as Stein points out, even my use of the term "the other sex" invokes a problematic binary (that between male and female). Many people are intersexed—they have biological characteristics of males and females. See E. Stein, *The Mismeasure of Desire* (New York: Oxford University Press, 1999).

9. See Stein, *Mismeasure of Desire.*

10. See M. Hunt, *The Natural History of Love* (New York: Anchor Books, 1994).

11. See E. K. Sedgwick, *Epistemology of the Closet* (Berkeley and Los Angeles: University of California Press, 1990).

12. See A. C. Kinsey, W. B. Pomeroy, and C. E. Martin, *Sexual Behavior in the Human Male* (Philadelphia: W. B. Saunders, 1948).

13. M. Storms, "Theories of Sexual Orientation," *Journal of Personality and Social Psychology* 38 (1980): 783–92; Stein, *Mismeasure of Desire.*

14. A. Watts, *The Book* (New York: Vintage Books, 1989).

15. D. Harris, *The Rise and Fall of Gay Culture* (New York: Hyperion, 1997).

16. See M. Warner, *The Trouble with Normal* (New York: Free Press, 1999).

17. K. Weston, *Families We Choose* (New York: Columbia University Press, 1991).

18. See C. Thomas, "Introduction: Identification, Appropriation, Proliferation," in *Straight with a Twist,* ed. C. Thomas (Urbana: University of Illinois Press, 2000), 1–7.

19. Fee, "Coming Over"; M. W. Kirch, "Cross-Sexually Oriented Male Friendship: An Initial Exploration" (paper presented at the annual meeting of the National Communication Association, Chicago, November 1997). See also P. M. Nardi, *Gay Men's Friendships* (Chicago: University of Chicago Press, 1999); and J. Price, *Navigating Differences* (New York: Harrington Park Press, 1999).

20. C. Hassett and T. Owen-Towle, *Friendship Chronicles* (San Diego: Bald Eagle Mountain Press, 1994).

21. See P. J. Stein, "Men and Their Friendships," in *Men in Families,* ed. R. A. Lewis and R. E. Salt (Beverly Hills, Calif.: Sage, 1986), 261–70.

22. J. T. Wood, *Gendered Lives,* 2d ed. (Belmont, Calif.: Wadsworth, 1997).

23. For a compelling analysis of the Western genre, see J. Tompkins, *West of Everything* (New York: Oxford University Press, 1992).

Notes   235

24. For an exception, see Dan Woog's story of Stefan Lynch in *Friends and Family* (Los Angeles: Alyson Books, 1999). Lynch is a straight man whose mother and father are gay. "I've never seen myself as separate from the gay community" (77) he says. In fact, Lynch considers himself "erotically straight and culturally queer" (72).

25. Kirch, "Cross–Sexually Oriented Male Friendship"; M. Rowe, "Looking for Brothers: Barney, Chris, and Me," in *Friends and Lovers*, ed. J. Preston and M. Lowenthal (New York: Plume, 1996), 177–88.

26. Fee, "Coming Over."

27. T. K. Fitzgerald, *Metaphors of Identity* (Albany: State University of New York Press, 1993).

28. C. Thomas and C. A. F. MacGillivray, "Afterword(s): A Conversation," in *Straight with a Twist*, ed. Thomas, 253–80.

29. J. Malone, *Straight Women/Gay Men* (New York: Dial Press, 1980); G. G. Pearlberg and S. Wilder, "The Cultural Exchange," in *Sister and Brother*, ed. J. Nestle and J. Preston (San Francisco: HarperSanFrancisco, 1995), 323–31.

30. S. Miller, *Men and Friendship* (Boston: Houghton Mifflin, 1983); Hasset and Owen-Towle, *Friendship Chronicles*; Kirch, "Cross–Sexually Oriented Male Friendship."

31. Fee, "Coming Over."

32. However, the frequency of these friendships is difficult to ascertain; see K. Werking, *We're Just Good Friends* (New York: Guilford Press, 1997). In *Straight Women/Gay Men*, Malone says that "large numbers of straight women from widely different backgrounds form close friendships with gay men" (4), but the term "large numbers" is left ambiguous. Later, this author reports that the average gay man has between three and four straight women friends (50), but he gives no comparable statistic for straight women. Of Nardi's 161 gay male respondents, 10 percent said that their best friend was a heterosexual woman; about 60 percent reported having two or fewer close female friends (of any sexual identity); and only around 3 percent indicated that the majority of their friends were women. See Nardi, *Gay Men's Friendships*.

33. See Herek and Capitanio, "'Some of My Best Friends.'"

34. K. Rauch and J. Fessler, *Why Gay Guys Are a Girl's Best Friend* (New York: Fireside, 1995).

35. Wood, *Gendered Lives*.

36. G. Bateson, *Steps to an Ecology of Mind* (San Francisco: Chandler, 1972).

37. See M. F. Shyer and C. Shyer, *Not Like Other Boys* (Boston: Houghton Mifflin, 1996), 193.

38. See M. Kirk and H. Madsen, *After the Ball* (New York: Plume, 1990), 187.

39. See Shyer and Shyer, *Not Like Other Boys*, 258.

40. Kirk and Madsen, *After the Ball*, 146 (emphasis in original).

41. Hassett and Owen-Towle, *Friendship Chronicles*.

42. See J. J. Brumberg, *The Body Project* (New York: Random House, 1997).

43. E. Becker, *The Denial of Death* (New York: Free Press, 1973).

44. T. A. Schwandt, "Constructivist, Interpretivist Approaches to Human Inquiry," in *Handbook of Qualitative Research*, ed. N. K. Denzin and Y. S. Lincoln (Thousand Oaks, Calif.: Sage, 1994), 118–37.

45. C. Geertz, *The Interpretation of Cultures* (New York: Basic Books, 1973).

46. N. K. Denzin, *Interpretive Ethnography* (Thousand Oaks, Calif.: Sage, 1997).

47. J. A. Cook and M. M. Fonow, "Knowledge and Women's Interests: Issues of Epistemology and Methodology in Feminist Sociological Research," *Sociological Inquiry* 56 (1986): 2–27; S. Reinharz, *Feminist Methods in Social Research* (New York: Oxford University Press, 1992); H. Roberts, ed., *Doing Feminist Research* (London: Routledge & Kegan Paul, 1981). On emotional sharing, see C. Ellis, C. E. Kiesinger, and L. M. Tillmann-Healy, "Interactive Interviewing: Talking about Emotional Experience," in *Reflexivity and Voice*, ed. R. Hertz (Thousand Oaks, Calif.: Sage, 1997), 119–49. On vulnerability, see R. Behar, *The Vulnerable Observer* (Boston: Beacon Press, 1996).

48. See, e.g., P. H. Collins, "Learning from the Outsider Within: The Sociological Significance of Black Feminist Thought," *Social Problems* 33 (1986): 514–32; and S. G. Harding, *Whose Science? Whose Knowledge?* (Ithaca, N.Y.: Cornell University Press, 1991).

49. See J. Butler, *Gender Trouble*, 10th anniv. ed. (New York: Routledge, 1999); and Thomas, "Introduction."

50. See, e.g., Sedgwick, *Epistemology of the Closet*; and Stein, *Mismeasure of Desire.*

51. J. Gamson, *Freaks Talk Back* (Chicago: University of Chicago Press, 1998), 222.

52. M. Fine, "Working the Hyphens: Reinventing Self and Other in Qualitative Research," in *Handbook of Qualitative Research*, ed. Denzin and Lincoln, 70–82.

53. P. Reason, "Three Approaches to Participative Inquiry," in *Handbook of Qualitative Research*, ed. Denzin and Lincoln, 324–39.

54. P. A. Lather, *Getting Smart* (New York: Routledge, 1991).

55. See Ellis, Kiesinger, and Tillmann-Healy, "Interactive Interviewing."

56. See A. P. Bochner, C. Ellis, and L. M. Tillmann-Healy, "Mucking Around Looking for Truth," in *Dialectical Approaches to Studying Personal Relationships*, ed. B. M. Montgomery and L. A. Baxter (Mahwah, N.J.: Lawrence Earlbaum Associates, 1998), 41–62.

57. See L. M. Tillmann-Healy, "A Secret Life in a Culture of Thinness: Reflections on Body, Food, and Bulimia," in *Composing Ethnography*, ed. C. Ellis and A. P. Bochner (Walnut Creek, Calif.: AltaMira Press, 1996), 76–108.

58. M. Jackson, *Paths toward a Clearing* (Bloomington: Indiana University Press, 1989).

59. See Warner, *Trouble with Normal.*

60. See A. P. Bochner, "It's about Time: Narrative and the Divided Self," *Qualitative Inquiry* 3 (1997): 418–38.

Epilogue

I would like to thank Dave Deitz and Lowell Harris for serving as videographers of my dissertation defense. The tapes proved invaluable in writing this section.

1. See J. Van Maanen, *Tales of the Field* (Chicago: University of Chicago Press, 1988).

2. See J. R. King, "Am Not! Are Too! Using Queer Standpoint in Postmodern Critical Ethnography," *Qualitative Studies in Education* 12 (1999): 473–90.

3. See M. Warner, *The Trouble with Normal* (New York: Free Press, 1999). One privilege that Warner critiques is normativity. The more "passable" a gay man or lesbian is, the more s/he is perceived as "normal" (read also "heterosexual"). While normativity raises one's social and political status, it also complicates the process of making peace with a sexual orientation constructed as deviant (because there will be dissonance between one's public, "normal" self and one's private, "deviant" self). One who cannot or does not pass will more easily reject the normal/deviant binary and thus won't experience the attendant discord.

4. See J. Wypijewski, "A Boy's Life: For Matthew Shepard's Killers, What Does It Take to Pass as a Man?" *Harper's Magazine*, September 1999, 61–74.

5. See D. Cullen, "Gay Panic," *Salon.com News*, www.salon.com/news/feature/1999/10/26/trial/index.html (accessed June 15, 2000).

6. More recent examples of movies include *The Object of My Affection, Trick,* and *The Next Best Thing*. The sit-com *Will and Grace* centers on the best-friendship between the title characters, a gay man and a straight woman. In 2000, *Will and Grace* won the Emmy for best comedy.

7. See K. Kumashiro, "Toward a Theory of Anti-Oppressive Education" (paper presented at the Review of Educational Research Symposium, University of South Florida, Tampa, 2000).

8. See Kumashiro, "Anti-Oppressive Education."

Postscript

1. See D. Cullen, "A Dramatic Moment of Mercy," *Salon.com News*, www.salon.com/news/feature/1999/11/05/shepard/index/html (accessed June 15, 2000).

Bibliography

Angrosino, M. V. *Opportunity House: Ethnographic Stories of Mental Retardation.* Walnut Creek, Calif.: AltaMira Press, 1998.

Austin, D. A. "Kaleidoscope: The Same and Different." Pp. 206–30 in *Composing Ethnography: Alternative Forms of Qualitative Writing,* ed. C. Ellis and A. P. Bochner. Walnut Creek, Calif.: AltaMira Press, 1996.

Bateson, G. *Steps to an Ecology of Mind: Collected Essays in Anthropology, Psychiatry, Evolution, and Epistemology.* San Francisco: Chandler, 1972.

Becker, E. *The Denial of Death.* New York: Free Press, 1973.

Behar, R. *The Vulnerable Observer: Anthropology That Breaks Your Heart.* Boston: Beacon Press, 1996.

"Billy Jack Gaither: Assault on Gay America." www.pbs.org/wgbh/pages/frontline/shows/assault/billyjack/. Accessed June 15, 2000.

Bochner, A. P. "Perspectives on Inquiry 2: Theories and Stories." Pp. 21–41 in *Handbook of Interpersonal Communication,* ed. M. L. Knapp and G. R. Miller. 2d ed. Thousand Oaks, Calif.: Sage, 1994.

———. "It's about Time: Narrative and the Divided Self." *Qualitative Inquiry* 3 (1997): 418–38.

———. "Criteria against Ourselves." *Qualitative Inquiry* 6 (2000): 266–72.

Bochner, A. P., and C. Ellis. "Introduction: Talking over Ethnography." Pp. 13–45 in *Composing Ethnography: Alternative Forms of Qualitative Writing,* ed. C. Ellis and A. P. Bochner. Walnut Creek, Calif.: AltaMira Press, 1996.

Bochner, A. P., C. Ellis, and L. M. Tillmann-Healy. "Mucking Around Looking for Truth." Pp. 41–62 in *Dialectical Approaches to Studying Personal Relationships,* ed. B. M. Montgomery and L. A. Baxter. Mahwah, N.J.: Lawrence Earlbaum Associates, 1998.

Breald, K. S. "Falwell, Gays Pray for End to Violence." *Detroit News,* October 25, 1999. http://detnews.com/1999/nation/9910/25/10250136htm. Accessed June 15, 2000.

Brumberg, J. J. *The Body Project: An Intimate History of American Girls.* New York: Random House, 1997.

Bruner, E. M. "Experience and Its Expressions." Pp. 3–30 in *The Anthropology of Experience,* ed. V. W. Turner and E. M. Bruner. Urbana: University of Illinois Press, 1986.

———. "Introduction: The Ethnographic Self and the Personal Self." Pp. 1–26 in *Anthropology and Literature,* ed. P. Benson. Urbana: University of Illinois Press, 1993.

Bull, C. "Disclosure." *Advocate,* March 21, 1995, 28–34.

Butler, J. *Gender Trouble: Feminism and the Subversion of Identity.* 10th anniversary ed. New York: Routledge, 1999.

Cherry, K. "Ain't No Grave Deep Enough." *Journal of Contemporary Ethnography* 25 (1996): 22–57.

Coles, R. *The Call of Stories: Teaching and the Moral Imagination.* Boston: Houghton Mifflin, 1989.

Collins, P. H. "Learning from the Outsider Within: The Sociological Significance of Black Feminist Thought." *Social Problems* 33 (1986): 514–32.

Conquergood, D. "Rethinking Ethnography: Towards a Critical Cultural Politics." *Communication Monographs* 58 (1991): 179–94.

Cook, J. A., and M. M. Fonow. "Knowledge and Women's Interests: Issues of Epistemology and Methodology in Feminist Sociological Research." *Sociological Inquiry* 56 (1986): 2–27.

Cullen, D. "The Reluctant Activist." *Salon.com News,* October 15, 1999. www.salon.com/news/feature/1999/10/15/laramie/index.html. Accessed June 20, 2000.

———. "Gay Panic." *Salon.com News,* October 26, 1999. www.salon.com/news/feature/1999/10/26/trial/index.html. Accessed June 15, 2000.

———. "A Dramatic Moment of Mercy." *Salon.com News,* November 5, 1999. www.salon.com/news/feature/1999/11/05/shepard/index.html. Accessed June 15, 2000.

Delsohn, G., and S. Stanton. "'I'm Guilty of Obeying the Laws of the Creator.'" *Salon.com News,* November 8, 1999. www.salon.com/news/feature/1999/11/08/hate/index.html. Accessed June 15, 2000.

Denzin, N. K. *Interpretive Ethnography: Ethnographic Practices for the Twenty-first Century.* Thousand Oaks, Calif.: Sage, 1997.

Denzin, N. K., and Y. S. Lincoln. "Introduction: Entering the Field of Qualitative Research." Pp. 1–17 in *Handbook of Qualitative Research,* ed. N. K. Denzin and Y. S. Lincoln. Thousand Oaks, Calif.: Sage, 1994.

Elliot, D. "One Year. Twenty Dead. No Action." *National Gay and Lesbian Task Force News and Views,* October 11, 1999. www.ngltf.org/news/release.cfm?releaseID=13. Accessed June 15, 2000.

———. "Murder of Gay, African-American Man Reflects Twin Diseases of Racism, Homophobia, NGLTF Says." *National Gay and Lesbian Task Force News and Views,* March 24, 2000. www.ngltf.org/news/release.cfm?releaseID=277. Accessed June 15, 2000.

Ellis, C. "Emotional Sociology." Pp. 123–45 in *Studies in Symbolic Interaction,* vol. 12, ed. N. K. Denzin. Greenwich, Conn.: JAI Press, 1991.

———. "Sociological Introspection and Emotional Experience." *Symbolic Interaction* 14 (1991): 23–50.

———. "Speaking of Dying: An Ethnographic Short Story." *Symbolic Interaction* 18 (1995): 73–81.

Ellis, C., and A. P. Bochner. "Telling and Performing Personal Stories: The Constraints of Choice in Abortion." Pp. 79–101 in *Investigating Subjectivity: Research on Lived Experience,* ed. C. Ellis and M. G. Flaherty. Newbury Park, Calif.: Sage, 1992.

———. "Autoethnography, Personal Narrative, Reflexivity: Researcher as Subject." Pp. 733–68 in *Handbook of Qualitative Research,* ed. N. K. Denzin and Y. S. Lincoln. 2d ed. Thousand Oaks, Calif.: Sage, 2000.

Ellis, C., C. E. Kiesinger, and L. M. Tillmann-Healy. "Interactive Interviewing: Talking about Emotional Experience." Pp. 119–49 in *Reflexivity and Voice,* ed. R. Hertz. Thousand Oaks, Calif.: Sage, 1997.

Fee, D. "Coming Over: Friendship between Straight and Gay Men." Ph.D. diss., University of California, Santa Barbara, 1996.

Fine, M. "Working the Hyphens: Reinventing Self and Other in Qualitative Research." Pp. 70–82 in *Handbook of Qualitative Research,* ed. N. K. Denzin and Y. S. Lincoln. Thousand Oaks, Calif.: Sage, 1994.

Fitzgerald, T. K. *Metaphors of Identity: A Culture–Communication Dialogue.* Albany: State University of New York Press, 1993.

Foucault, M. *The History of Sexuality: An Introduction.* Vol. 1. New York: Vintage Books, 1990.

Gamson, J. *Freaks Talk Back: Tabloid Talk Shows and Sexual Nonconformity.* Chicago: University of Chicago Press, 1998.

———. "Sexualities, Queer Theory, and Qualitative Research." Pp. 347–65 in *Handbook of Qualitative Research,* ed. N. K. Denzin and Y. S. Lincoln. 2d ed. Thousand Oaks, Calif.: Sage, 2000.

Geertz, C. *The Interpretation of Cultures.* New York: Basic Books, 1973.

GLSEN (Gay, Lesbian, and Straight Education Network). www.glsen.org. Accessed June 20, 2000.

Harding, S. G. *Whose Science? Whose Knowledge? Thinking from Women's Lives.* Ithaca, N.Y.: Cornell University Press, 1991.

Harris, D. *The Rise and Fall of Gay Culture.* New York: Hyperion, 1997.

Hassett, C., and T. Owen-Towle. *Friendship Chronicles: Letters between a Gay and a Straight Man.* San Diego: Bald Eagle Mountain Press, 1994.

Herek, G. M., and J. P. Capitanio. "'Some of My Best Friends': Intergroup Contact, Concealable Stigma, and Heterosexuals' Attitudes toward Gay Men and Lesbians." *Personality and Social Psychology Bulletin* 22 (1996): 412–24.

Hopcke, R. H., and L. Rafaty. *A Couple of Friends: The Remarkable Friendship between Straight Women and Gay Men.* Berkeley, Calif.: Wildcat Canyon Press, 1999.

Hunt, M. *The Natural History of Love.* New York: Anchor Books, 1994.

Jackson, M. *Paths toward a Clearing: Radical Empiricism and Ethnographic Inquiry.* Bloomington: Indiana University Press, 1989.

"Journey to a Hate-Free Millennium." 1999. www.newlightmedia.com. Accessed June 20, 2000.

Katz, J. N. *The Invention of Heterosexuality.* New York: Plume, 1996.

King, J. R. "Am Not! Are Too! Using Queer Standpoint in Postmodern Critical Ethnography." *Qualitative Studies in Education* 12 (1999): 473–90.

Kinsey, A. C., W. B. Pomeroy, and C. E. Martin. *Sexual Behavior in the Human Male.* Philadelphia: W. B. Saunders, 1948.

Kirch, M. W. "Cross–Sexually Oriented Male Friendship: An Initial Exploration." Paper presented at the annual meeting of the National Communication Association, Chicago, November 1997.

Kirk, M., and H. Madsen. *After the Ball: How America Will Conquer Its Fear and Hatred of Gays in the Nineties.* New York: Plume, 1990.

Kumashiro, K. "Toward a Theory of Anti-Oppressive Education." Paper presented at the Review of Educational Research Symposium, University of South Florida, Tampa, 2000.

Lather, P. A. *Getting Smart: Feminist Research and Pedagogy with/in the Postmodern.* New York: Routledge, 1991.

Lincoln. Y. S., and N. K. Denzin. "The Seventh Moment: Out of the Past." Pp. 1047–65 in *Handbook of Qualitative Research,* ed. N. K. Denzin and Y. S. Lincoln. 2d ed. Thousand Oaks, Calif.: Sage, 2000.

Malone, J. *Straight Women/Gay Men: A Special Relationship.* New York: Dial Press, 1980.

Mann, W. J. "One of Us." Pp. 167–77 in *Sister and Brother: Lesbians and Gay Men Write about Their Lives Together,* ed. J. Nestle and J. Preston. San Francisco: HarperSanFrancisco, 1995.

Marriage Project—Hawaii. 2000. http://members.tripod.com/~MPHAWAII/. Accessed June 15, 2000.

Miller, S. *Men and Friendship.* Boston: Houghton Mifflin, 1983.

Mohr, R. D. *A More Perfect Union: Why Straight America Must Stand Up for Gay Rights.* Boston: Beacon Press, 1994.

Mushroom, M. "Gay Girls and Gay Guys: An Old Past, a New Future." Pp. 65–72 in *Sister and Brother: Lesbians and Gay Men Write about Their Lives Together.* San Francisco: HarperSanFrancisco, 1995.

Myerhoff, B. *Number Our Days.* New York: Simon & Schuster, 1980.

Nahas, R., and M. Turley. *The New Couple: Women and Gay Men.* New York: Seaview Books, 1979.

Nardi, P. M. *Gay Men's Friendships: Invincible Communities.* Chicago: University of Chicago Press, 1999.

National Coming Out of Homosexuality Day. 2000. www.kerusso.org/. Accessed June 20, 2000.

Newport, F. "Some Change over Time in American Attitudes towards Homosexuality, but Negativity Remains." *Gallup Organization.* 1999. www.gallup.com/poll/releases/pr990301b.asp. Accessed June 15, 2000.

NGLTF (National Gay and Lesbian Task Force). 2000. www.ngltf.org/index/cfm. Accessed June 20, 2000.

Pallone, D. *Behind the Mask: My Double Life in Baseball.* New York: Viking, 1990.

Pearlberg, G. G., and S. Wilder. "The Cultural Exchange." Pp. 323–31 in *Sister and Brother: Lesbians and Gay Men Write about Their Lives Together,* ed. J. Nestle and J. Preston. San Francisco: HarperSanFrancisco, 1995.

Phillips, A. *On Flirtation: Psychoanalytic Essays on the Uncommitted Life*. Cambridge: Harvard University Press, 1994.

Poynter, C. "Soldier to Be Tried in Slaying." *Courrier Journal*, September 25, 1999. www.temenos.net/winchell/news0925.htm. Accessed June 15, 2000.

Price, J. *Navigating Differences: Friendships between Gay and Straight Men*. New York: Harrington Park Press, 1999.

Punch, M. "Politics and Ethics in Qualitative Research." Pp. 83–97 in *Handbook of Qualitative Research*, ed. N. K. Denzin and Y. S. Lincoln. Thousand Oaks, Calif.: Sage, 1994.

Rauch, K., and J. Fessler. *Why Gays Are a Girl's Best Friend*. New York: Fireside, 1995.

Reason, P. "Three Approaches to Participative Inquiry." Pp. 324–39 in *Handbook of Qualitative Research*, ed. N. K. Denzin and Y. S. Lincoln. Thousand Oaks, Calif.: Sage, 1994.

Reinharz, S. *Feminist Methods in Social Research*. New York: Oxford University Press, 1992.

Rich, A. "Compulsory Heterosexuality and Lesbian Existence." Pp. 227–54 in *The Lesbian and Gay Studies Reader*, ed. H. Abelove, M. A. Barale, and D. M. Halperin. New York: Routledge, 1993.

Richardson, L. "The Consequences of Poetic Representation: Writing the Other, Rewriting the Self." Pp. 125–37 in *Investigating Subjectivity: Research on Lived Experience*, ed. C. Ellis and M. G. Flaherty. Newbury Park, Calif.: Sage, 1992.

Roberts, H., ed. *Doing Feminist Research*. London: Routledge & Kegan Paul, 1981.

Rodi, R. *Fag Hag*. New York: Dutton, 1992.

Ronai, C. R. "Multiple Reflections of Child Sex Abuse: An Argument for a Layered Account." *Journal of Contemporary Ethnography* 23 (1995): 395–426.

Rowe, M. "Looking for Brothers: Barney, Chris, and Me." Pp. 177–88 in *Friends and Lovers: Gay Men Write about the Families They Create*, ed. J. Preston and M. Lowenthal. New York: Plume, 1996.

Russo, V. *The Celluloid Closet: Homosexuality in the Movies*. New York: Harper & Row, 1987.

Schwandt, T. A. "Constructivist, Interpretivist Approaches to Human Inquiry." Pp. 118–37 in *Handbook of Qualitative Research*, ed. N. K. Denzin and Y. S. Lincoln. Thousand Oaks, Calif.: Sage, 1994.

Sedgwick, E. K. *Epistemology of the Closet*. Berkeley and Los Angeles: University of California Press, 1990.

Shyer, M. F., and C. Shyer. *Not Like Other Boys: Growing Up Gay—A Mother and Son Look Back*. Boston: Houghton Mifflin, 1996.

Singer, B. L., and D. Deschamps, eds. *Gay and Lesbian Stats*. New York: New Press, 1994.

Spence, D. P. *Narrative Truth and Historical Truth: Meaning and Interpretation in Psychoanalysis*. New York: W. W. Norton, 1982.

Stein, E. *The Mismeasure of Desire: The Science, Theory, and Ethics of Sexual Orientation*. New York: Oxford University Press, 1999.

Stein, P. J. "Men and Their Friendships." Pp. 261–70 in *Men in Families*, ed. R. A. Lewis and R. E. Salt. Beverly Hills, Calif.: Sage, 1986.

Stoller, P. *The Taste of Ethnographic Things: The Senses in Anthropology*. Philadelphia: University of Pennsylvania Press, 1989.

Storms, M. "Theories of Sexual Orientation." *Journal of Personality and Social Psychology* 38 (1980): 783–92.

Stux, L., ed. *Imagine That: Letters from Russell*. Chicago: Lambda Publications, 1999.

Tedlock, B. "From Participant Observation to the Observation of Participation: The Emergence of Narrative Ethnography." *Journal of Anthropological Research* 47 (1991): 69–94.

Thomas, C. "Introduction: Identification, Appropriation, Proliferation." Pp. 1–7 in *Straight with a Twist: Queer Theory and the Subject of Heterosexuality*, ed. C. Thomas. Urbana: University of Illinois Press, 2000.

Thomas, C., and C. A. F. MacGillivray. "Afterword(s): A Conversation." Pp. 253–80 in *Straight with a Twist: Queer Theory and the Subject of Heterosexuality*, ed. C. Thomas. Urbana: University of Illinois Press, 2000.

Tillmann-Healy, L. M. "A Secret Life in a Culture of Thinness: Reflections on Body, Food, and Bulimia." Pp. 76–108 in *Composing Ethnography: Alternative Forms of Qualitative Writing*, ed. C. Ellis and A. P. Bochner. Walnut Creek, Calif.: AltaMira Press, 1996.

"Tinky Winky Comes Out of the Closet." *NLJ online*, February 1999. www.liberty.edu/chancellor/nlj/feb99/politics2.htm. Accessed June 15, 2000.

Tompkins, J. *West of Everything: The Inner Life of Westerns*. New York: Oxford University Press, 1992.

Van Maanen, J. *Tales of the Field: On Writing Ethnography*. Chicago: University of Chicago Press, 1988.

Wallace, S. B. "Kids' Town Hall Airs Opinions on Tolerance." *DenverPost.com*, October 27, 1999. www.denverpost.com/news/news1027g.htm. Accessed June 15, 2000.

Warner, M. *The Trouble with Normal: Sex, Politics, and the Ethics of Queer Life*. New York: Free Press, 1999.

Warren, C. A. B. "Women among Men: Females in the Male Homosexual Community." *Archives of Sexual Behavior* 5 (1976): 157–69.

Watts, A. *The Book: On the Taboo against Knowing Who You Are*. New York: Vintage Books, 1989.

Werking, K. *We're Just Good Friends: Women and Men in Nonromantic Relationships*. New York: Guilford Press, 1997.

Weston, K. *Families We Choose: Lesbians, Gays, Kinship*. New York: Columbia University Press, 1991.

Whitney, C. *Uncommon Lives: Gay Men and Straight Women*. New York: New American Library, 1990.

Wood, J. T. *Gendered Lives: Communication, Gender, and Culture*. 2d ed. Belmont, Calif.: Wadsworth, 1997.

Woog, D. *School's Out: The Impact of Gay and Lesbian Issues on America's Schools*. Los Angeles: Alyson Publications, 1995.

———. *Friends and Family: True Stories of Gay America's Straight Allies*. Los Angeles: Alyson Books, 1999.

"Words of Dr. Laura." 2000. www.stopdrlaura.com/laura/index.htm. Accessed June 15, 2000.

Wypijewski, J. "A Boy's Life: For Matthew Shepard's Killers, What Does It Take to Pass as a Man?" *Harper's Magazine*, September 1999, 61–74.

About the Author

Lisa M. Tillmann-Healy is an assistant professor of communication at Rollins College. She is a graduate of Marquette University (B.A.) and the University of South Florida (Ph.D.). She has authored and contributed to articles and book chapters on relationship narratives and dialectics, interactive interviewing, and the lived, emotional experiences of family dissolution and eating disorders. Anyone with questions or comments about this project should contact the author at ltillmann@rollins.edu.